The *Sams Teach Yourself in 24 Hours* Series

Sams Teach Yourself in 24 Hours books provide quick and easy answers in a proven step-by-step approach that works for you. In just 24 sessi[...] hour or less, you will tackle every task you need to get the result[...] Let our experienced authors present the most accurate informati[...] reliable answers—fast!

Windows users should use Control instead of Command and Alt i[...] Option.

VIEWING

Command-Y	Preview/Artwork mode
F	Toggle through Screen Viewing modes
Command-R	Show/Hide Rulers
Command-Control-U	Cycle through measurement systems (Macintosh only)
Command-Slash	Online Help
Command-Quote (")	Show/Hide Grid
Command-Shift-Quote (")	Toggle Snap to Grid
Command-Semicolon (;)	Show/Hide Guides
Command-Option-Semicolon (;)	Lock/Unlock Guides
Command-H	Hide/Show Edges
Command-Plus Sign (+)	Zoom In
Command-Minus Sign (-)	Zoom Out
Command-0	Fit in Window
Command-1	Actual Size
Command-5	Make Guides
Command-Option-5	Release Guides

SELECTING

Command-2	Lock All
Command-Option-2	Unlock All
Command-3	Hide Selection
Command-Option-3	Show Selection
Command-Tab	Toggle between Selection and Direct Selection tools
Command-A	Select All
Command-Shift-A	Deselect All
Command-G	Group
Command-Shift-G	Ungroup

TRANSFORMATIONS

Command-D	Repeat Transform
Command-Tilde (~)	Puts Focus in last-used palette
Tilde (~)	When used with polygon tools, create duplicates; when used with transformation tools, transforms only pattern fills
Command-Option-B	Make Blend
Command-Option-Shift-B	Release Blend

TYPE

Option-Right Arrow	Open Kerning
Option-Left Arrow	Close Kerning
Option-Command-Right Arrow	Open Kerning in increments of 5
Option-Command-Left Arrow	Close Kerning in increments of 5
Option-Up Arrow	Close Leading
Option-Down Arrow	Open Leading
Command-Shift-L	Align Flush Left
Command-Shift-R	Align Flush Right
Command-Shift-C	Align Center
Command-Shift-Less Than (<)	Down in Point Size
Command-Shift-Greater Than (>)	Up in Point Size
Option-Shift-Up Arrow	Baseline Shift Up
Option-Shift-Down Arrow	Baseline Shift Down
Option-Shift-Command-Up Arrow	Baseline Shift Up in increments of 5
Option-Shift-Command-Down Arrow	Baseline Shift Down in increments of 5
Command-Shift-J	Justifies Area Text
Command-Shift-F	Force Justifies Area Text
Command-Shift-X	Resets Horizontal Scale to 100%

SAMS

Illustrator® 8

in 24 Hours

FUNCTIONS

Command-Shift-Q	Resets Tracking to 0
Command-J	Join
Command-Option-J	Average
Command-Z	Undo
Command-Shift-Z	Redo
Command-X	Cut
Command-C	Copy
Command-V	Paste
Command-4	Repeat Pathfinder
Command-F	Paste in Front
Command-B	Paste in Back
Command-Open Bracket	Send Backward
Command-Shift-Open Bracket	Send to Back
Command-Closed Bracket	Bring Forward
Command-Shift-Closed Bracket	Bring to Front
Command-7	Make Mask
Command-Option-7	Release Mask
Command-8	Make Compound Path
Command-Option-8	Release Compound Path
Command-Shift-0	Convert text to outlines
Command-E	Apply last filter
Command-Option-E	Last Filter (brings up dialog box)

PALETTES

Command-I	Toggles Color palette
Tab	Hides all palettes
Shift-Tab	Hides all palettes except toolbar
Command-T	Toggles Character palette
Command-M	Toggles Paragraph palette
F-5	Toggles Swatches palette

PALETTES (CONTINUED)

F-6	Toggles Color palette
F-7	Toggles Layers palette
F-8	Toggles Info palette
F-9	Toggles Gradient palette
F-10	Toggles Stroke palette
F-11	Toggles Attribute palette
Command-Shift-I	Toggles Attributes palette

SHORTCUTS

Control (Macintosh)	Activates context-sensitive pop-up menu
Right mouse button (Windows)	Activates context-sensitive pop-up menu
Command-Option	Toggles the Convert Direction Point tool
Command	Toggles the last-used Selection tool
Spacebar	Toggles the Hand tool
Command-Spacebar	Toggles the Zoom tool
Command-Option-Spacebar	Toggles the Zoom Out tool
Comma (,)	Color
Period (.)	Gradient
Slash (/)	None attribute
X	Toggles between Fill and Stroke
Shift-X	Swaps Fill and Stroke
D	Sets Fill and Stroke to default (White Fill, Black Stroke)

TOOLS

(add Shift key to access tools with same shortcut)

V	Selection
A	Direct Selection/Group Selection
P	Pen/Add Anchor Point/Delete Anchor Point/Convert Direction Point
T	Type/Area Type/Path Type/Vertical Type/Vertical Area Type/Vertical Path Type
L	Ellipse/Polygon/Star/Spiral
M	Rectangle/Rounded Rectangle
B	Paintbrush
N	Pencil/Smooth/Erase

TOOLS (CONTINUED)

(add Shift key to access tools with same shortcut)

R	Rotate Twirl
S	Scale/Reshape
O	Reflect/Shear
E	Free Transform
W	Blend/Auto Trace
J	All Graph
U	Gradient Mesh
G	Gradient
I	Eyedropper/Paint Bucket
C	Scissors/Knife
H	Hand/Page/Measure
Z	Zoom

SAMS

Who Should Read This Book

If you've already picked up the book and started reading, you're probably interested in learning Illustrator, and Behold! This book was written for anyone who wants to learn Illustrator! Whether you're an experienced Photoshop user who wants to enjoy the precise illustration benefits of Illustrator, a FreeHand convert, an experienced Illustrator user who wants to get up to speed with the new version, or a beginner, this book is a great way to quickly learn Illustrator.

Can This Book Really Teach Illustrator in 24 Hours?

I think the comic Steven Wright said it best: A guy walks down to a 24-hour convenience store at 2:00 a.m. to see the owner locking up the store. The guy incredulously says, "But it says you're open 24 hours!" The owner replies, "Yeah, but not in a row."

You do yourself a tremendous disservice if you try to read this entire book in one day (to say nothing of the disservice you'd be doing to your social life). It is impossible to learn a complex illustration program in one sitting. By spending a few solid hours at comfortable intervals, however, you can.

This book has been carefully organized so that you can systematically progress, learning more and more about Illustrator—whether you do it in a few days, weeks, or even months. As with the great sage who observed the little drops of water that eventually bored through the rock, each hour you spend in Illustrator brings you that much closer to mastering the program.

Mordy Golding

SAMS
Teach Yourself
Illustrator® 8
in 24 Hours

SAMS

201 West 103rd St., Indianapolis, Indiana 46290

Sams Teach Yourself Illustrator 8 in 24 Hours

Copyright © 1999 by Sams

International Standard Book Number: 0-672-31354-5x

Library of Congress Catalog Card Number: 98-85237

Printed in the United States of America

First Printing: October 1998

00   99   98   4   3   2   1

Trademarks

Warning and Disclaimer

EXECUTIVE EDITOR
Beth Millett

ACQUISITIONS EDITOR
Karen Whitehouse

DEVELOPMENT EDITOR
Juliet MacLean

MANAGING EDITOR
Patrick Kanouse

PROJECT EDITOR
Andrew Cupp

COPY EDITOR
Charles Hutchinson

INDEXER
Kelly Talbot

PROOFREADERS
Kim Cofer
Gene Redding

TECHNICAL EDITOR
Jay Nelson

INTERIOR DESIGN
Gary Adair

COVER DESIGN
Aren Howell

LAYOUT TECHNICIANS
Tim Osborn
Staci Somers
Mark Walchle

Contents at a Glance

Contents

About the Author

MORDY GOLDING is a trainer, consultant, writer, graphic designer, production artist, network manager, husband, and father (not necessarily in that order). Mordy resides on Long Island in NY, where he spends too much time sitting in front of a computer, fiddling with his Web site (`http://www.mordy.com`), and not enough time with his loving family. With a strong technical background, Mordy has been designing on computers since 1990, and has been a featured panelist at *Macworld*. Mordy also loves replying to email (`mordy@mordy.com`).

Dedication

To my loving wife, Batsheva.

Acknowledgments

To Beth, Karen, Julie, and all the great folks at Macmillan for keeping the faith and for turning yet another dream into a reality.

To Ted and Jen Alspach for their warm friendship and never-ending advice. It's the little things in life—right, guys?

To Sandee Cohen for taking me by the hand and bringing me into the fold. For all those hours on the phone, and for a friend who doesn't know how to say no.

To Sharon Steuer for constantly reminding me to spend more time with my family. If only I had listened to her more.

To all my "Illustrator Buddies" on AOL. There are too many to mention, but you all know who you are :)

To the 7:58 "train gang": Danny, Stuie, Michael, and the Daf for keeping me sane.

To Yisroel Golding, who started it all when, in a cramped little room in St. Louis, he showed me Adobe Illustrator 88 on something called Macintosh. I still remember the day clearly…

To my parents, who always knew that I could do it, but just never thought that I actually would.

To the Wrotslavsky family for still believing in me.

Most of all, to my dearest wife Batsheva, my daughter Chayala, and my son Simcha, whose support, love, and most importantly, smiles keep me going every day of my life.

Tell Us What You Think!

As the reader of this book, *you* are our most important critic and commentator. We value your opinion and want to know what we're doing right, what we could do better, what areas you'd like to see us publish in, and any other words of wisdom you're willing to pass our way.

As the Executive Editor for the Web Graphics and Design team at Macmillan Computer Publishing, I welcome your comments. You can fax, email, or write me directly to let me know what you did or didn't like about this book—as well as what we can do to make our books stronger.

Please note that I cannot help you with technical problems related to the topic of this book and that, due to the high volume of mail I receive, I might not be able to reply to every message.

When you write, please be sure to include this book's title and author as well as your name and phone or fax number. I will carefully review your comments and share them with the author and editors who worked on the book.

Fax: 317-817-7070

Email: desktop_pub@mcp.com

Mail: Executive Editor
            Web Graphics and Design
            Macmillan Computer Publishing
            201 West 103rd Street
            Indianapolis, IN 46290 USA

Introduction

"Teach yourself Illustrator in 24 hours?" Yeah, right. I'll bet you're thinking you could probably learn how to do a triple-bypass open heart procedure before you could learn Adobe Illustrator (those guys on *E.R.* make it look so easy). But it can be done, and this book is the perfect way to learn how. I've broken down the entire application into easy-to-understand chapters, and before you know it, you'll be a proficient Illustrator user. Trust me, it's a lot simpler than medical school....

What This Book Assumes

This book was written on the assumption that you are already familiar with certain concepts, ideas, and techniques.

I will take it for granted that you already know how to use your computer—turning it on and off, launching applications, choosing printers, and other basic computer functions. You should also already be familiar with using the mouse (if you just dropped the book, let out a shriek, and ran, this book is not for you).

Typographical Conventions

- Accessing commands on menus or submenus is shown with the name of the menu, an arrow, then the command or submenu. For example: "Choose File➡Open" means choose Open from the File menu.
- Macintosh keyboard shortcuts appear in parentheses, and Windows keyboard shortcuts appear in brackets, like this (Command+A)[Command+A].

Terminology

Throughout the book, I may ask you to perform certain functions, which I will list below to avoid any confusion.

- Click—Press the mouse button and release it quickly.
- Double-click—Press the mouse button twice in rapid succession and release it.
- Drag—Simply move the mouse.
- Press and drag—Press the mouse button and, without releasing it, drag the mouse. Release the button only when instructed.

Now, let's learn a little more about what Illustrator is and how it works.

HOUR 1

Getting to Know Illustrator

Adobe has put together a tightly integrated trio of applications (Photoshop, PageMaker, and Illustrator) that all work in the same intuitive way. Most key commands are the same across all applications, and palettes look and work the same. The applications are truly *cross-platform*, working virtually identically on both the Macintosh and Windows platforms. If you are already familiar with Photoshop, many features will be familiar to you as you learn Illustrator.

If you are already an Illustrator user, you will need to adjust to the new features and workflow in version 8. For those of you new to Illustrator in general, this chapter deals with how Illustrator works and how it differs from other graphics programs.

In this hour, you will learn about the following:

- Raster and vector images
- Illustrator's environment
- Illustrator's tools and palettes
- Views in Illustrator

Raster Versus Vector

In the ever-growing world of computer graphics, you will find two types of images: raster and vector. Some programs that create raster images (also known as pixel or paint images) are Photoshop, MacPaint, PC Paintbrush, and Painter. Some programs that create vector art (also known as object-oriented art) are Illustrator (that's us!), FreeHand, MacDraw, and Expression. Other programs, such as Canvas and CorelDRAW, have tools to create both raster and vector images.

Raster Images

NEW TERM *Raster images* are made up of a whole lot of tiny dots, called *pixels*. The number of pixels determines the resolution of your file. To illustrate this concept, think of a sheet of graph paper. Each square on the sheet represents one pixel (see Figure 1.1). Start simple and create a black and white circle that is 20 pixels in diameter (see Figure 1.2). The computer stores this file by recording the exact placement and color of each pixel (see Figure 1.3). The computer has no idea that it is a circle, only that it is a collection of little dots.

FIGURE 1.1

Each square in the raster represents one pixel.

FIGURE 1.2

A raster circle.

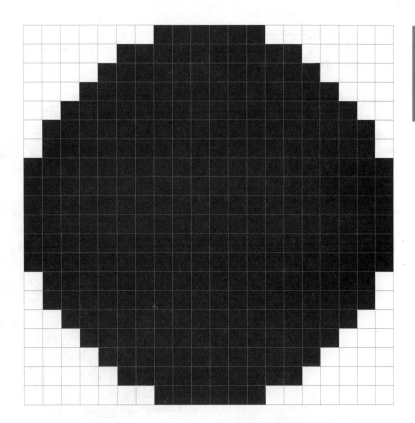

FIGURE 1.3

Each pixel has a coordinate, and the contents of that pixel are recorded and saved in a file.

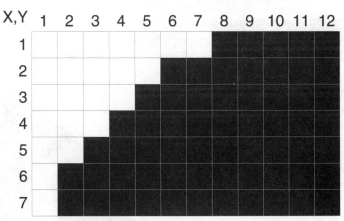

In this example, you can see each individual pixel, and the circle is very blocky. By adding more pixels, thereby increasing the resolution, you can make that same circle appear smoother because the pixels are much smaller (see Figure 1.4). Of course, the higher your resolution, the larger your file size will be because the computer has many more pixels to keep track of.

FIGURE 1.4

By creating a circle with a higher resolution, you can make edges appear smoother at the cost of having a larger file size.

NEW TERM The problem arises when you try enlarging a raster image. Because the resolution is set, when you scale the art, in reality, you are just enlarging the pixels (see Figure 1.5), which results in a jaggy (or *pixelated*) image.

FIGURE 1.5

At 100% (left), the circle appears to have a smooth edge. Enlarging the circle, however, reveals the jaggy edges (right).

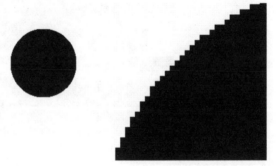

Vector Images: An Objective Approach

 Vector art is different; instead of creating individual pixels, you create objects, such as rectangles and circles. By noting the mathematical coordinates of these shapes, a vector program can store files in a fraction of the space as raster images and, more importantly, can scale images to virtually any size without any loss in detail (see Figure 1.6).

FIGURE 1.6

Unlike raster images, the vector circle appears smooth at 100% (left) and just as smooth when enlarged 800% (right).

The Illustrator Workplace

Now that you understand the differences between raster and vector images, you can actually open Illustrator and see what it has to offer. If you haven't already installed it, follow the instructions that came with Illustrator to install it on your computer. Now, launch Adobe Illustrator.

If you've launched Illustrator before, or if you're working on someone else's computer, it's a good idea to trash your Preferences file so that what you see pictured in this book matches what you see onscreen. Follow these steps to trash your files.

On a Macintosh:

1. In the Finder, open your System folder.
2. In your System folder is a folder called Preferences. Open it.
3. Find and select the file called Adobe Illustrator 8 Prefs in your Preferences folder.
4. Drag it to the Trash, and empty the Trash.

On Windows:

1. Locate the Illustrator application folder.

2. Within the Illustrator application folder is a folder called Preferences. Open it.

3. Find and select the AIPREFS file.

4. Drag it to the Recycle Bin, and empty the Recycle Bin.

The next time you launch Illustrator, a sparkling new Preferences file is automatically created.

Did you know that you can edit Illustrator's Preferences file? If you're the daring type, open the file in a text editor. There, you can make changes, such as turning off warning dialog boxes.

You should learn how to trash your Preferences file, because it is a great troubleshooting tip. If Illustrator seems to be acting weird, or even crashing often, trashing the preferences and restarting Illustrator usually clears up any problems.

After viewing the beautiful Illustrator splash screen and trying to read all the names of the programmers to see whether you know any of them, you are presented with Illustrator's working environment and an open Untitled document. Now, you're ready for action.

The Illustrator Window

First, take a tour of the Illustrator window. You can start with a general look at Illustrator (see Figure 1.7) and then examine each part in more detail.

- Menu bar—Across the top of the screen is the menu bar, which contains Illustrator's commands and essentials such as printing, saving, copying, and pasting.

- Document window—Directly beneath the menu bar, the document window is the actual Illustrator file. In the title bar of the document window is the filename and the percentage at which it is currently being viewed.

- Toolbox—This narrow strip of boxes on the far left of the screen contains the tools you will use to work in Illustrator.

- Page border—In the center of your screen, you can see the page border of your document. You can change the page size to fit whatever you might need—anywhere from 2×2 inches to 227.54×227.54 inches.

Menu bar   Page border   Print area   Document window

FIGURE 1.7

Welcome to Illustrator. Illustrator looks like this when you open it for the first time.

Toolbox

Floating palettes

Zoom magnification window

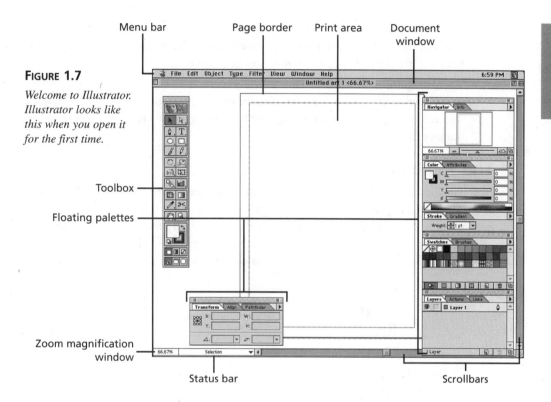

Status bar

Scrollbars

- Print area—Right inside the page border is a dotted line that represents the physical print area of the printer. Illustrator determines this area by taking information from the PostScript Printer Description (PPD) file of your currently selected printer.

- Floating palettes—Along the right side and across the bottom of the screen, you can find some of Illustrator's many floating palettes: Color, Attributes, Stroke, Gradient, and more. They are clustered and docked, which you will soon see when you examine palettes in detail in "The Many Palettes of Illustrator," later in this hour.

- Scrollbars—At the very bottom of the document window, as well as along the right side, are scrollbars. By clicking the arrows at each end, or by dragging the box within the scrollbar, you can move your page around within the document window. Now that you've learned what it is, don't ever use it. You will learn far more efficient ways to move around as you progress.

- Status bar—To the left of the scrollbar at the bottom of the document window is the status bar. Clicking the mouse on the status bar enables you to choose to have

Illustrator display important information for you as you work. Alternatively, you can hold down the (Option)[Alt] key while pressing the mouse button on the status bar for a list of not-so-important things to keep track of.

- Zoom magnification window—Immediately to the left of the status bar is the zoom magnification window, which identifies the current zoom percentage of your file. You can quickly zoom to any percentage by clicking this window and typing any number from 6.25 to 6400.

The Toolbox

How can you keep track of Illustrator's different tools (see Figure 1.8)? Well, I can give you a hint: Look at your *cursor*. Sometimes it's an arrow; other times, a crosshair, a paintbrush, or different variations of a pen (see Figure 1.9). By recognizing the different cursors, you can concentrate more on what you're drawing than on how to draw it. Wherever appropriate, I will bring these tell-tale cursors to your attention.

FIGURE 1.8

The Illustrator Toolbox.

FIGURE 1.9

Depending on circumstances, the Pen tool cursor changes to help you complete your drawing quickly.

I strongly suggest that you learn the keyboard shortcuts for the Toolbox (for example, the keyboard shortcut for the Rectangle tool is "M"). Adobe has made this task easy by assigning single keystrokes to every tool (see Figure 1.10). For tools that have several options (such as the Rectangle tool), hold down the Shift key and the shortcut key to cycle through the tools.

FIGURE 1.10

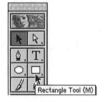

When you drag the mouse cursor over the Toolbox, a ToolTip pops up, identifying the tool and the keyboard shortcut for it.

The following is a brief description of the tools found in the Illustrator Toolbox. The keyboard shortcut for each tool appears in parentheses following the tool name.

Notice that many more tools are included in the list than appear in the Illustrator Toolbox. To make life easier for you, tools that are similar in function are grouped together in the Toolbox. Those tools with a little black arrow in the lower-right corner of the box have other tools in their space. You can access these tools either by clicking and dragging the tool, which brings up a pop-up box of the tools in that group, or by using the Shift+keyboard shortcut key as just mentioned.

Do not be alarmed if you find a tool in the Toolbox that is not listed here. Illustrator enables the addition of third-party plug-ins and the capability to place those plug-ins directly into the Illustrator Toolbox. VectorTools from Extensis, for instance, adds a Magic Wand selection tool to the Toolbox, and ILLOM Toolbox 1 adds a Lasso selection tool to the Toolbox.

Selection Tools

Used most often, the selection tools tell Illustrator which objects you are working on. The selection tools are as follow

- Selection tool (V)—Used to select and move objects
- Direct Selection tool (A)—Used to select parts of an object
- Group Selection tool (A)—A variation of the Direct Selection tool, used to select grouped items

Creation Tools

It would be kind of silly if you couldn't create anything in Illustrator, right? The creation tools enable you to create your artwork, each tool serving a specific drawing task. The creation tools are as follows:

- Pen tool (P)—Creates Bézier paths
- Add Anchor Point tool (P)—Adds an anchor point to an existing path
- Delete Anchor Point tool (P)—Removes an existing anchor point
- Convert Direction Point tool (P)—Changes a selected anchor point of one type into another
- Type tool (T)—Creates headline or point type
- Area Type tool (T)—Creates area or paragraph type
- Path Type tool (T)—Creates type on a path
- Vertical Type tool (T)—Creates vertical headline or point type
- Vertical Area Type tool (T)—Creates vertical area or paragraph type
- Vertical Path Type tool (T)—Creates vertical text on a path
- Ellipse tool (N)—Creates circles and ovals
- Polygon tool (N)—Creates polygons
- Star tool (N)—Creates multipointed stars
- Spiral tool (N)—Creates spirals
- Rectangle tool (M)—Creates squares and rectangles
- Rounded Rectangle tool (M)—Creates squares and rectangles with rounded corners
- Paintbrush tool (B)—Creates filled variable-width objects and paints with defined brushes; also supports pressure-sensitive tablets
- Pencil tool (Y)—Draws freehand path lines
- Smooth tool (Y)—Smoothes out path lines
- Erase tool (Y)—Erases path lines

Transformation Tools

Power is being able to change that which you have. Illustrator's transformation tools give you the power you need to perfect your art. The transformation tools are as follow:

- Rotate tool (R)—Rotates selected objects
- Twirl tool (R)—Distorts selected objects in a circular fashion
- Scale tool (S)—Resizes selected objects

1

- Reshape tool (S)—Makes simple changes in the shape of a Bézier segment
- Reflect tool (O)—Mirrors selected objects
- Shear tool (O)—Skews or slants selected objects
- Free Transform tool (E)—Performs multiple transformations on a selection in one step

Assorted Tools

Some tools just can't be categorized. Illustrator contains a wealth of task-specific tools to assist you in your quest for the perfect art. Illustrator's remaining tools are as follows:

- Blend tool (W)—Creates blends between objects
- Autotrace tool (W)—Traces bitmapped art and converts it to vector
- Graph tool (J)—Creates an assortment of different graphs
- Gradient Mesh tool (U)—Creates mesh gradients
- Gradient tool (G)—Controls the way gradients are filled within an object
- Eyedropper tool (I)—Samples fill and stroke attributes for use with the Paint Bucket tool
- Paint Bucket tool (K)—Copies fill and stroke attributes from one object to another
- Scissors tool (C)—Splits a path at a selected point
- Knife tool (C)—Splits objects by slicing through them
- Hand tool (H)—"Grabs" the page and moves it within the document window
- Page tool (H)—Positions artwork on the printed page
- Measure tool (H)—Measures distance and angles
- Zoom tool (Z)—Zooms both in and out of your document

Underneath the tools are two swatches depicting the currently selected fill and stroke colors, with a small icon on the lower left to quickly set the fill and stroke back to the default white fill, black stroke (D), and a small icon on the upper right to swap the fill and stroke (see Figure 1.11). Using the X key toggles *focus* between fill and stroke. You'll learn more about these features in Hours 10, "Fills," and 11, "Strokes."

FIGURE 1.11

The fill and stroke selectors. If you use Photoshop, they are identical to the foreground and background swatches.

— Switch Fill and Stroke

— White Fill, Black Stroke

w the fill and stroke selectors are three buttons (as shown in Figure 1.12) that you can use to quickly access the Color (,) and Gradient (.) palettes and the None attribute (/).

FIGURE 1.12

Quick-click shortcuts to the Color and Gradient palettes, as well as the None attribute.

— None
— Gradient
— Color

Finally, at the bottom of the Toolbox are three options for document viewing: standard screen mode, full screen mode with menu bar, and full screen mode (see Figure 1.13).

FIGURE 1.13

Also similar to Photoshop are options to hide the menu bar and view a file full screen.

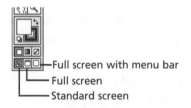

— Full screen with menu bar
— Full screen
— Standard screen

The Many Palettes of Illustrator

NEW TERM I think the development of palettes all began when someone said, "Hey, the Toolbox is always visible; why can't we have other stuff also always be visible?" Thanks to that one person, you now have floating palettes. They're called *floating palettes* because no matter what you are working on, they still remain in the foreground, accessible at all times. You can also move them around by clicking and dragging the mouse cursor over the title bar at the top of each palette.

The people at Adobe must really like floating palettes, because Illustrator now has 18 of them (see Figure 1.14):

- Info palette
- Transform palette
- Align palette
- Color palette
- Gradient palette
- Stroke palette
- Swatches palette

- Layers palette
- Attributes palette
- Links palette
- Navigator palette
- Actions palette
- Pathfinder palette
- Brushes palette
- Character palette
- Paragraph palette
- Multiple Master Design palette
- Tab palette

FIGURE 1.14

If you opened every Illustrator palette onscreen, you wouldn't have much room left to draw anything.

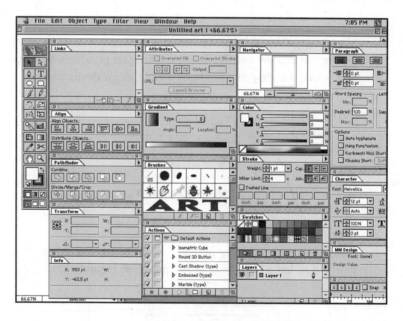

Throughout the book, you will learn how to use each of these palettes to your advantage.

Screen real estate is really valuable, so the fact that you can quickly hide all palettes at any time by pressing the Tab key is nice. To hide all palettes except the Toolbox, press Shift+Tab.

Working with Palettes

Well, if you want to criticize Illustrator for having too many floating palettes, then you must also praise Illustrator for making it so easy to manage them. All of Illustrator's palettes "stick" to one another like magnets. They also stick to the edge of the screen, which makes positioning them easy.

Working with the palettes gets even better than that. Double-click the tab (the tab is the area where the actual name of the palette appears) of a floating palette, and the palette collapses, showing you only the tab (see Figure 1.15). Double-click the tab again to expand the palette.

FIGURE 1.15

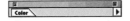

Double-clicking a tab collapses the palette.

You already know that you can position a floating palette by grabbing the top bar of the palette, but you get an extra surprise when you grab the tab of a palette. Clicking the tab of a palette and dragging produces the outline of the palette (see Figure 1.16).

FIGURE 1.16

Dragging a palette by its tab.

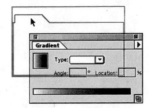

Now drag the outline right over the middle of another palette. Notice that the underlying palette now has a black outline around it (see Figure 1.17).

FIGURE 1.17

Notice how the palette underneath becomes "selected" with a black outline.

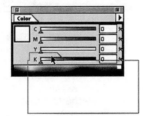

Let go of the mouse button, and both palettes are now clustered (see Figure 1.18). Click the tab to bring that palette to the foreground. This capability gives you unlimited possibilities to configure your palettes.

FIGURE 1.18

The new clustered palette.

Believe it or not, you have yet another way to configure palettes; this method is called *docking*. Grab the tab from a palette, and drag it over so that your mouse cursor just touches the bottom of another palette (see Figure 1.19). Notice the black outline only along the bottom of the underlying palette.

FIGURE 1.19

Positioning a palette for docking.

When you release the mouse button, the two palettes are docked (see Figure 1.20). You can now move the entire palette as one, but still collapse and cluster each palette individually. Cool, huh?

FIGURE 1.20

The palettes, docked.

Views in Illustrator

Illustrator has three viewing modes: Preview, Artwork, and Preview Selection. You can toggle between Preview and Artwork viewing modes by pressing (Command+Y) [Control+Y]. In Preview mode, you see the file as it would print, with colored fills and strokes (see Figure 1.21). Sometimes you need to view your file in Artwork mode, in which you see only the outline of each object (see Figure 1.22). Finally, the last view mode, Preview Selection—which you access by pressing (Command+Shift+Y) [Control+Shift+Y]—is a combination of the two (see Figure 1.23). Whichever object you have selected shows in Preview mode, and all other artwork appears in Artwork mode. This mode is useful when you are working on large files that seem to take years for your monitor to redraw.

FIGURE 1.21

A page viewed in Preview mode.

FIGURE 1.22

A page viewed in Artwork mode.

FIGURE 1.23

A page viewed in Preview Selection mode.

Things That Make You Go Zoom!

Illustrator enables you to zoom in and out of your page, letting you view the entire page for layout and giving you an up-close view for detail work. You can change the zoom percentage of a document in the following ways:

- Use the Zoom tool. Select the Zoom tool from the Toolbox (see the following Time Saver), and click the place you want to zoom into; or even better, click and drag a marquee where you want to zoom (see Figure 1.24), and Illustrator tries to make that selected area fill the screen. Hold down the (Option)[Alt] key, and notice that the little plus sign inside the magnifying glass turns to a minus sign, which will zoom out, letting you see more of your document, only smaller.

FIGURE 1.24

Zooming in using the marquee method, as you did with the Selection tool.

- Use the keyboard. Pressing (Command+hyphen)[Control+hyphen] zooms out or down one increment, and pressing (Command+=)[Control+=] zooms in (or up) one increment.
- Use the Navigator palette. This option is discussed later, in the section "The Navigator Palette."
- Select a custom view. This option is discussed later in the section "Custom Views."

> To access the Zoom tool instantly at any time, no matter what tool you are using, simply press (Command+Spacebar)[Control+Spacebar], and your cursor changes to the magnifying glass. By also holding down the (Option)[Alt] key, you can zoom out, seeing more of your image. When you release these keys, Illustrator brings you right back to the tool you were using.

Moving Around Your Page

When you zoom in really close to work on an image, only a small portion of the image is visible. Here, the Hand tool (see Figure 1.25) comes into play. Select the Hand tool from the Toolbox. Press the mouse button and drag. The little hand "grabs" the page and moves it so that you can see other parts of the image.

FIGURE 1.25

The Hand tool.

> To quickly zoom to fit your page in your document window, double-click the Hand tool. To quickly go to 100% magnification, double-click the Zoom tool.

The Navigator Palette

Many times, especially on slower computers, scrolling around can be tedious—especially in large and complex files. To help make your viewing easier, Illustrator provides a Navigator palette to help you "get around." By moving the proxy within the palette (see Figure 1.26), you can quickly move to that part of your artwork. Dragging on the Zoom Slider enables you to zoom in and out (see Figure 1.27), or you can click the percentage at the lower left of the palette and type in any value from 6.25 to 6400.

FIGURE 1.26

Moving the proxy to scroll.

FIGURE 1.27

Dragging the Zoom Slider.

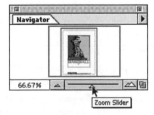

Custom Views

If you work with large, complex images, you will be very happy that you took the time to read this chapter. I'll explain why. Everyone is always complaining about how slow computers are for graphics and that you need expensive multiprocessor computers to keep up with today's work. Well, I'll let you in on a little secret. One of the biggest bottlenecks in computer graphics today is screen redraw. An accelerated graphics card can do wonders for your application speed, but these cards can be costly. Illustrator has a secret weapon, however, that costs a lot less than a graphics accelerator: custom views.

Imagine yourself in a TV recording studio. One show is being performed on center stage, and five different cameras are aimed at this stage. This setup gives the person in the recording studio the ability to jump from camera to camera, to seeing different views, instantaneously. Illustrator's custom views work in a similar fashion.

To create a custom view, simply choose New View from the View menu (see Figure 1.28). Whatever your current view is, it is automatically added to the Views list in the View menu. Attributes such as zoom percentage, viewing mode (Preview or Artwork), and window position are all saved, enabling you to jump quickly from an extreme close-up in Artwork mode, for example, to something such as a fit-in-window view in Preview mode. The first 10 views you define are also automatically assigned keyboard shortcuts (Command+Option+Shift)[Control+Alt+Shift] and 1 through 0.

FIGURE 1.28

Creating a new custom view.

New Window

Illustrator has a feature in which you can create two different windows that contain the same artwork. It's the same file, but you can view it in two windows. You can, for example, work in Artwork mode in one window and have another, smaller window in Preview mode so that you can see changes as you work.

To use this feature, choose New Window from the Window menu (see Figure 1.29), and a new window opens. Of course, whatever you do in one window automatically happens in the other.

Figure 1.29

Creating a new window.

Another great way to use the New Window feature is if you have two monitors. By set-ting one of the monitors to 256 colors, you can see how your artwork will look if viewed at two different color settings. This capability can be useful when you are designing art for the World Wide Web.

Context-Sensitive Menus

A new feature recently added to Illustrator is context-sensitive menus. From anywhere on the screen, hold down the (Control key)[right mouse button] and click the screen. You get a pop-up list of the most common functions, depending on what you currently have selected (see Figure 1.30).

Figure 1.30

Illustrator's new context-sensitive menus offer you a slew of relevant and useful commands, right where you want them, all at the touch of a key.

Summary

Congratulations! You've spent your first hour in Illustrator. That wasn't so bad now, was it? You learned how Illustrator is different from paint programs such as Photoshop, and you learned all about Illustrator's palettes and tools. In the next hour, you will learn how to customize Illustrator to your needs and tastes, as well as learn how to set up a document to work in.

Workshop

The Workshop contains quiz questions to help you solidify your understanding of the material covered in this hour and exercises to provide you with experience using what you have learned. You can find the answers to the quiz questions at the end of the hour.

Quiz

1. The Navigator palette enables you to do what?
   a. Surf the Web
   b. Quickly scroll and zoom
   c. Find due south on your screen

2. How many floating palettes does Illustrator 8 have?
   a. 6
   b. 11
   c. 18

3. A pixel is
   a. The physical print area of the printer
   b. A figment of your imagination
   c. One dot in a raster image

4. What is the keyboard shortcut to toggle the focus between fill and stroke?
   a. X
   b. F
   c. S

5. A cluster is
   a. Chocolate and caramel with nuts
   b. Several palettes combined in one window
   c. A group of tools in the Toolbox

Exercises

1. Can you remember any of the keyboard shortcuts for the tools in the Illustrator Toolbox? Try switching among tools just by using the keyboard and not the mouse.

2. Practice hiding and showing your palettes. Press the Tab key to hide them all, and press Tab again to bring them back. Use Shift+Tab to hide everything but the Toolbox.

3. Customize your palettes by mixing and combining them. Use the Dock and Cluster features to see how they "stick" to each other and to the edge of the screen.

Term Review

Cross-platform—Term used to describe software that runs on multiple operating systems, such as Mac OS and Windows 98.

Cursor—The icon on your screen that indicates the position of your mouse or selection point.

Floating palettes—Palettes that are always visible (remain in front) even though the Document window is selected.

Focus—The active part of the screen. Because of all the new keyboard shortcuts in version 8, Illustrator might not know when you are entering data in a palette or when you are trying to invoke a keyboard shortcut. By making a palette the active part of your screen—making it the focus—you are telling Illustrator exactly what you plan to do.

Palettes—Small windows that contain settings such as colors or fonts.

Pixel—A square that is the smallest part of an image.

Pixelated—An image enlarged to the point that you can see the individual pixels.

Raster image—A graphic consisting of a collection of dots, or pixels (*see* Pixel).

Vector image—A graphic defined by a scalable, mathematical outline.

Answers to Quiz Questions

1. b
2. c
3. c
4. a
5. b

Hour 2

Customizing Illustrator

When you move into a new house or apartment, you feel a kind of excitement, yet you also feel a bit uncomfortable because everything is new and different to you. Only after you've arranged things the way you like, making adjustments and finding your favorite "spot," do you get that warm comfortable feeling.

The same holds true with Illustrator (although Illustrator is a lot cheaper than a new house). In the beginning, Illustrator might feel foreign—even overwhelming—but as you progress, you will find yourself getting comfortable working in Illustrator. One way to get comfortable is by setting Illustrator's preferences.

In this chapter, you will learn about the following:

- Setting Document Setup options
- Setting Illustrator preferences
- Using guides and grids
- Creating an Illustrator Startup file

Document Setup

The first step in creating a document is setting up the correct page size. Do so by selecting Document Setup from the File menu. You're presented with a dialog box with four sections: Artboard, View, Paths, and Options (see Figure 2.1).

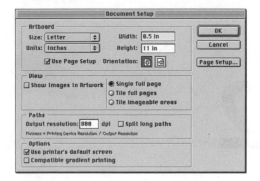

Artboard

In the Artboard section of the Document Setup dialog box, you specify the size of your page. You can choose from the sizes listed in the Size pop-up menu, or you can enter a custom size manually in the Width and Height boxes. Illustrator supports page sizes anywhere from 2×2 inches up to 227.54×227.54 inches. Clicking either Orientation icon swaps the width and height values, so you can quickly change from Portrait (tall) to Landscape (wide) format (see Figure 2.2).

FIGURE 2.2

Simply clicking the Tall or Wide icon automatically swaps the Width and Height settings.

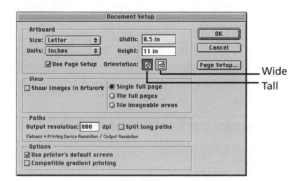

From the Units pop-up menu (see Figure 2.3), you can select any of Illustrator's five supported measurement systems to specify page sizes. If you check the box marked Use Page Setup, Illustrator uses the page size that is currently selected in Page Setup. You can change the setting by clicking the Page Setup button beneath the Cancel button.

FIGURE 2.3

Selecting a measurement system.

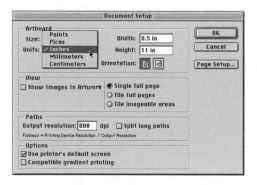

View

The first option in the View section of the Document Setup dialog box is Show Images in Artwork. By enabling this setting, you can view placed images when in Artwork mode. You can always see placed images in Preview mode.

Often, Illustrator is used as a tool to create art that will then be placed into another program for final layout, such as PageMaker or QuarkXPress. In such cases, you don't need to create more than one page. When creating complex layouts and spreads, however, you can set Illustrator to create a number of pages in your document. Unlike other programs, however, Illustrator makes multiple pages in a document by splitting one large page into smaller pseudo-pages. You can select either Single Full Page; Tile Full Pages, which creates the most possible full-sized pages on your *artboard* (see Figure 2.4); or Tile Imageable Areas, for which Illustrator creates tiles to fill the entire artboard (see Figure 2.5).

FIGURE 2.4

Only two 8.5×11-inch pages fit onto this 20×20-inch artboard using the Tile Full Pages option.

FIGURE 2.5

If you use the Tile Imageable Areas option, Illustrator maps out tiles for the entire 20×20-inch art-board.

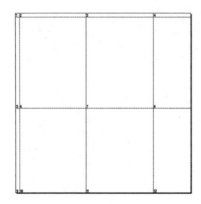

Paths

NEW TERM In the Paths section of the Document Setup dialog box, you can choose a printer resolution, which helps Illustrator determine smooth *gradients* and clean curves. Plus, you have the option Split Long Paths. This means that sometimes paths become very long and complex, filled with many anchor points (*anchor points* are part of a Bézier object, as you will learn in Hour 6, "Drawing Bézier Paths"). When a path has so many points, its complexity can cause problems at print time (see Figure 2.6).

FIGURE 2.6

For demonstration pur-poses, a path with sev-eral hundred unneces-sary anchor points has been created. This image will "choke" on an imagesetter and will not print.

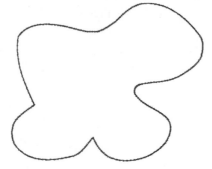

In such cases, to print the file, you can select Split Long Paths to have Illustrator split the one big path into several smaller ones, which makes printing them possible (see Figure 2.7). Always save and keep a copy of your file before you split long paths for future edit-ing purposes; after a path is split, editing it is difficult.

FIGURE 2.7

After selecting Split Long Paths, saving the file, closing it, and reopening the file, you can see how Illustrator splits up the one large object into several smaller ones and, more importantly, makes the file printable.

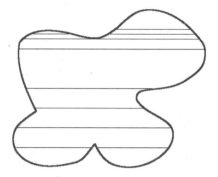

Options

In the Options section of the Document Setup dialog box, you can choose to use the printer's default *line screen* setting or, if you're printing to a PostScript Level 1 device, check the box marked Compatible Gradient and Gradient Mesh Printing. (If you're not sure about this, leave this box unchecked, and if you have problems printing a file, try turning it on.)

You can change any settings that you set in the Document Setup dialog box or those that you will be setting in the Preferences dialog box (coming up next) at any time, even after you've saved the document, closed it, and opened it again. Changes will take effect when you close either dialog box, except for the Split Long Paths option, which takes effect only when you save and close the file, and then reopen it.

Setting Preferences

Okay, so you've decided where all the furniture goes, but you still have more to do. As I've come to realize, the smaller things really make a difference in my daily life. It isn't the bed or the refrigerator that gives that homey feeling; it's the rug on the floor or that cute little end table with the lava lamp on it. It's the pictures and paintings on the walls and the potpourri in the bathroom that create a comfortable, safe feeling.

As you set Illustrator's preferences to your tastes, you will be creating your own little environment—your custom workspace—which enables you to use Illustrator comfortably, as well as conveniently.

Illustrator has seven screens of preferences, all located in the Preferences dialog box, found in the File menu (see Figure 2.8). The seven screens are General, Type & Auto Tracing, Units & Undo, Guides & Grid, Smart Guides, Hyphenation Options, and Plug-ins & Scratch Disk.

FIGURE 2.8

Choosing Preferences from the File menu.

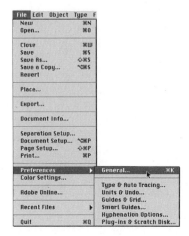

To cycle through each of the seven Preferences screens, you can either select them from the pop-up menu at the top of the Preferences dialog box or you can use the Previous and Next buttons found on the far right of the dialog box (see Figure 2.9).

FIGURE 2.9

Selecting a preference screen from the pop-up menu. Also notice the Previous and Next buttons on the far right.

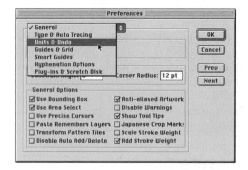

General Preferences

The General Preferences dialog box has three sections: Keyboard Increment, Tool Behavior, and General Options (see Figure 2.10).

Keyboard Increment

NEW TERM The mouse is a nice little gadget, but when you need to position something precisely, controlling it can be a bit difficult. For that reason, Illustrator lets you "nudge" objects by using the arrows on your keyboard. The Cursor Key setting in the Keyboard Increment section of the General Preferences dialog box determines just how much each *nudge* is.

FIGURE 2.10

The General Preferences dialog box.

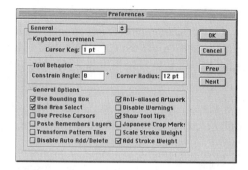

Tool Behavior

Constrain Angle, the first option in the Tool Behavior section of the General Preferences dialog box, is a really cool feature that sets the default angle of your document, which means that if you set the angle to 30 degrees and draw a square while holding the Shift key, the square is drawn on a 30-degree angle. This feature is great for creating 3D drawings, as well as for creating isometric drawings.

You also can set the Corner Radius in the Tool Behavior section; you use it when drawing with the Rounded Rectangle tool. This setting can be overridden when drawing the rectangle (see Hour 3, "Drawing Basic Objects"), and the number here is only the default setting.

General Options

In the General Options section of the General Preferences dialog box, Use Bounding Box refers to the box that appears when you select an object. With this option enabled, you can quickly transform selected objects (such as resizing them or rotating them) in the same way that you can in other popular graphics programs.

Use Area Select enables you to specify how Illustrator selects objects via the selection tools. With this option turned on, you can select objects by clicking anywhere within the object (if it is filled). With this option turned off, you must click the point or border of an object to select it (see Figure 2.11).

FIGURE 2.11

The box on the left is selected with Use Area Select activated, whereas the box on the right is selected with Use Area Select deactivated.

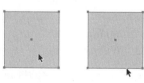

You can choose Use Precise Cursors, which replaces Illustrator's tool cursors with crosshairs, allowing for more precise control. You can toggle this setting to see the standard cursors while working by using the Caps Lock key. If Use Precise Cursors is not checked, then pressing Caps Lock while working changes the cursor to a crosshair cursor.

Paste Remembers Layers keeps layer information intact when you are moving artwork to and from the Clipboard. You can set this option from within the Layers palette as well.

When performing transformations on objects, you can choose to Transform Pattern Tiles as well as the object (see Figure 2.12). Say that you have a square that is filled with a pattern, for example. If you have Transform Pattern Tiles activated and then you rotate the square, the pattern fill rotates as well. But if you have Transform Pattern Tiles turned off, the Rotate function affects the square, but the pattern tiles remain unchanged. This setting is only a default and can be overridden from within a Transformation dialog box.

FIGURE 2.12

The first box is the original item, and the center box has been rotated without Transform Pattern Tiles selected. The third box was rotated with Transform Pattern Tiles selected.

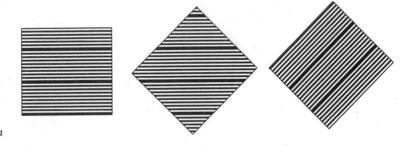

Disable Auto Add/Delete is a preference setting for the Pen tool. As you will see later in Hour 7, "Editing Bézier Paths," Illustrator automatically selects the Add Anchor Point tool or the Delete Anchor Point tool for you at certain times, unless you disable that option here.

With Anti-aliased Artwork turned on, objects appear onscreen with smooth, soft edges. Usually, text appears jagged onscreen because of a computer monitor's low screen resolution (72 dpi). This setting is purely aesthetic and has no bearing when you print your file because all type prints with smooth, sharp edges from your PostScript printer. This capability should not be confused with antialiasing for Web and raster images; you'll learn about that capability in Hour 23, "Web Graphics."

If you've used Illustrator before, you probably have seen those annoying dialog boxes telling you that you can't perform certain operations or functions (which was usually because you clicked just a few pixels too far). Well, enabling Disable Warnings sends those dialog boxes home crying, and Illustrator will then alert you with a simple beep upon encountering any violations.

Did you forget the keyboard shortcut for a tool? Or did you forget which tool was the Scale tool? Illustrator makes remembering easy with ToolTips. When this setting is activated (the default is set with ToolTips on), simply drag your mouse cursor over a tool and wait a second. A teeny box pops up, telling you the name of the tool or function, and it also lists the keystroke command, if one exists.

Japanese Cropmarks are simply a different kind of crop mark, obviously used in Japan.

Scale Stroke Weight determines whether *stroke weights* are scaled when you transform objects. In other words, with Scale Stroke Weight activated, enlarging a box with a 1-point rule to 200 percent results in a box with a 2-point rule. With Scale Stroke Weight turned off, the rule remains at 1 point.

NEW TERM Add Stroke Weight is an option that is reflected in the *Transform* palette. When you choose this option, Illustrator includes the width of a stroke in the size measurement of that object. For example, with the option enabled, a 10-point box with a 1-point rule will register in the Transform palette as a 12-point box.

Type & Auto Tracing

In the Type & Auto Tracing Preferences dialog box, you can refine how some keyboard shortcuts for these controls are implemented (see Figure 2.13). You can enter numerical input by using any of Illustrator's measurement systems.

FIGURE 2.13

The Type & Auto Tracing Preferences dialog box.

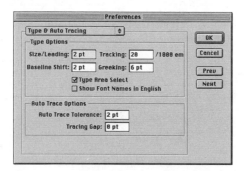

Type Options

In the Type Options section of the Type & Auto Tracing Preferences dialog box, the Size/Leading (pronounced "ledding") option specifies how much *leading* is added or removed from a line of type when you use the leading keyboard shortcut (Option+up arrow and Option+down arrow)[Alt+up arrow and Alt+down arrow].

Baseline Shift specifies the increment when you use the Baseline Shift keyboard shortcut (Option+Shift+up arrow and Option+Shift+down arrow)[Alt+Shift+up arrow and Alt+Shift+down arrow].

The Tracking increment, measured in ems (literally, the width of the letter "M"), determines the amount of *tracking* added or removed when you apply the tracking keyboard shortcut (Option+left arrow, Option+right arrow)[Alt+left arrow, Alt+right arrow].

See Hour 15, "Advanced Typography," to learn more about the three preceding features.

NEW TERM   The Greeking Type Limit sets the size at which text is *greeked*. When small type is rendered onscreen, the computer has to work hard to calculate the letterforms. Because very small type is not readable onscreen anyway, the computer "greeks" the type by simply drawing gray bars where the type should appear (see Figure 2.14). Of course, if you zoom in closer, Illustrator renders the type correctly. Type greeking applies only to the screen; when you are printing, all text appears correctly.

FIGURE 2.14

The three gray bars are greeked text.

Hello There!

How Are you?

Type Area Select is basically the same as Use Area Select, mentioned earlier. You can select type by clicking anywhere within the bounding box of the type (see the following Just a Minute). With Type Area Select turned off, you can select type only by selecting it on the baseline (see Figure 2.15).

FIGURE 2.15

The top word has the type bounding box visible, and clicking anywhere within it with Type Area Select enabled selects the word. The bottom word shows the type's baseline, which you must click to select type if Type Area Select is turned off.

Prefere
Guides & Grid
Guides
Color: Other...
Style: Lines
Grid
Color: Other...
Style: Lines
Gridline every: 1 in
Subdivisions: 8

If you have special multilingual fonts installed, Show Font Names in English does just what its name implies.

> When you are using the Baseline Shift option with type, keep in mind that although you can't see it, the bounding box still takes up all the space, and clicking what might seem like whitespace selects the type. Of course, only the type prints. By the same token, when you are selecting type by the baseline, if a baseline shift was applied, the baseline may be well above or below the type. In these cases, selecting the type when you are in Artwork mode is easiest.

Auto Trace Options

In the Auto Trace Options section of the Type & Auto Tracing dialog box, the Auto Trace Tolerance defines how closely Illustrator traces the object. A lower number produces a tighter path, whereas a higher number produces a smoother, looser path.

The Tracing Gap helps Illustrator determine when two shapes that are close together should be traced as two separate objects. For example, with a high Tracing Gap setting, even if two objects are separated, Illustrator still traces it as one object. This capability is helpful when you are tracing scans that are broken up and are not solid throughout.

Units & Undo

Rather straightforward, the Units & Undo Preferences dialog box contains two sections: Units & Undo and simply Undo (see Figure 2.16).

FIGURE 2.16

The Units & Undo Preferences dialog box.

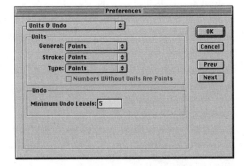

Units & Undo

Illustrator can use five different measurement systems: inches, millimeters, centimeters, picas, and points. In the Units & Undo section of the Units & Undo Preferences dialog box, you can set Illustrator to use any of these measurements.

You can also enter any mathematical function within any of Illustrator's palettes and dialog boxes, and Illustrator does the math for you on the fly. You can also mix measurement systems in dialog boxes. You can, for example, enter 4 in. + 3p2 - 12mm, and Illustrator automatically does the math for you.

You will be doing several exercises later in the chapter, so setting Illustrator's units to Inches for now would be a good idea.

> Here's a tip for Macintosh users: If you're working with one measurement system, and you want to switch quickly to another, press Command+Control+U to toggle through all five measurement systems. This shortcut works directly in the document, so you don't need to open the Preferences dialog box.

Undo

New Term Hey, everyone makes mistakes sometimes, and that's okay because Illustrator has *multiple undos*. Just how many, you ask? Well, the answer depends on how much RAM you have allocated to Illustrator. Illustrator keeps track of as many undos as memory allows, but it never goes below the amount that you set in the Undo section of the Units & Undo Preferences dialog box. Remember, though, the more undos you have, the less RAM Illustrator has for other tasks. Illustrator's default setting is 5, and unless you're working on really large files, I don't recommend using anything higher than 10.

Guides & Grid

An important feature of almost any program, the Guides & Grid Preferences dialog box helps you easily align objects and create perfect layouts and art. Guides are vertical or horizontal lines that you can place anywhere on your page. These guides do not print; they are only visible onscreen. The grid is similar to graph paper—a set of nonprinting boxes that fill your page, making for easier layout. The Guides & Grid Preferences dialog box contains two sections: Guides and Grid (see Figure 2.17).

In this dialog box, you can specify what color guides should be, either by choosing from the pop-up list of predefined colors Illustrator provides or by choosing Other and selecting any other color from the Color Picker. You also have the option of having Illustrator render guides as solid lines or dotted lines.

You have the same options with Illustrator's Grid settings as you have with Guides. You can choose any color that pleases you, as well as specify a solid or dotted line.

Figure 2.17

The Guides & Grid Preferences dialog box.

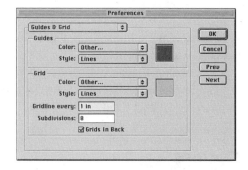

You can also specify how the grid is drawn, with main gridlines at any increment and multiple subdivisions.

Smart Guides

Smart Guides, which are a new feature in version 8, give you visual feedback as you work in Illustrator. The two sections in the Smart Guides Preferences dialog box are Display Options and Angles (see Figure 2.18).

Figure 2.18

The Smart Guides Preferences dialog box.

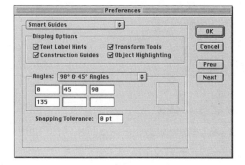

Display Options

In the Display Options section of the Smart Guides Preferences dialog box, you have a choice of telling Illustrator exactly when you want the Smart Guides feature to appear. Text Label Hints identify objects and functions as you work with them. Construction Guides are helpful indicators that appear when you are creating and editing art. Transform Tools help you to move and align objects on the fly, and Object Highlighting helps you determine which object your mouse cursor is over, aiding you in selecting and editing.

Angles

In the Angles section of the Smart Guides Preferences dialog box, you can define exactly at what increments Smart Guides appear by choosing from the pop-up menu or entering any angles in the boxes. The Snapping Tolerance determines how close your cursor is to an angle before the Smart Guides feature is activated. A low number here makes Smart Guides appear less often, whereas a higher number means you'll see them a lot more often.

Hyphenation Options

Rather simple, the Hyphenation Options screen of the Preferences dialog box lets you select a default language, as well as add and delete entries in the dictionary (see Figure 2.19).

FIGURE 2.19

The Hyphenation Options Preferences dialog box.

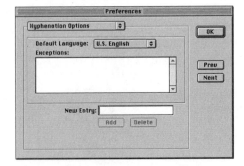

Plug-ins & Scratch Disk

The Plug-ins & Scratch Disk Preferences dialog box (see Figure 2.20) has two sections: Plug-ins Folder and Scratch Disks.

FIGURE 2.20

The Plug-ins & Scratch Disk Preferences dialog box.

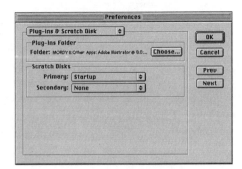

Plug-ins Folder

The Plug-ins folder is the place where Illustrator keeps all its "extensions" or add-ons, including third-party filters and *plug-ins*. Sometimes, Illustrator might "lose touch" with its Plug-ins folder. If this happens, you need to remind Illustrator where to find the Plug-ins folder in the Plug-ins Folder section of the Plug-ins & Scratch Disk Preferences dialog box. You might also want to retain more than one Plug-ins folder, and this dialog box enables you to switch between the two.

To specify the Plug-ins folder, do the following:

1. Select Preferences from the File menu (Command+K)[Control+K].
2. Select Plug-ins & Scratch Disk from the pop-up menu.
3. Click the Choose button to locate the Plug-ins folder.
4. Click OK.
5. Quit and relaunch Illustrator.

Scratch Disks

NEW TERM Those of you familiar with Photoshop are probably familiar with the term *scratch disk*. A scratch disk is like Illustrator's scrap paper, where it temporarily holds data to perform operations. As the default, your scratch disk is your startup drive. When you are working with large files, your scratch disk can fill up rather quickly.

In the Scratch Disks section of the Plug-ins & Scratch Disk Preferences dialog box, Illustrator enables you to specify which disk should be the scratch disk, and it also enables you to specify a secondary scratch disk where Illustrator goes if the primary scratch disk is full. If you have only one hard drive, you can specify a removable disk, such as a Syquest, Jaz, or Zip, to be your secondary scratch disk.

To specify a scratch disk, follow these steps:

1. Select Preferences from the File menu.
2. Select Plug-ins & Scratch Disk from the pop-up menu.
3. Select a primary and a secondary scratch disk.
4. Click OK.

You need to restart Illustrator for both plug-ins and scratch disk information to take effect.

Working with Guides, Smart Guides, and Illustrator's Grid

If you've worked in any page layout program, such as PageMaker or QuarkXPress, you know how important guides are. They help you in laying out and designing pages and aligning objects.

Because guides and the grid are important, I want to leave the preferences alone for a moment and talk about how to use these features in Illustrator. If you have the Preferences dialog box open, close it now because you will be working in Illustrator for a little while.

Rulers

When Illustrator opens, you are presented with a new blank file. Now, turn on your rulers. From the View menu, select Show Rulers (see Figure 2.21). Notice that your rulers appear across the top and left side of your screen. If you set them earlier, they should be set in inches. If not, Mac users can use the keyboard shortcut (Command+Control+U) to toggle over to inches; Windows users have to return to Preferences and choose Inches in the Units & Undo dialog box.

FIGURE 2.21

Turning Illustrator's rulers on. (I still wonder why Adobe doesn't have Illustrator launch with rulers on as a default.)

Creating Guides

You can easily create guides in Illustrator by following these steps:

1. Drag your mouse so that your cursor is directly on the ruler (see Figure 2.22).

2. Press the mouse button and drag the mouse onto the artboard.

3. After you position your guide, release the mouse button.

FIGURE 2.22

Preparing to drag a guide.

In its default setting, guides are always locked. After you place them, you cannot select them, move them, or delete them. To do so, you must unlock the guides by choosing Lock Guides from the View menu or pressing (Command+Option+;)[Control+Alt+;] (see Figure 2.23).

FIGURE 2.23

Choosing Lock Guides toggles between locked and unlocked guides.

You can also turn any Illustrator object (such as a square, a star, or an ellipse) into a guide by simply selecting it and choosing Make Guides from the View menu or pressing (Command+5)[Control+5] (see Figure 2.24). You can return a guide to its original state as an object by selecting it and then choosing Release Guides from the View menu or pressing (Command+Option+5)[Control+Alt+5].

Illustrator's Grid

A recent addition to Illustrator is the Grid feature. Turn on the grid by selecting Show Grid from the View menu (see Figure 2.25). Your screen should now look like a sheet of graph paper. To change how the grid appears, select Guides & Grid from the Preferences submenu, as mentioned before.

Besides helping with layout, Illustrator's grid serves another great purpose. With the grid as the backmost object (which you can set in Preferences), you can quickly tell whether an object is filled with None or white.

FIGURE 2.24

Making an Illustrator object into a guide.

FIGURE 2.25

Turning on Illustrator's grid.

Snap To Grid

The grid is nice, but what makes it powerful is that Illustrator snaps to it. Gridlines act as a kind of magnet, and your mouse "sticks" to them when it gets near them. Sometimes this feature can get annoying, though, so you can turn off the Snap To feature by unchecking Snap To Grid in the View menu (see Figure 2.26).

Now that you've learned how to work with guides and the grid, you can get back to the rest of Illustrator's preferences by selecting Preferences from the File menu or pressing (Command+K)[Control+K]. On with the show!

FIGURE 2.26

The Snap To Grid toggle in the View menu.

Creating an Illustrator Startup File

When you quit Illustrator, it "remembers" the position of the palettes, and the next time you open Illustrator, it looks just like it did when you quit it. All the other settings, such as colors, page size, default typeface, and so on, are defined by a file called the Illustrator startup file, and those settings revert to match the startup file every time you launch Illustrator. Whatever is in this file appears whenever you launch Illustrator.

To create a customized Illustrator startup file, follow these steps:

1. Create a document with whatever settings you want to make the default.
2. Save the file in Illustrator format, and name it `Adobe Illustrator Startup`.
3. Place the file in the Illustrator Plug-ins folder.
4. Restart Illustrator.

Summary

You're learning more and more about Illustrator, and the dust is beginning to settle as you become more familiar with Illustrator's feel and metaphors. In this hour, you learned how to customize Illustrator to fit your needs, and you learned how to set up a file, ready for use, with guides and grids. Next, you will begin learning how to draw simple shapes, using Illustrator's primary drawing tools.

Workshop

The Workshop contains quiz questions to help you solidify your understanding of the material covered in this hour and exercises to provide you with experience using what you have learned. You can find the answers to the quiz questions at the end of the hour.

Quiz

1. What is the keyboard shortcut for Preferences?

    a. (Command+P)[Control+P]

    b. (Command+K)[Control+K]

    c. (Option+K)[Alt+K]

2. The Keyboard Increment setting lets you

    a. Set the nudge amount

    b. Choose different language sets

    c. Fight Carpal Tunnel Syndrome

3. How many screens of preferences are in Illustrator?

    a. 6

    b. 5

    c. 7

4. Smart Guides are

    a. Guides that appear to help you align objects

    b. Guides in the shape of circles

    c. Kinda like laser-guided smart bombs, only a lot cheaper

5. How many measurement systems does Illustrator support?

    a. 4

    b. 5

    c. 6

Exercises

1. Practice changing the nudge setting by pressing (Command+K)[Control+K], entering a number, and then pressing Enter. See how quickly you can change it again and again.

2. Experiment setting up different size pages by using the different Tiling options.

3. Practice creating, moving, locking, and deleting guides and grids.

Term Review

Anchor point—The heart of a Bézier curve. You can find more details on this term in Hour 6, "Drawing Bézier Paths."

Artboard—Illustrator's term for the actual page you work on.

Baseline shift—Typographical term for the vertical movement of text relative to the base.

Gradient—An attribute referring to the blending of colors into each other.

Greeked type—Gray lines used to substitute for small type onscreen.

Line screen—Printing term referring to the number of dots per inch.

Nudge—The act of moving a selection incrementally using the keyboard arrow keys.

Leading—Typographical term for the space between lines of text.

Multiple undos—An undo is the act of deleting the last thing you did, as if it never happened (something everyone needs in real life). Multiple undos means that you can go back several steps.

Plug-ins—Adobe or third-party add-ons or extra features for Illustrator. Extensis VectorTools is an example of a set of plug-ins.

Scratch disk—A temporary area on your hard drive that Illustrator uses to calculate operations.

Stroke weight—The stroke is the outline of a shape, and the weight refers to the thickness of the outline.

Tracking—Typographical term for the addition or removal of space between letters.

Transform—A function, such as scaling, rotating, or moving, performed on an object.

Answers to Quiz Questions

1. b
2. a
3. c
4. a
5. b

Hour **3**

Drawing Basic Objects

Now the fun begins: You actually start drawing something. You will start with the easy shapes, such as rectangles and ovals, and move up to polygons, stars, and spirals. One of the great things about Illustrator is that you usually can accomplish the same thing in more than one way. As you progress, you will get a feel for using different techniques and determining when one might be better in certain situations than another.

Specifically, this hour covers the following topics:

- Drawing rectangles
- Drawing ellipses
- Drawing polygons, stars, and spirals
- Saving your work

Probably the most important thing about Illustrator—let me correct myself—*one* of the most important things about Illustrator is the modifier keys—Shift, (Option)[Alt], and (Command)[Control]. Using combinations of these keys when you are drawing with the mouse controls different options. It's important that you become familiar with these key combinations to the point where they become second nature, and you don't even think about them. You just do it.

Working with Rectangles and Ellipses

The most primitive shapes, rectangles, and ellipses are also the easiest shapes to create in Illustrator. You can draw these shapes in several different ways, each a slight variant of the other, and as you work more in Illustrator, you'll get a better feel for when to use each method.

As you learned in the first hour, Illustrator is a vector art program. A vector rectangle or ellipse consists of three elements: a starting point, an ending point, and a center point. You define the start and end points, and Illustrator calculates the center point for you automatically. As the saying goes, the best way to learn is to do it yourself, so get ready to draw.

Drawing Rectangles

Start by drawing a rectangle as shown here:

1. Select the Rectangle tool (see Figure 3.1). Notice your cursor becomes a crosshair (see Figure 3.2).

FIGURE 3.1

The Rectangle tool.

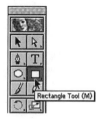

FIGURE 3.2

The Rectangle tool's cursor.

2. Position your cursor to the place where you want the upper-left corner of the rectangle.

3. Press and hold the mouse button, and drag down and to the right (see Figure 3.3). Do not let go of the mouse button until the end of this exercise.

FIGURE 3.3

Dragging to draw a rectangle.

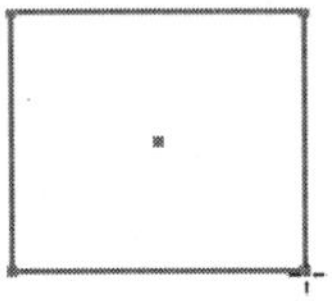

4. Hold the Shift key while dragging, and Illustrator forces your box, or *constrains* it, to be a perfect square—with even lengths on all sides.

5. Press and hold the Option button while dragging, and Illustrator draws your shape out from the center, as opposed to from the upper-left corner.

6. Press and hold the Spacebar while dragging, and Illustrator "freezes" the state of the shape you are drawing. While you're still dragging the mouse, you can position the shape you're drawing anywhere on the screen. Release the Spacebar to continue changing the shape of your rectangle.

7. Release the mouse button. You have now drawn your first shape.

In Illustrator, the Shift key is almost always the constrain key. Using it often takes the guesswork out of creating and manipulating your illustrations, as Illustrator does the work for you.

Using the Rounded Rectangle Tool

A rounded rectangle is one in which the corners don't come to a point but are rounded. Now that you've drawn a regular rectangle, you can draw a rounded rectangle as follows:

1. Select the Rounded Rectangle tool (see Figure 3.4).

2. Position your cursor to the place where you want the upper-left corner of the rounded rectangle.

3. Press and hold the mouse button, and drag down and to the right (see Figure 3.5). Do not release the mouse button until the end of this exercise.

FIGURE 3.4

*The Rounded
Rectangle tool.*

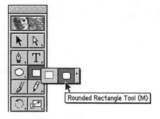

FIGURE 3.5

*Dragging to draw a
rounded rectangle.*

4. Hold the Shift key while dragging, and Illustrator constrains the rounded rectangle to be the same length on all sides.

5. Press and hold the Option button while dragging, and Illustrator draws your shape out from the center, as opposed to from the upper-left corner.

6. Press and hold the Spacebar while dragging, and Illustrator "freezes" the state of the shape you are drawing. While you are still dragging the mouse, you can position the shape you're drawing anywhere on the screen. Release the Spacebar to continue changing the shape of your rounded rectangle.

7. Release the mouse button.

 NEW TERM   To change the *corner radius* of the rounded rectangle (how rounded the corners are), see "Drawing Rectangles Numerically," next.

> If you have the Rectangle tool selected, and you want to draw a box out from the center, hold down the (Option)[Alt] key before dragging. See how your cursor changes between the regular and centered crosshairs.

Drawing Rectangles Numerically

The previously mentioned ways of drawing a box are great when you want to draw something freely, but often you need to create a rectangle or square with exact proportions. You can do so as follows:

1. Select the Rectangle or Rounded Rectangle tool.
2. Click once anywhere on the screen, and let go of the mouse button. Illustrator opens the Rectangle dialog box (see Figure 3.6).

FIGURE 3.6
The dialog box for drawing a rounded rectangle numerically.

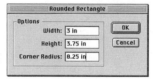

3. Enter the width and height (and corner radius if necessary); then click OK.

If you click while holding the (Option)[Alt] key, Illustrator places the center of the rectangle where you clicked. If not, Illustrator makes the spot you click the upper-left corner of the rectangle.

Ellipses

Ellipses (also known as ovals or circles) are slightly different from the rectangles you've been drawing. Whereas a rectangle is made up of four straight line segments, an ellipse is made up of four curved segments. In Hour 6, "Drawing Bézier Paths," I'll talk in more detail about straight and curved segments. Actually, drawing an ellipse in Illustrator is similar to drawing a rectangle.

To draw an ellipse, follow these steps:

1. Select the Ellipse tool (see Figure 3.7). Notice that your cursor becomes a crosshair (see Figure 3.8).

FIGURE 3.7
The Ellipse tool.

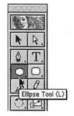

FIGURE 3.8
The cursor for the Ellipse tool.

2. Position your cursor to the place where you want the upper-left edge of the ellipse.

3. Press and hold the mouse button, and drag down and to the right (see Figure 3.9). Do not let go of the mouse button until the end of this exercise.

FIGURE 3.9

Dragging to draw an ellipse.

4. Press and hold the Shift key while dragging, and Illustrator constrains the ellipse to be a perfect circle.

5. Press and hold the Option button while dragging, and Illustrator draws your ellipse out from the center, as opposed to from the upper-left corner.

6. Press and hold the Spacebar while dragging, and Illustrator "freezes" the state of the shape you are drawing. While you are still dragging the mouse, you can position the shape you're drawing anywhere on the screen. Release the Spacebar to continue changing the shape of your ellipse.

7. Release the mouse button.

Drawing an Ellipse Numerically

As with the rectangles, you can create an ellipse numerically. You can do so as follows:

1. Select the Ellipse tool.

2. Click once anywhere on the screen, and let go of the mouse button. Illustrator opens the Ellipse dialog box (see Figure 3.10).

FIGURE 3.10

Creating an ellipse numerically.

3. Enter the width and height; then click OK.

If you click while holding the (Option)[Alt] key, Illustrator places the center of the circle where you clicked. If not, Illustrator makes the spot you click the upper-left of the circle.

Now that you can draw primitive shapes such as rectangles and ovals, you're ready to move on to drawing more complex shapes. Of course, after you create a shape in Illustrator, you can edit it in all sorts of ways. You get to editing and transformations in Hours 7, "Editing Bézier Paths," and 13, "Transformations."

Drawing Other Shapes

NEW TERM The next three creation tools—the Polygon tool, the Star tool, and the Spiral tool—are really cool. They first appeared in Illustrator 6 as plug-in tools, in their own little palette. Now they are fully integrated into the interface (grouped with the Ellipse tool in the Toolbox), with all their coolness intact. These *interactive tools* create complex shapes in a fraction of the time it would take to draw them manually.

The Polygon Tool

The Polygon tool is used to create shapes such as triangles, pentagons, and octagons (for those of you who like making stop signs). Here's how to get started with this tool:

1. Select the Polygon tool (see Figure 3.11).

FIGURE 3.11

The Polygon tool.

2. Because the Polygon tool always draws out from the center, press and hold the mouse button and drag outward (see Figure 3.12). Do not let go of the mouse button until the last step of this exercise.

FIGURE 3.12

Dragging to draw a polygon.

3. Rotate the polygon by moving your mouse in a circular motion (see Figure 3.13).

FIGURE 3.13

Rotating the polygon in real-time as you're creating it.

4. Add more sides to the polygon by pressing the up-arrow key on your keyboard (see Figure 3.14). If you hold the key down, it adds sides repeatedly.

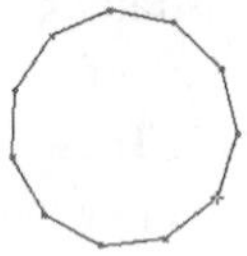

FIGURE 3.14

Adding sides to your polygon.

5. Remove sides from the polygon by pressing the down-arrow key on your keyboard (see Figure 3.15). Holding the key removes sides repeatedly.

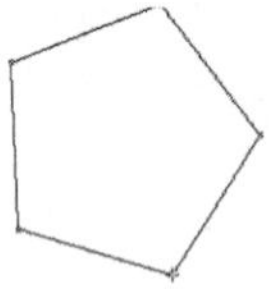

FIGURE 3.15

Removing sides from your polygon.

6. To keep the polygon straight (constrained at 90° or whatever the Constrain Angle is set to in Preferences), press the Shift key.

7. Press the Spacebar, and the polygon "freezes," enabling you to move the mouse and position the polygon on the page.

8. Press the tilde key (~) to create duplicates of the polygon as you drag and move it.

9. Release the mouse button.

You can use any combination of the modifier keys simultaneously as you create your polygon.

Creating a Polygon Numerically

You can also create a polygon numerically. Just follow these steps:

1. Select the Polygon tool.

2. Click the mouse button once, anywhere on the screen. Illustrator opens the Polygon dialog box (see Figure 3.16).

FIGURE 3.16

Creating a polygon numerically.

3. Enter the radius size and the number of sides.

4. Click OK.

The Star Tool

The Star tool is one of the great timesavers. Creating stars and starbursts used to be a real drag. Now it really is just a drag!

1. Select the Star tool (see Figure 3.17).

FIGURE 3.17

The Star tool.

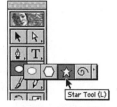

2. Because stars are always drawn from the center, press and hold the mouse button and drag outward (see Figure 3.18). Do not let go of the mouse button until the end of this exercise.

FIGURE 3.18

Dragging to create a star.

3. Rotate the star as you are dragging it by moving the mouse in a circular motion (see Figure 3.19).

FIGURE 3.19

Rotating the star in real-time, as you draw it.

4. Press the up-arrow key to add points to the star (see Figure 3.20).

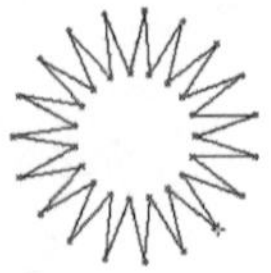

FIGURE 3.20

Adding points to your star.

5. Press the down-arrow key to remove points from the star (see Figure 3.21).

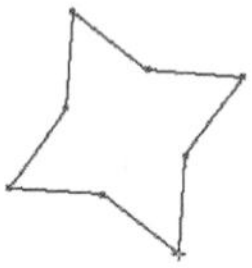

FIGURE 3.21

Removing points from your star.

6. Press the Shift key to keep the star straight and aligned with the baseline.

7. Press the (Option)[Alt] key to align the segments on either side of each point of the star—the point's shoulders—with each other so that they form a straight line (see Figure 3.22).

FIGURE 3.22

Aligning the shoulders on your star.

8. Press the (Command)[Control] key to adjust the inner radius of the star (see Figure 3.23). This step controls how "pointy" the star is.

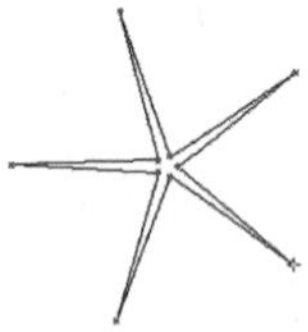

FIGURE 3.23

Changing the inner and outer radius with the (Command) [Control] key.

9. Press and hold the Spacebar to "freeze" the star, and position it on the page.

10. Press the tilde (~) key to make numerous copies of your star as you drag (see Figure 3.24).

FIGURE 3.24

This figure was created by holding down the Option, Shift, Spacebar, and tilde keys simultaneously while dragging the mouse.

You can use any combination of the modifier keys simultaneously as you create your star.

Creating a Star Numerically

You can also create a star numerically by following these steps:

1. Select the Star tool.
2. Click the mouse once, anywhere on the screen, and release the button to open the Star dialog box, as shown in Figure 3.25.

FIGURE 3.25

Drawing a star numerically.

3. Enter values for the outer and inner radius (Radius 1 and 2, respectively) and the number of points. The outer radius, Radius 1, is the place where the points facing outward extend to, whereas the inner radius, Radius 2, is the place where the points facing inward extend to.
4. Click OK.

The Spiral Tool

At one time, drawing spirals was very difficult, but it's easy now, thanks to the Spiral tool. By simply clicking and dragging, you can create interesting spirals while controlling the number of winds (how many times it goes around) and attributes, such as whether the spiral goes clockwise or counterclockwise. Do not confuse the Spiral tool with the Twirl tool, which looks similar. I'll cover the Twirl tool (and accompanying filter) later in Hour 17, "Vector Filters."

Follow these steps to use the Spiral tool:

1. Select the Spiral tool (see Figure 3.26).

FIGURE 3.26

The Spiral tool.

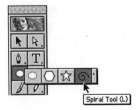

2. Because spirals are always drawn from the center, press and hold the mouse button and drag outward (see Figure 3.27). Do not let go of the mouse button until the end of this exercise.

FIGURE 3.27

Dragging to create a spiral.

3. Rotate the spiral as you are dragging it by moving the mouse in a circular motion (see Figure 3.28).

FIGURE 3.28

Rotating the spiral as you draw.

4. Press the up-arrow key to add segments (or winds) to the spiral (see Figure 3.29).

FIGURE 3.29

Adding segments to your spiral.

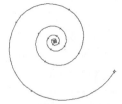

5. Press the down-arrow key to remove segments from the spiral (see Figure 3.30).

FIGURE 3.30

Removing segments from your spiral.

6. Press the Shift key to constrain the rotation of the spiral to 45-degree increments.

7. Press the (Option)[Alt] key to control the style of the spiral. This action determines whether the winds go clockwise or counterclockwise.

8. Press the (Command)[Control] key to adjust the decay of the spiral (see Figure 3.31). This step controls how tightly the spiral winds.

FIGURE 3.31

Adjusting the decay of the spiral with the (Command)[Control] key.

9. Press and hold the Spacebar to "freeze" the spiral, and position it on the page.

10. Press the tilde (~) key to make numerous copies of your spiral as you drag (see Figure 3.32).

FIGURE 3.32

Many spirals can look like waves.

You can use any combination of the modifier keys simultaneously as you create your spiral.

Creating a Spiral Numerically

You can also create a spiral numerically by following these steps:

1. Select the Spiral tool.

2. Click the mouse and release the button to open the Spiral dialog box, as shown in Figure 3.33.

FIGURE 3.33

*Creating a spiral
numerically.*

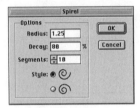

3. Enter values for the radius, decay, and segments, and choose a style (clockwise or counterclockwise).

4. Click OK.

Saving Your Work

No doubt, after this lesson, you have created a masterpiece that you want to keep forever, so be sure to save your work. Here's how:

1. Choose Save from the File menu.

2. Select a location for your file.

3. Give the file a name and click OK.

You just learned to save a file. The very nature of a computer is to crash when you least expect it to, and when you are relying on it most. So, it's a good idea to get into the habit of saving your files frequently and keeping backups of them in case you lose them or they become corrupt.

Summary

After this hour, your feet are definitely wet, as you learned to draw simple shapes. You created polygons, stars, and spirals, and you learned about the power of using the modifier keys as you draw. Next, you'll learn to edit and manipulate the shapes you created today.

Workshop

The Workshop contains quiz questions to help you solidify your understanding of the material covered in this hour and exercises to provide you with experience using what you have learned. You can find the answers to the quiz questions at the end of the hour.

Quiz

1. Holding down the (Option)[Alt] key while drawing a shape
   a. Constrains it
   b. Draws it out from the center
   c. "Freezes" it to allow for repositioning

2. Holding down the Spacebar while drawing a shape
   a. Constrains it
   b. Draws it out from the center
   c. "Freezes" it to allow for repositioning

3. Holding down the Shift key while drawing a shape
   a. Constrains it
   b. Draws it out from the center
   c. "Freezes" it to allow for repositioning

4. When you are using the Star tool, pressing the up-arrow key does what?
   a. Adds points
   b. Removes points
   c. Makes duplicates

5. You can rotate a rectangle as you are drawing it.
   a. True
   b. False

Exercises

1. The keyboard shortcuts for the Rectangle and Ellipse tools are M and L, respectively. Practice drawing rectangles, squares, ovals, and circles without going back to the toolbar; use only the keyboard shortcuts.

2. Get comfortable using the modifier keys while drawing your shapes. Keep your left hand over the bottom-left part of the keyboard while holding the mouse in your right hand.

3. See how many modifier keys you can use at one time while drawing a star. Can you use the Shift, Option, Command, Spacebar, and tilde keys all at once while dragging? It's like playing Twister with your fingers!

Term Review

Corner radius—The amount of curve at the corners of a rounded rectangle.

Interactive tools—Tools that let you change options on-the-fly as you are drawing with them.

Modifier keys—The Shift, Control, (Option)[Alt], and (Command)[Control] keys found on your keyboard.

Answers to Quiz Questions

1. b
2. c
3. a
4. a
5. b

Hour 4

Working with Selections

Besides actually drawing your illustration, the most important things to master in Illustrator are the selection tools. Please allow me to explain. Illustrator can do lots of things, but it has to know where and when to do them. For example, say you have a picture of a face. If you want to make the eyes smaller, you have to select the eyes before you perform the transformation; otherwise, Illustrator scales the whole face. By selecting only certain objects, or even just certain parts of an object, you can tell Illustrator exactly what you want it to do and, more important, have complete control over your illustration (see Figure 4.1).

In this hour, you'll learn all about selecting objects, including the following:

- Using the selection tools
- Grouping objects
- Locking and hiding objects
- Arranging objects

FIGURE 4.1

The image on the left is the original. You see the image in the middle when you scale the entire illustration, and the image on the right just has the eyes reduced.

The Selection Tools

The three selection tools in Illustrator are the Selection tool, the Direct Selection tool, and the Group Selection tool. In this hour, you'll learn about each of them in detail, as well as learn how to use each of them effectively.

Before you begin, however, I'd like to take you back to a topic covered in Hour 2, "Customizing Illustrator." One of the settings in General Preferences was Use Bounding Box. To avoid confusion in the beginning of this hour, open the Preferences dialog box by pressing (Command+K)[Control+K], and turn off the Use Bounding Box option. Later in this hour, you'll turn it back on to see the difference.

The Selection Tool

The Selection tool (or the black arrow, as it is most commonly called because of its appearance) is used to select entire objects (see Figure 4.2). You select an object simply by clicking it (see the section "Area Select," later in this hour). After an object is selected, you can move it by clicking the mouse button and dragging the object.

FIGURE 4.2

The Selection tool, also referred to as the black arrow.

Why don't you give the Selection tool a whirl right now? Make sure you have Illustrator open, and if you don't already have an empty file opened, select New from the File menu or press (Command+N)[Control+N] (see Figure 4.3).

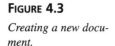

FIGURE 4.3

Creating a new document.

Follow these steps to practice using the Selection tool:

1. Press D to set your colors to the default setting of a white fill and a black stroke. Don't worry about the details right now; you'll learn about fills and strokes in Hours 10, "Fills," and 11, "Strokes."

2. Draw several rectangles on your page (see Figure 4.4).

3. After you draw the last rectangle, choose the Selection tool from the Toolbox.

4. Click any rectangle. Notice that the object is now selected (see Figure 4.5). You can see the four anchor points of the rectangle, and its Bézier path is highlighted in light blue. (When I discuss layers in the next hour, I'll talk more about what color selected objects are.)

5. Now that the rectangle is selected, click and drag the rectangle to move it to a new position (see Figure 4.6). Release the mouse button after you have moved the rectangle to its new home.

6. Deselect the rectangle by clicking any blank space on the page.

Now select and move more than one object at a time:

1. Click any rectangle to select it.

2. Press and hold down the Shift key.

3. Click another rectangle to add it to your selection (see Figure 4.7).

FIGURE 4.4

Your screen should look something like this.

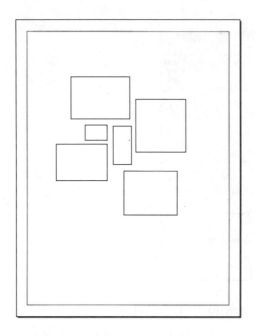

FIGURE 4.5

The selected rectangle.

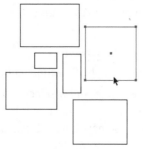

FIGURE 4.6

Dragging the rectangle to move it.

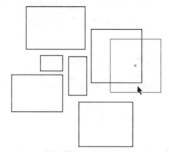

FIGURE **4.7**

With the first rectangle still selected, clicking the second rectangle while pressing the Shift key adds the second rectangle to your selection.

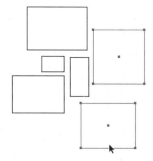

4. Click and drag one of the rectangles. You'll see that both selected rectangles move together (see Figure 4.8).

FIGURE **4.8**

Moving both rectangles simultaneously.

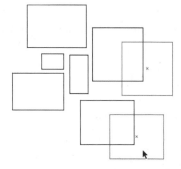

4

5. Deselect the rectangles by pressing (Command+Shift+A)[Control+Shift+A], or by clicking any blank space on the page.

The Shift key is actually a toggle that adds or subtracts from your selection. In the preceding example, you selected rectangle number one and then selected rectangle number two while holding down the Shift key. Now, with both rectangles selected, if you were to Shift+select rectangle number two again, it would become deselected (go ahead and try it). The Shift key makes an unselected item selected, or a selected item unselected.

The Shift key technique can really save time when you're making certain selections, too, as in the following exercise, where you will select all the rectangles except for the one in the middle. From what you've learned until now, you would Shift+select each rectangle until all were selected except the one in the center. Depending on how many rectangles you have, that approach could be a lot of work! However, you can do it in two easy steps:

1. Using the same rectangles as in the preceding exercise, press (Command+A)[Control+A] to select all.

2. Hold down the Shift button and, using the Selection tool, click the center rectangle.

Sure, this trick may not seem like such a big deal now, when you have just a few rectangles on your page, but imagine if you had 50 or even 100 rectangles. Imagine how much time you would save then.

You can select objects in yet another way. This one is called the *marquee* method, which defines a selection by drawing a bounding box around what you want selected. Anything that falls within the bounding box becomes selected. For this example, continue to work on the same file with all the rectangles, as I am becoming rather fond of them.

1. Click any blank area onscreen, or press (Command+Shift+A)[Control+Shift+A] to make sure that nothing is selected.

2. Position your mouse cursor to the upper left of the object(s) you want to select (see Figure 4.9).

FIGURE 4.9

Position the mouse cursor to begin the marquee.

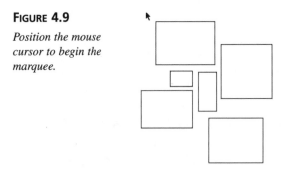

3. Press and drag the mouse down and to the right. As you drag, a dotted line appears (see Figure 4.10). Any object that falls within this "bounding box" is selected. If you have multiple objects, you do not need to hold down the Shift key.

FIGURE 4.10

Defining the marquee.

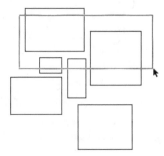

4. Release the mouse button, and the objects are selected (see Figure 4.11).

FIGURE 4.11

The selected objects.

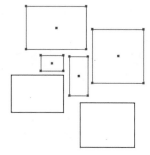

Sometimes, using the marquee method saves a lot of time, as in the case presented earlier in which you select all rectangles except for the middle one. You can marquee-select all the rectangles and then Shift+click the center one to deselect it. This trick is especially useful when you're working on one portion of a page, where using (Command+A) [Control+A] would select other unwanted objects.

Okay, go back into General Preferences (by pressing (Command+K)[Control+K]), and turn on the Use Bounding Box option. Click OK, go back to the rectangles, and select one of them. Notice that a "bounding box" appears around the rectangle, with square "handles" at the corners and also along the top and the sides (see Figure 4.12).

4

FIGURE 4.12

*A rectangle selected
with the Use Bounding
Box option turned on.*

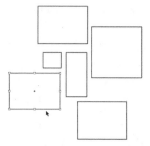

Now you can move and resize these rectangles as follows:

1. To move the selected rectangle, click and drag from the center of the rectangle, or click and drag from the edge of the rectangle, but not from one of the handles.

2. While holding down the Shift key, select another rectangle, and the bounding box grows to include both rectangles (see Figure 4.13).

FIGURE 4.13

Two rectangles are now selected.

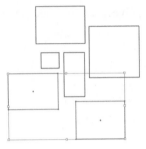

3. Click and drag on one of the handles. As you drag, Illustrator resizes the rectangles (see Figure 4.14).

FIGURE 4.14

Resizing both rectangles.

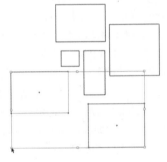

4. Hold down the Shift key after you start dragging, and the objects will scale in proportion to their original sizes.

Some people prefer to have the Use Bounding Box option turned on, and others feel it gets in the way. In truth, Adobe included this functionality only because some other illustration programs have it, and some users had asked for it. (That's right; Adobe actually *does* listen to your suggestions.) I'll leave the decision whether to leave it on or not up to you, okay?

The Direct Selection Tool

NEW TERM The *Direct Selection tool*, or as I like to call it, the white arrow, is the selection tool used the most in Illustrator (see Figure 4.15). In a few moments, you will see why. As you just learned, the black arrow is used to select entire objects. The white arrow, on the other hand, is used to select parts of an object. Although you can move only an entire object with the black arrow, the white arrow enables you to move parts of an object individually.

FIGURE 4.15

*The Direct Selection
tool, also referred to as
the white arrow.*

Now go back to the file with all the rectangles, and try to move a single point:

1. Click any blank area on the screen, or press (Command+Shift+A)
   [Control+Shift+A] to make sure that nothing is selected.

2. Choose the Direct Selection tool from the Toolbox.

3. Carefully select the lower-right corner of one of the rectangles (see Figure 4.16).

FIGURE 4.16

*When you select just
one corner, notice that
the selected point you
clicked is solid, where-
as the other, unselected
points are hollow.*

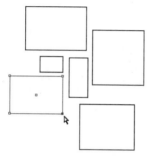

4. Press and drag down and to the right. Notice that only the point that you selected is
   moving; the rest of the object stands still (see Figure 4.17). Release the mouse
   button.

FIGURE 4.17

*Moving part of an
object.*

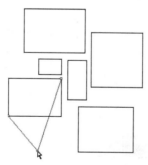

Try something a little different now, and move a single line segment:

1. Carefully move your mouse cursor right over the edge of one of the rectangles (see
   Figure 4.18).

FIGURE 4.18

Selecting just one of the rectangle's line segments.

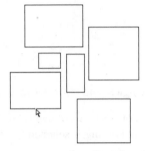

2. Press and drag outward (see Figure 4.19). Notice how just the one side moves.

FIGURE 4.19

Moving the line is really like moving two points with one click.

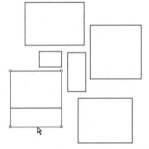

3. Press and hold the Shift key as you drag to constrain your move to 45° angles.

You're doing great! You can apply what you've learned up to now and move multiple points:

1. Click and select one of the corners (anchor points) of a rectangle.

2. Hold down the Shift key, and click the anchor point directly opposite that point (see Figure 4.20).

FIGURE 4.20

Using Shift+click to add anchor points to the selection.

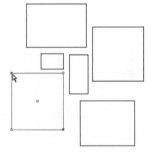

3. Click and drag one of the points. Because both points are selected, they both move as you drag (see Figure 4.21).

FIGURE 4.21

Moving both selected points.

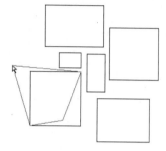

4. Release the mouse button.

Marquee selecting works here as well. Try it:

1. Deselect any objects by pressing (Command+Shift+A)[Control+Shift+A].

2. Marquee-select the bottom two points of a rectangle (see Figure 4.22).

FIGURE 4.22

Marquee-selecting multiple anchor points.

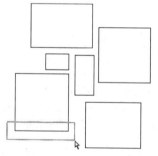

4

3. Press and drag on one of the points.

Now that you are familiar with the black and white arrows, you can go on to grouping objects, where you'll learn about the Group Selection tool, which is a variation of the white arrow. I mentioned before that the white arrow is the most used selection tool in Illustrator, and if you hang in there just a few more minutes, you'll see the light.

Grouping Objects

Now for a little fun! Create a new document by choosing New from the File menu. Draw 10 rectangles randomly on the screen. Then draw 10 circles (see Figure 4.23). Okay, now imagine you are showing this incredible work of art to your boss. I can just hear your boss say it now: "That's not what I wanted! I want you to shift all the circles over one inch to the left!"

FIGURE 4.23

Picasso would be proud.

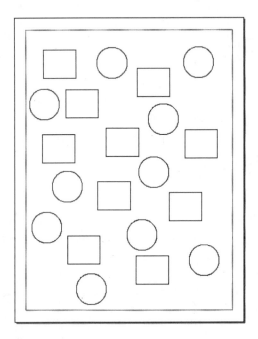

Your boss leaves in a huff, and now you must make a change. So you begin the wonderful chore of moving each circle one inch to the left—a time-consuming task, I assure you. So what do you do? I was hoping you would ask that question....

1. Using the black arrow, select one circle (see Figure 4.24).

2. While holding down the Shift key, click and select the rest of the circles (see Figure 4.25).

3. Choose Group from the Object menu (see Figure 4.26).

FIGURE 4.24

Selecting the first circle.

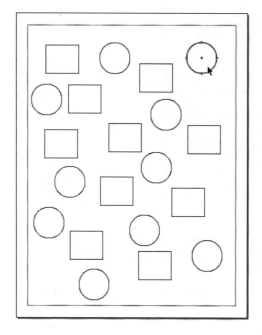

FIGURE 4.25

Selecting the remaining circles while holding the Shift key.

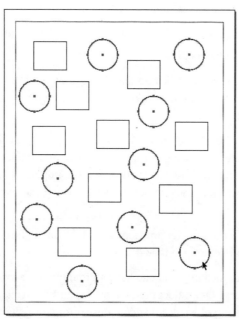

4

FIGURE **4.26**

*Choosing Group from
the Object menu.*

NEW TERM You've just created a *group*. To see what you've actually done, deselect everything by pressing (Command+Shift+A)[Control+Shift+A] and then, using the
black arrow, select just one of the circles. You'll be pleasantly surprised to see that all the
circles have now become selected. Now you can easily move all the circles together. In
fact, because you're anticipating even more changes from your favorite boss, grouping
the rectangles as well might be a good idea. However, before you begin selecting all the
rectangles, I think I feel another step-by-step coming on:

1. Choose Select All from the Edit menu, or press (Command+A)[Control+A].

2. While holding down the Shift key, click a circle.

All the rectangles are selected. Because the circles are a group, deselecting one of them
deselects all of them. Now would be a good time to group the rectangles by pressing
(Command+G)[Control+G].

Groups are extremely helpful when you are working in complex documents, and grouping items as you create them is a good idea. After you create a logo, for instance, group
it. This way, you can move it around easily, and more important, you won't accidentally
lose parts by trying to select each and every piece, every time (inevitably, you'll forget
one or two).

To break up a group, choose Ungroup from the Object menu (see Figure 4.27), or press
(Command+Shift+G)[Control+Shift+G].

Groups can be nested, meaning you can have a group within a group, and so on. To better demonstrate the next tool, select both the circles and the rectangles and group them.
You now have one group of shapes that contains a group of rectangles and a group of circles.

FIGURE 4.27

*Choosing Ungroup
from the Object menu.*

The Group Selection Tool

NEW TERM The *Group Selection tool* is a variation of the Direct Selection tool (the white arrow). You can find it by pressing and holding the mouse button on the white arrow in the Toolbox. In complex illustrations, you might have nested groups that contain many groups. The Group Selection tool makes working with these files easy. To demonstrate, follow these steps working in the same file as you did earlier with all the rectangles and circles:

1. Deselect everything by pressing (Command+Shift+A)[Control+Shift+A].

2. Using the Group Selection tool, click one of the circles. Only the circle you clicked becomes selected.

3. Click that same circle again. All the circles are now selected.

4. Click that same circle again, and all the rectangles become selected as well.

Each time you click with the Group Selection tool, it selects the next higher group, giving you easy access to any group within a nested group.

I promised earlier to tell you why the white arrow is so important in Illustrator. Switch back to the Direct Selection tool by selecting it from the Toolbox. Now press and hold down the (Option)[Alt] key. Notice that the Direct Selection tool changes to the Group Selection tool. Releasing the (Option)[Alt] key returns you to the Direct Selection tool. Now you have the power to select parts of an object, or simply by holding down the (Option)[Alt] key, you can select an entire object or entire groups. For 90 percent of your work, you never have to go back to the black arrow.

Working with Selections

You can already see that selecting objects can become complicated. Now you will learn how Illustrator can help you select objects with certain settings and functions.

Area Select

I briefly mentioned Area Select in Hour 2, "Customizing Illustrator." In Illustrator's General Preferences, you have the option of activating Area Select, which makes selecting objects easier. (By default, Area Select is turned on.)

With Area Select turned on, you can select filled objects by clicking anywhere within the object. When Area Select is turned off, you must click an anchor point or the Bézier path of an object to select it (see Figure 4.28). An object filled with the None attribute is considered unfilled and can be selected only by clicking its Bézier path.

FIGURE 4.28

The box on the left is selected with Area Select activated, whereas the box on the right is selected with Area Select deactivated.

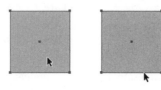

NEW TERM   Area Select works only in Preview mode. When you're working in Artwork mode, you must click an object's Bézier path (or *center point*—see the following sidebar) to select it.

Another option, called Type Area Select, is covered in Hour 14, "Adding Text." Similar to Area Select, Type Area Select enables you to select type by clicking anywhere on the text.

JOURNEY TO THE CENTER OF THE VECTOR

One of the characteristics of PostScript art is that each object has a center point. When you select an object or view a page in Artwork mode, you can usually see an object's center point. Illustrator has the capability to show or hide the center point of any object via the Attributes palette (see Figure 4.29). Simply click the Don't Show Center or the Show Center button. When Snap-To-Point is turned on, using the center point of an object can be a big timesaver and also make for easier alignment of objects.

FIGURE 4.29

By clicking the center point buttons, you can have Illustrator display or hide an object's center point.

Locking Objects

Illustrator enables you to lock items. Locked items cannot be selected, moved, or edited until they are unlocked. This feature is important when files get complex, and you don't want to accidentally select objects you are not working on. Sometimes several objects are very close to one another (or even overlaying), so selecting the right one can be very difficult. By locking items that are not being edited, you can quickly select and edit the correct objects.

To use the lock and unlock feature, select an object and then choose Lock from the Object menu (see Figure 4.30), or press (Command+2)[Control+2]. You can lock several objects at a time, or you can keep locking items separately. To unlock all your locked items, choose Unlock All from the Object menu, or press (Command+Option+2) [Control+Alt+2].

4

FIGURE 4.30

Choosing Lock from the Object menu.

Hiding Selections

If locking items won't do the trick, Illustrator also lets you hide objects from view. This capability has several uses. When you're working on one section of a complex file, hiding other parts makes it easier to concentrate on what you are working on, as well as makes it easier for you to view what you are drawing onscreen. Even more important, hiding certain objects can give you a big speed boost. Placed images, objects filled with gradients or patterns, and other such items can severely slow down your screen redraw. If seeing those items is not critical to what you are working on, you can choose to hide those items, saving Illustrator from having to constantly redraw them.

To hide a selection, choose Hide Selection from the Object menu (see Figure 4.31), or press (Command+3)[Control+3]. You can keep hiding objects as often as you like, individually or in groups, but when you choose Show All from the Object menu or press (Command+Option+3)[Control+Alt+3], all hidden objects become visible. You cannot reveal only certain hidden objects.

FIGURE 4.31

Hiding a selection by choosing Hide Selection from the Object menu.

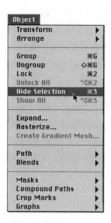

Hiding Edges

If you have used Photoshop, you are probably familiar with the function that allows you to hide edges. When you select an object, its path becomes highlighted in a color, and the object's anchor points become visible. This color can sometimes interfere with viewing the object and can make editing and creating artwork difficult, as well as annoying.

To hide a selected object's edges, choose Hide Edges from the View menu (see Figure 4.32), or press (Command+H)[Control+H]. With edges turned off, you cannot see which item is selected, so make sure you pay attention to what you click.

The Hide Edges command is a toggle, which means that it stays on until you turn it off by pressing (Command+H)[Control+H] again. Too many times, it's easy to forget that you turned edges off, and then you go crazy trying to figure out why nothing can be selected, when in reality, you just can't see that they're being selected.

FIGURE 4.32

Choosing the Hide Edges command from the View menu.

Arranging Items

Although all drawn objects in Illustrator are on the same screen, they appear in the order that they were drawn. In other words, if you were to draw two rectangles, one on top of another, the second rectangle would cover the first one and hide it from view. This concept is similar to having a stack of papers on your desk. If you want to shuffle the order of pages, you would take a paper from the bottom or middle of the pile and put it on top. Or you might take a paper from the top of the pile and move it to the bottom.

Illustrator enables you to move objects all throughout the "pile." Under the Object menu, you can find the Arrange submenu, which contains four commands (see Figure 4.33).

FIGURE 4.33

The Arrange submenu.

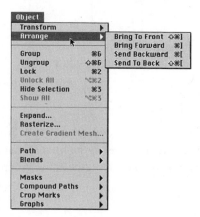

- Bring To Front—Brings the selected object to the front, similar to putting a paper on the top of the pile (see Figure 4.34).

FIGURE 4.34

Starting out as the back-most object, the black square gets sent to the front with the Bring To Front command.

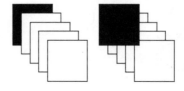

- Bring Forward—Brings the selected object forward one level, similar to moving a paper over the one directly above it (see Figure 4.35).

FIGURE 4.35

The black square starts out as the back-most object (left). After you apply Bring Forward, the black square moves forward one level (right).

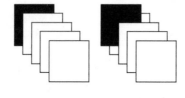

- Send Backward—Sends the selected object one level backward, similar to putting a paper directly under the one it's resting on (see Figure 4.36).

FIGURE 4.36

Here the black square begins as the topmost object (left) and is sent back one level by using the Send Backward command (right).

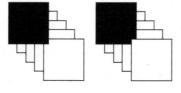

- Send To Back—Sends the selected object to the rear, similar to putting a paper on the bottom of the pile (see Figure 4.37).

When you're using groups, each group has its own set of levels. So, if you bring an object that is part of a group to the front, it goes to the front of that group. To bring the object to the front of everything, you need to select the entire group and bring the whole group to the front.

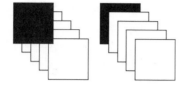

FIGURE 4.37

Starting out as the top-most object (left), the black square gets sent to the back with the Send To Back command (right).

Summary

After learning all about selections and how they work, you should be feeling comfortable with moving things around, and you should know how to work with groups. You should also be able to lock and hide objects to make working easier. In this hour, you also learned about arranging items and how objects are layered. In the next hour, I'll discuss Illustrator's layers, which provide a powerful step above the kind of layering you just learned.

Workshop

The Workshop contains quiz questions to help you solidify your understanding of the material covered in this hour and exercises to provide you with experience using what you have learned. You can find the answers to the quiz questions at the end of the hour.

4

Quiz

1. Which selection tool would you use to select only part of an object?

    a. Selection tool

    b. Direct Selection tool

    c. Group Selection tool

2. With Area Select turned on, you can

    a. Screen your phone calls

    b. Select part of an object

    c. Select a filled object from the inside

3. Dragging on a bounding box handle does what?

    a. Scales the object

    b. Rotates the object

    c. Moves the object

4. If you have an item already selected, and then you Shift+click it, what happens?

    a. It becomes deselected.

    b. It is constrained.

    c. Nothing happens.

5. You cannot have a group within another group.

    a. True

    b. False

Exercises

1. The keyboard shortcuts for locking and hiding are (Command+2)[Control+2] and (Command+3)[Control+3], respectively. Notice how accessible they are when you have your left hand at the lower-left side of the keyboard. Practice the key combinations repeatedly.

2. Spend 10 minutes practicing with selections by using only the Direct Selection tool and switching to the Group Selection tool by using the (Option)[Alt] key when necessary.

3. Practice using the marquee method for making selections.

Term Review

Center point—A noneditable point that appears at the center of a vector object.

Direct Selection tool—The tool that looks like a white arrow; used to select parts of an object.

Fill—The attribute that determines a color, gradient, or pattern for the interior of a shape.

Group—A collection of objects that all become selected when just one item in the group is selected.

Group Selection tool—The tool that looks like a white arrow with a plus sign next to it; used for selecting groups.

Marquee—A rectangular-shaped bounding box indicating an area to be selected.

Selection tool—The tool that looks like a black arrow; used to select entire objects.

Stroke—The attribute that determines the outline of an object.

Answers to Quiz Questions

1. b
2. c
3. a
4. a
5. b

4

HOUR 5

Working with Layers

In the preceding hour, you learned about moving objects to the front and to the back. You discovered that each object is on its own level. Continuing on the topic of levels, you're now ready to learn about the king of all levels in Illustrator: layers. If you've worked in Photoshop, you're probably familiar with the concept of layers. If you'll forgive me for using the analogy, layers are similar to mechanical overlays. Clear sheets of acetate, mechanical overlays contain parts of artwork, and when they are laid over one another, they form the complete art. Layers are extremely versatile and can really help keep complex illustrations under control and manageable. By viewing only certain layers, you can concentrate more completely on the task at hand.

In this hour, you will learn all about these layers, including the following:

- Using the Layers palette
- Shuffling layers
- Hiding and locking layers
- Moving artwork between layers

The Layers Palette

Illustrator's layers are specified in the Layers palette. When you start working in a new document, all artwork is automatically placed on a layer (see Figure 5.1). To open the Layers palette, choose Show Layers from the Window menu (see Figure 5.2).

FIGURE 5.1

Illustrator's Layers palette.

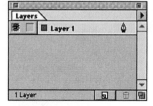

FIGURE 5.2

Choosing Show Layers from the Window menu.

Version 8 gives you the capability to export Illustrator files in Photoshop format while *keeping layer information intact.* This feature is spectacular because it allows you to edit each layer individually in Photoshop and use each shape layer as a selection as well. It's also a wonderful feature for those who create animations for Web pages. You'll learn more about the ability to export layers in Hour 20, "Saving/Exporting Files."

Editing Layers

A small controversy is going on between designers as to when to create layers. Some artists prefer to create several layers before they begin working, adding the art to each layer as they progress. Others prefer to add or delete layers as necessary, as they work on a project. Still others like to create the entire piece and then chop it up into different layers. No matter which way you do it, though, you have to learn how to add and discard layers.

Creating a New Layer

The easiest way to create a new layer is to click the New Layer button at the bottom of the Layers palette (see Figure 5.3). Illustrator creates the layer and assigns it a name. Don't worry, you won't have to keep the assigned names "Layer 1" and "Layer 2." You'll learn how to change them later in this hour in the "Layer Options" section.

FIGURE 5.3

The New Layer button.

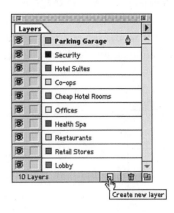

Another way to create a new layer is to select New Layer from the Layers palette menu (see Figure 5.4).

FIGURE 5.4

Choosing New Layer from the Layers palette menu.

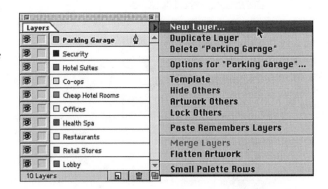

5

Deleting a Layer

To delete a layer, click the name of a layer, and drag it to the Trash icon in the lower-right corner of the Layers palette (see Figure 5.5). Alternatively, you can delete a layer via the Layers palette menu. But what if the layer you are deleting contains artwork? It turns out that Illustrator is keeping a watchful eye out for you. If you try to delete a layer with art on it, a warning message appears, alerting you about the situation, and Illustrator proceeds to delete the layer and its contents only if you click OK. Otherwise, Illustrator returns you to the document with the layer intact, where you can copy the art to another layer (see "Moving or Copying Items Between Layers," later in this hour).

Duplicating a Layer

Sometimes you want to make a copy of an entire layer. You can easily create a duplicate of a layer by clicking the name of an existing layer and dragging it to the New Layer icon on the bottom of the Layers palette (see Figure 5.6). Again, you can also create a duplicate by selecting Duplicate Layer from the Layers palette menu. The attributes, as well as all the artwork contained on that layer, are duplicated, and Illustrator adds the word "copy" to the layer name.

FIGURE 5.5

Deleting a layer with the Layers palette Trash icon.

FIGURE 5.6

Creating a duplicate layer by dragging an existing layer on top of the New Layer icon.

Layer Options

Each layer has several attributes that facilitate your work, as well as add functionality to the layers. Double-clicking the name of a layer brings up the Layer Options dialog box (see Figure 5.7). Here you can name the layer, which is an important step. As you add more and more layers, remembering which items are on Layer 23 and Layer 14 becomes increasingly difficult. By giving intuitive names to layers (such as "Template," "Wheels," or "Ad Copy"), you can quickly identify where items are. In the Layer Options dialog box, you can also assign a selection color (see "Layer Colors," later in this hour) and choose to show, preview, or lock the layer (these tasks are also discussed later in this hour).

FIGURE 5.7

Double-clicking the name of a layer brings up the Layer Options dialog box.

Three more options are located in the Layer Options dialog box:

- Template—Making a layer a template automatically locks the layer and activates the Dim Images option.

- Print—By unchecking the Print box, you are telling Illustrator that you do not want the objects in this layer to print. You might want to create a layer where you write notes to yourself or a colleague, and putting it on a nonprinting layer assures that the text won't print when you send it to a client or for film separations. Sometimes you also might have a complex illustration but want to print only specific parts of it.

5

 Forgetting if you've made a particular layer nonprinting can be easy, and that could lead to embarrassing and costly printouts. To make your job easier, any layer that is set not to print appears italicized in the Layers palette.

In today's fast-paced world, a designer is sometimes forced to send a fax of a design to a client for instant approval. Fancy backgrounds and tints, however, can make text very difficult—if not impossible—to read when faxed. If you create your text and backgrounds on separate layers, you can use Layer Options to print only the text layer so that your client can read the clear text without the background. Just remember to set the background layer to print again before you send for final output.

- Dim Images—Use the Dim Images button when you want to use placed images as a template. Upon placing a bitmapped image, Illustrator dims the image to make it easier to trace over it. You can specify how dark or light you want the image to appear by changing the tint percentage. Try to avoid using this feature if possible, as it slows screen redraw. Of course, if you have no other choice, remember to turn off the option when you are done tracing. For more details on tracing images, see Hour 21, "Working Smart in Illustrator."

Layer Colors

If you have one or two layers in your document, keeping track of which objects are on which layer is pretty simple. However, in a document with many layers, remembering which objects are on each layer becomes increasingly difficult. To make it easier to identify which object is on which layer, a *color* is defined for each layer. When an object is selected, it is highlighted in the color of its layer. When you create a new layer, Illustrator automatically assigns a new unique color to that layer. To change the color of a layer, simply double-click the layer to bring up the Layer Options dialog box, choose a new color (see Figure 5.8), and click OK.

FIGURE 5.8

Choosing a new layer color.

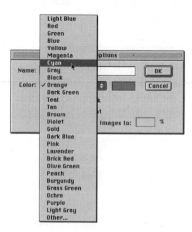

Arranging Layers

What good would layers be if you couldn't shuffle the *order* of them around? By simply clicking and dragging the layer name, you can change the order of the layers (see Figure 5.9). The order of layers determines which objects are in front of others. The objects of a layer closer to the top of the list in the Layers palette appear on top of those objects in layers closer to the bottom of the list.

> If you have many layers, you can drag a layer to the top or bottom of the palette, and the layers will scroll. Adobe has ingeniously created a variable-speed scroll in the Layers palette. At first, scrolling goes slowly, but as you hold the mouse, the scrolling rate speeds up.

FIGURE 5.9

You can change the order of layers by simply dragging them.

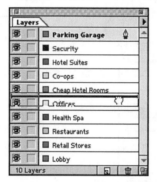

Moving or Copying Items Between Layers

Many times you need to move objects from one layer to another. Instead of making you copy and paste objects, Illustrator has an intuitive feature built into the Layers palette specifically for the purpose of moving and copying objects between layers.

When an object is selected, look for a little dot on the far right of the layer name in the Layers palette (see Figure 5.10). To move your selected object to another layer, simply click and drag the dot to another layer (see Figure 5.11), and the object is transferred to the new layer. The selection color changes to the new layer's color, too.

To copy objects to another layer, press and hold the (Option)[Alt] key as you drag the dot. A copy of your selection is put into the new layer.

5

FIGURE 5.10

The little dot on the far right indicates your selection.

You can quickly select all the objects on a layer by pressing the (Option)[Alt] key while clicking the layer name in the Layers palette.

FIGURE 5.11

Dragging the dot to a different layer.

Locking and Hiding Layers

One of the advantages of using layers is the capability to lock or hide the objects on each layer quickly. Notice that to the left of each layer are two boxes (see Figure 5.12). The left box controls the view, whereas the right box controls locking. An eye in the left box indicates that the layer is fully visible in your document.

To hide the layer, click the eye, and the objects in that layer aren't visible in your document. Clicking again in the left box makes the layer visible. If you press and hold down the (Command)[Control] key while you click in the left box, you set the layer to Artwork mode, as opposed to Preview mode. The little eye icon is hollow, indicating the change (see Figure 5.13). Simply (Command+click)[Control+click] again to return the layer to Preview mode.

FIGURE 5.12

The visibility and lock boxes are on the far left of the Layers palette.

FIGURE 5.13

A hollow eye in the visibility box indicates the layer is in the Artwork view mode.

Click in the right box, and a pencil with a line through it appears, indicating that the layer is locked (see Figure 5.14). Objects in a locked layer are visible in your document but cannot be selected. To unlock the layer, click again in the right box.

FIGURE 5.14

In this document, layers Parking Garage, Cheap Hotel Rooms, and Health Spa are locked. Hotel Suites, Offices, and Restaurants are hidden, and Parking Garage, Security, and the Lobby layers are in Artwork mode.

5

Remember that regardless of whether a layer is visible or locked, it prints unless you specify it as a nonprinting layer in the Layer Options dialog box.

Pressing the (Option)[Alt] key while clicking the eye icon on a layer hides all layers except for the one you clicked. (Option+click)[Alt+click] again to show all layers again.

Merging Layers

You can merge any selected layers by simply choosing Merge Layers from the Layers palette menu. Select layers by holding down the Shift key while clicking the layer names, or hold down the (Command)[Control] key while clicking the layer names to select noncontiguous layers. You also can combine all layers (they do not have to all be selected) by selecting Flatten Artwork from the Layers palette menu.

Extra Room Anyone?

In version 7, Adobe was criticized for "jazzing" up the Layers palette by making each layer take up more space. People who work with many layers (cartographers commonly use over 60 layers in a document) found that they had to constantly scroll through the palette. In version 8, Adobe has included an option called Small Palette Rows in the Layers palette menu (see Figure 5.15). Selecting this option allows more layers to be visible in the Layers palette at one time.

FIGURE 5.15

The Layers palette with the Small Palette Rows option active.

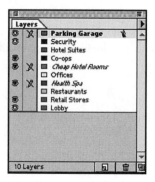

Hands-On

After you learn all about the different things you can do with layers, figuring out how to work with them in the most beneficial way might become confusing. Think you're ready for a step-by-step lesson?

1. Open a fresh new document by pressing (Command+N)[Control+N].

2. If it isn't open already, open the Layers palette by pressing the F7 key.

3. Using the Rectangle tool, draw several rectangles (see Figure 5.16).

4. Double-click Layer 1 in the Layers palette, and rename the layer `Rectangles` (see Figure 5.17).

5. Create a new layer by clicking the Create New Layer icon in the Layers palette.

FIGURE 5.16

Drawing rectangles on Layer 1.

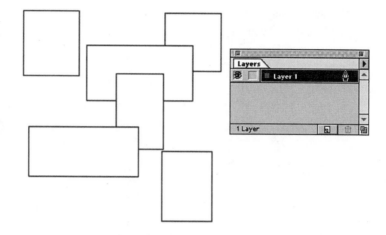

FIGURE 5.17

Renaming the layer.

6. Using the Ellipse tool, draw several circles. Feel free to draw them on top of the rectangles (see Figure 5.18).

7. Double-click Layer 2 in the Layers palette, and rename the layer Circles.

FIGURE 5.18

Drawing circles on Layer 2.

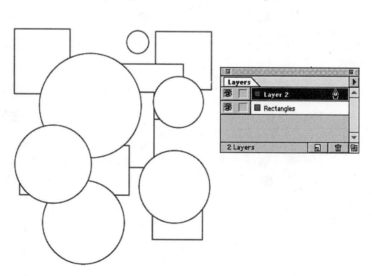

5

8. Use the Star tool to draw a single star (see Figure 5.19). Notice the star drawn on the Circles layer. Next, you'll move the star to its own layer.

FIGURE 5.19

Adding the star.

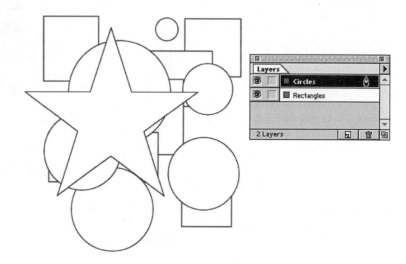

9. Create a new layer, and immediately double-click it to rename it Star.

10. Using the Selection tool, select the star. Notice that you are now back on the Circles layer (see Figure 5.20).

FIGURE 5.20

The star selected. Notice the Circles layer is currently selected.

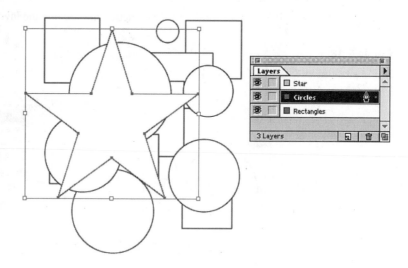

11. With the star still selected, click the selection dot, and drag it up onto the Star layer (see Figure 5.21). The star is now on the Star layer.

FIGURE 5.21

Dragging the selection dot to the Star layer.

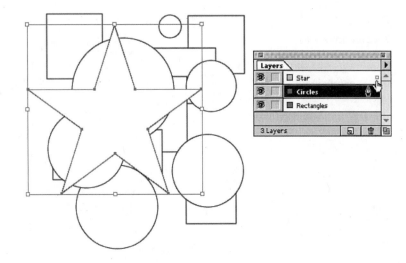

12. Deselect the star by clicking a blank area on the screen.

13. Rearrange some layers. For this example, drag the Star layer between the Circles and Rectangles layers. Notice how the star is now behind the circles (see Figure 5.22).

FIGURE 5.22

The star is now behind the circles.

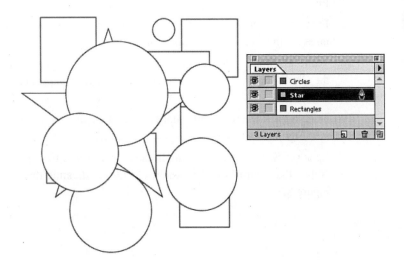

5

14. Double-click the Star layer, uncheck the Print box, and click OK. Notice how the layer name is now italicized, indicating it is a nonprinting layer (see Figure 5.23).

FIGURE 5.23

The Star layer name appears in italics, indicating at a glance that it is a nonprinting layer.

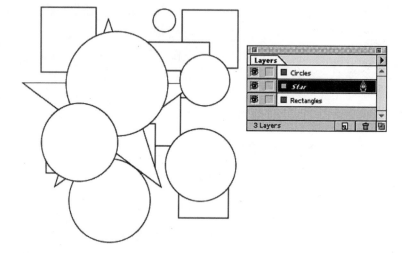

15. Click the black eye icon in the rectangles to hide the Rectangles layer. Notice all the rectangles are no longer visible.

16. Click again to show the Rectangles layer. Now select the Rectangles layer, and while holding down the (Command)[Control] key, also select the Circles layer (see Figure 5.24).

17. From the Layer pop-up menu, select Merge Layers. Notice the new merged layer takes on the name of the topmost layer, Circles.

18. With the Circles layer selected, click the Trash icon in the Layers palette to delete the Circles layer. Illustrator warns you that artwork appears on that layer (see Figure 5.25).

19. Double-click the remaining Star layer, and change the layer color to Dark Green (see Figure 5.26).

20. Lock the Star layer by clicking in the empty box to the right of the black eye icon. Notice that your arrow cursor now changes, indicating the layer is locked (see Figure 5.27).

FIGURE 5.24

Both the Circles and the Rectangles layers selected.

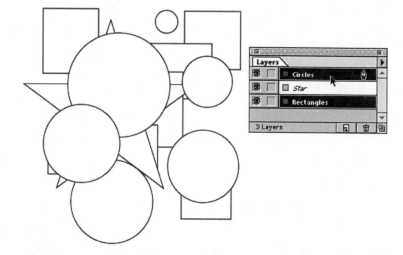

FIGURE 5.25

Illustrator's warning that you are about to delete art.

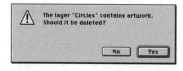

FIGURE 5.26

Changing the layer color to Dark Green.

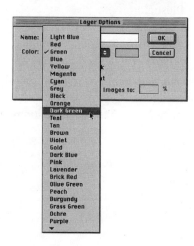

5

FIGURE 5.27

The crossed-pencil icon, indicating that you are working on a locked layer.

There now, that didn't hurt, did it? Working with layers can be easy.

Summary

Layers are an important part of Illustrator, and you learned about that topic in depth today. Although you might not use layers for simple illustrations, they can really come in handy as your illustrations become more complex. Speaking of complex, the next hour introduces you to the most difficult parts about Illustrator: the Pen tool and the Bézier curve, which are at the heart of Illustrator.

Workshop

The Workshop contains quiz questions to help you solidify your understanding of the material covered in this hour and exercises to provide you with experience using what you have learned. You can find the answers to the quiz questions at the end of the hour.

Quiz

1. Layers are good for

    a. Organizing art

    b. Reshaping objects

    c. Cold weather

2. Double-clicking a layer

    a. Turns it into a nonprinting layer

    b. Selects all objects on that layer

    c. Opens the Layer Options dialog box

3. You can delete a layer in two ways. Which of these is not one of them?

    a. Drag the layer to the palette Trash icon

    b. Press the Delete key with the layer highlighted

    c. Select Delete Layer from the palette pop-up menu

4. If a black eye icon appears on a layer, it means

    a. The layer is protected from evil spirits

    b. The layer is visible

    c. The layer is invisible

5. What happens when you flatten layers?

    a. All the layers are combined into one

    b. All 3D art becomes two dimensional

    c. The Layers palette becomes smaller

Exercises

1. Draw 10 objects and then create 10 layers. Now put each object on a different layer so that you have only one object on each layer.

2. Create two layers and practice moving artwork between them by using the selection dot. Now copy the objects from layer to layer by using the (Option)[Alt] key while dragging the selection dot to a different layer.

3. Practice merging noncontiguous layers by selecting several different layers while holding the (Command)[Control] key.

Term Review

Layer color—The selection color of items on a layer (that is, if an object is selected, its anchor points appear in the color of that object's layer color).

Layer order—The position of each layer in the Layers palette.

Answers to Quiz Questions

    1. a

    2. c

    3. b

    4. b

    5. a

5

HOUR 6

Drawing Bézier Paths

Strip away all of Illustrator's fancy features and new interface, and you're left with the heart of Illustrator: the Bézier path and the Pen tool. Since version 1.0, the Pen tool is probably the main reason that Illustrator has become one of today's best illustration programs. Comfortable, elegant, and functional, the Pen tool gives you complete control when you're creating and editing the base of all vector illustrations—the Bézier (pronounced *BEH-zee-ay*) path.

In this hour, you'll learn about the following:

- Working with the Bézier path
- Working with anchor points
- Drawing with the Pen tool
- Drawing with the Pencil tool

The Bézier Path

NEW TERM So what is a *Bézier path* anyway? It's a mathematical way of representing graphics, developed by Pierre Bézier. (It was originally created to put designs of aircraft on a computer; later, it was used for designing cars.) All vector objects are made up of Bézier path segments. Bézier paths come in two flavors: lines and curves.

NEW TERM The first type of Bézier path is a straight line; it contains two *anchor points* with a straight line connecting them (see Figure 6.1). This type is the simplest Bézier path and requires the least amount of memory to store and print. You just need the coordinates of the first point and the second point.

FIGURE 6.1

The simplest of Bézier paths: a straight line.

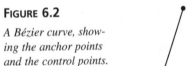

Anchor Point   Anchor Point

NEW TERM The second type of Bézier path is the curve, and here the description gets complicated. A curve consists of two anchor points, with a curved line connecting them. The curve is determined by *control points*, which are attached to each anchor point (see Figure 6.2). The control points (also called handles) define exactly how the curved line is drawn between the two anchor points.

FIGURE 6.2

A Bézier curve, showing the anchor points and the control points.

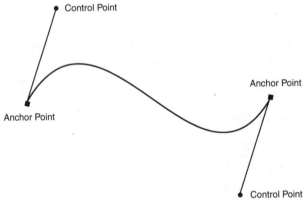

Of course, when the paths print, you don't see the anchor points or the handles. They just appear onscreen so that you can edit the paths, but when the paths print, all you see is the lines (see Figure 6.3).

FIGURE 6.3

When the files actually print, you don't see the anchor or the control points.

Up until now, you've been creating Bézier paths without even knowing it. The rectangles, ellipses, stars, polygons, and spirals that you've created are all made up of Bézier paths. You were doing fine until now, so why bring in all this complicated anchor point and control point stuff, you might ask? As the saying goes, ignorance is bliss. Sure, you could perform several tasks in Illustrator without knowing what Bézier paths are, but you lose out on all the power that Illustrator offers. Other programs have more features than Illustrator. In fact, I think it would be safe to say that of all the major illustration packages on the market, Illustrator has the fewest features. Illustrator's power lies within the Pen tool and the implementation of Bézier paths.

Before you begin learning how to create and edit Bézier paths and use the Pen tool, I want to make the following disclaimer:

Drawing and editing Bézier paths requires much patience and time. However, you have a lot to look forward to; you also get better with experience. I look back now at some of the art I created as a beginner, and I can't help but wonder, "What was I thinking?" I have no doubt that you will become comfortable with the Pen tool; you just have to give it time. Do the exercises listed here, practice a lot, and before you know it, you too will be looking back in wonder. More important, though, you will have harnessed the power of the Pen tool.

The Pen Tool

6

Illustrator's Pen tool is rumored to be the most inhumane torture tool ever devised by man. Fear not; there is a method to the madness and, with perseverance, you will prevail. The Pen tool is used to create precise Bézier paths of virtually any shape or form. It works by creating anchor points, which are the basis of Bézier paths.

If you have used Photoshop, you know that it has a Pen tool as well, for defining clipping paths and precise selections. Both the Photoshop and the Illustrator Pen tools work identically, and you can even move Bézier paths between the two programs easily using cut and paste or drag and drop. Integration such as this really makes for intuitive, useful, and practical applications.

The Anchor Points

NEW TERM   Illustrator has three different kinds of anchor points: the straight *corner point*, the *smooth point*, and the *combination point*. Each kind of anchor point has its specific attributes, and each is used to create different types of paths. A Bézier object can be made up of any of the three kinds of anchor points and can contain any combination as well. A square is made up of four straight corner anchor points, for example, whereas a circle is made up of four smooth anchor points. A shape such as a pie wedge contains both straight corner and combination anchor points. As you go through the following hands-on exercises, you'll get a better feel for anchor points and understand how they work.

Throughout this hour, and the rest of the lessons, you will be doing different exercises in Illustrator. Although you can use this book without them, the files that I have used for illustrations are available on the World Wide Web if you want to follow along. Simply direct your browser to http://www.mordy.com. I've also printed these illustrations in the book, preceding each exercise, to give you a better idea of the steps involved.

The Straight Corner Anchor Point

The straight corner is the simplest form of the anchor point, and it is used to define straight lines such as the ones shown previously in Figure 6.1. Before you begin using the Pen tool, I should mention again that Illustrator's cursors change to indicate the current status of a tool. I'll point out the subtle differences in the Pen tool cursor as they occur. If you goof anytime throughout the exercises, don't worry; just use the Undo command (Command+Z)[Control+Z]. In this first exercise, you will draw a triangle.

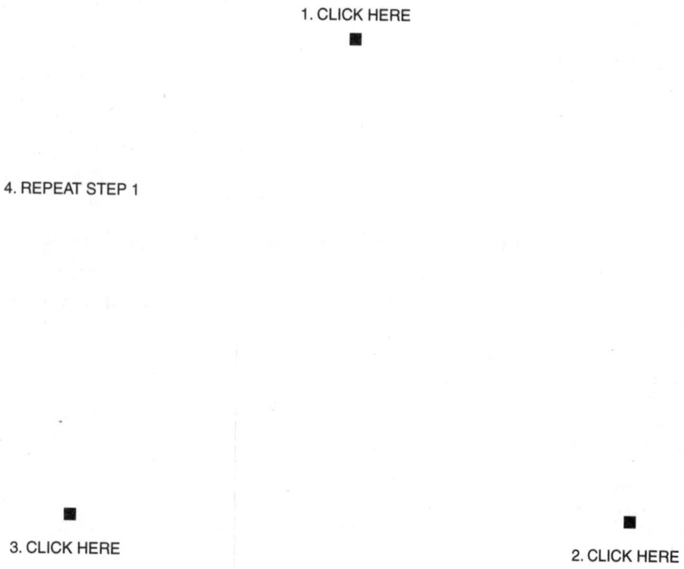

1. CLICK HERE
■

4. REPEAT STEP 1

■   ■
3. CLICK HERE   2. CLICK HERE

1. Start by opening a new Illustrator document; to do so, press (Command+N) [Control+N].

2. Select the Pen tool from the Toolbox (see Figure 6.4). Notice that the Pen tool cursor has a small "x" on the lower right (see Figure 6.5). This symbol indicates that you are starting a new path.

FIGURE 6.4

Selecting Illustrator's Pen tool.

FIGURE 6.5

The tell-tale cursor; the little "x" indicates that the Pen tool is ready to create a new path.

6

3. Create a triangle now. Click once. Click again to the lower right and again to the left (see Figure 6.6). Notice that the cursor changes to a plain Pen tool, indicating that you are in the midst of creating a path.

FIGURE 6.6

Two segments of the triangle are completed.

4. Drag your cursor up to the first point you created. Notice that when the cursor touches the point, a little "o" appears on the lower right of the Pen tool cursor (see Figure 6.7). This symbol indicates that you are about to close, or complete, a path.

FIGURE 6.7

By showing the little "o," the Pen tool indicates that clicking will complete and close the path.

5. Click the top anchor point to complete the triangle. The Pen tool cursor appears with the "x" again, ready to start a new path (see Figure 6.8).

FIGURE 6.8

After completing the triangle, the Pen tool is ready for its next assignment.

Congratulations! You have just created your first path with the Pen tool. Don't jump for joy just yet, however; the hard part comes next: the smooth anchor point.

The Smooth Anchor Point

The smooth anchor point contains two control points, or handles. By adjusting the control points, you determine the slope and sharpness of the curve on either side of the point. Because the path continues through the point without a sharp change in direction, it is called a smooth anchor point. Try drawing a circle so you can get a better idea of how it works.

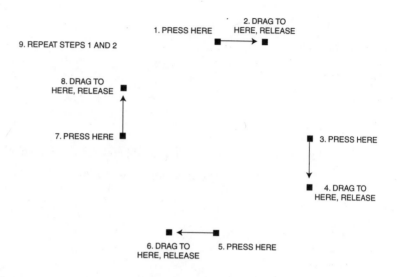

1. Using the Pen tool, press and drag a point to the right, about half an inch. When you drag, notice that you are pulling a control point out from the anchor point (see Figure 6.9).

FIGURE 6.9

When you press the mouse button, you define where the anchor point is. By dragging, you define where the control point is.

2. Release the mouse button.

3. Move your cursor about one inch down and to the right of the first anchor point, not the control point (see Figure 6.10).

FIGURE 6.10

Without clicking, you move your cursor to the place where the next anchor point will appear.

4. Press and drag down about half an inch (see Figure 6.11).

6

FIGURE 6.11

*While you're still hold-
ing down the mouse
button, drag as shown.*

5. Release the mouse button. You should now see the first arc of a circle.

6. Move your cursor one inch down and to the left of the last anchor point you created (see Figure 6.12).

FIGURE 6.12

*Repositioning the cur-
sor for the next step.*

7. Press and drag to the left about half an inch (see Figure 6.13).

FIGURE 6.13

*Dragging out another
control point.*

8. Release the mouse button. You're halfway there.

9. Move your cursor one inch up and to the left of the anchor point you just created
   (see Figure 6.14).

FIGURE 6.14

This one is the last anchor point, bringing the total number of anchor points in this shape to four.

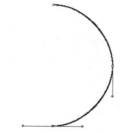

10. Press and drag up about half an inch (see Figure 6.15).

FIGURE 6.15

Dragging out another control point.

11. Release the mouse button.

12. To complete the circle, repeat step 1: click the first anchor point you created and drag about half an inch to the right (see Figure 6.16).

FIGURE 6.16

Completing the circle.

13. Release the mouse button, and voila, you have a circle.

So you see that by pressing and dragging a point, you can create a smooth anchor point with control handles. Control handles determine the direction of the curved path. To demonstrate, switch to the Direct Selection tool (the white arrow), and click the path of the circle. The control points are now visible for that section of the path. Press and drag on one of the control handles, and see how the path behaves when you move the control point.

6

Generally, the direction of the curve follows the control point. Try to avoid stretching the handles too far from the anchor point because doing so makes for difficult editing. (The ideal guideline shouldn't exceed one third the length of the curve.) Again, as you work more and more with control points, you will get a better idea of where to place them and how to achieve the curves you want.

The Combination Anchor Point

Okay, you're building confidence now, and you're really going to need it. The combination point is—get this—a combination of the straight anchor point and the smooth anchor point, so using these types of points can get a bit confusing. In this next exercise, you will create some waves.

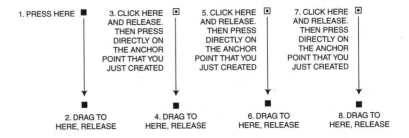

1. Press and drag a point down about one inch. Release the mouse button (see Figure 6.17).

FIGURE 6.17

Dragging the first point.

2. Position your cursor one inch to the right of the first anchor point.

3. Click the mouse button (see Figure 6.18).

FIGURE 6.18

A single click completes the path. The first anchor point was a smooth point; the second, a straight point.

4. Position your cursor directly atop the anchor point you just created. Notice that the pen cursor changes to show a small inverted "V" on the lower right (see Figure 6.19).

FIGURE 6.19

Notice the change in the Pen tool cursor.

5. Click the point, and drag down one inch (holding the Shift key while you drag the line straight).

6. Repeat steps 2 through 5 (see Figure 6.20).

FIGURE 6.20

Making waves.

In the preceding exercise, you created a straight anchor point, which has no control handles, when you clicked. By dragging out the straight point, you defined the next connecting path and anchor point. So, in reality, the combination point has two sides to it: a straight side (from the single click) and a curved side (from the click and drag).

True, in these examples, you were told where to place the anchor points and the control points. If you were creating any other random shape, you would have to decide where those points belong on your own. After getting a feel for how anchor points and control points affect the path, you will be able to make these decisions on your own. I've included several other templates, shown here, that you can use to get a better feel for the Pen tool.

6

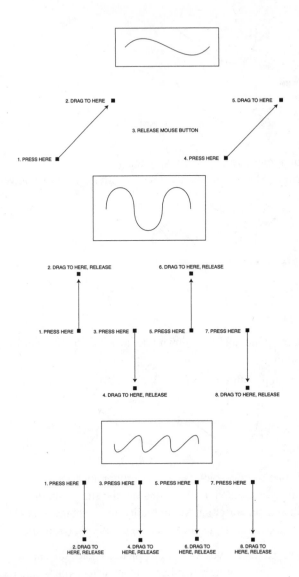

Open and Closed Paths

NEW TERM A path in Illustrator can be either open or closed. An *open path* has two endpoints, whereas a *closed path* has none (one end joins the other). As you draw
with the Pen tool, Illustrator uses the current fill and stroke attributes for your shape. As
you complete each click, Illustrator attempts to fill the path by using the current fill, so
don't be alarmed. Just continue following the steps in the exercise. I'll cover fills and
strokes in detail in Hours 10, "Fills" and 11, "Strokes."

The Pencil Tool

Now that you've learned how to draw with the Pen tool, I'll tell you about a much easier way to draw a Bézier path. The Pencil tool, shown in Figure 6.21, lets you click and drag on the screen to draw, and Illustrator places the anchor points for you (see Figure 6.22). So why bother with the Pen tool at all? Because creating precise drawings is very difficult with the Pencil tool. It's great, for say, signing your name or making quick sketch lines, but for most of your work, the Pen tool is better. Besides, after creating a path with the Pencil tool, you may still have to "clean it up" by editing the path. By learning the ways of the Pen tool, you can edit art no matter how it was created.

FIGURE 6.21

The Pencil tool.

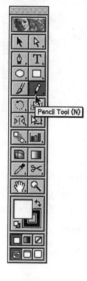

FIGURE 6.22

You just draw; Illustrator does the rest.

6

Drawing with the mouse (or even a tablet) is not anything like drawing with a real pencil, and getting comfortable with the way a mouse or tablet stylus feels takes time. To make life a bit easier, you can control how sensitive Illustrator's Pencil tool is by changing the settings in the Pencil Tool Preferences dialog box (see Figure 6.23). To open it, simply double-click on the Pencil tool in the Toolbox. The higher you set the Fidelity and the Smoothness, the cleaner and smoother your paths will be. If the Keep Selected option is on, Illustrator will leave the path selected right after you've drawn it.

FIGURE 6.23

The Pencil Tool Preferences dialog box.

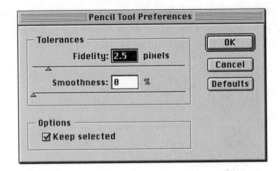

Summary

Whew! This hour was the hardest yet. Give yourself a big hand for making it through the horrors of using the Pen tool. But don't worry; using this tool will become second nature before you know it. In this hour, you also learned about Bézier paths, the different kinds of anchor points, and don't forget the Pencil tool. Next, you are going to work with Bézier paths after you've created them.

Workshop

The Workshop contains quiz questions to help you solidify your understanding of the material covered in this hour and exercises to provide you with experience using what you have learned. You can find the answers to the quiz questions at the end of the hour.

Quiz

1. What are the two types of Bézier paths?

   a. Round and straight

   b. Line and curve

   c. Right and wrong

2. Control points are also called

   a. Pressure points

   b. Hot spots

   c. Handles

3. A square is made up of four straight corner anchor points.

   a. True

   b. False

4. When you're drawing with the Pen tool, pressing and dragging creates

   a. A control point

   b. A straight line

   c. Havoc

5. A combination point is a combination of

   a. Corned beef and pastrami

   b. A straight anchor point and a smooth anchor point

   c. A vector and a raster image

Exercise

Draw a path with the Pencil tool, and then observe where Illustrator placed the anchor and control points. Now try to duplicate the path, using the Pen tool this time.

Term Review

Anchor point—A defined point on a Bézier path.

Bézier path—A mathematically defined line consisting of anchor points and control points.

Closed path—A Bézier path that encloses an area; it has no beginning and no end.

Combination point—An anchor point that shares the attributes of both a smooth point and a corner point.

Control point—A defined point that is part of an anchor point; it is used to control the curve of a path.

Corner point—An anchor point with no control points; it is used to define straight lines.

Open path—A Bézier path with two open (unconnected) endpoints.

Smooth point—An anchor point whose control points are tangent to the anchor point.

6

Answers to Quiz Questions

1. b
2. c
3. a
4. a
5. b

HOUR 7

Editing Bézier Paths

No one is perfect, so you always have times when you need to edit a path to get it just right. There are also plenty of times when you create a simple path and modify it to create a more complex path. Perhaps the greatest advantage a computer offers is the ability to easily make changes over and over again. In Illustrator, you can edit a path in several ways. In this hour, you'll learn about these issues, including the following:

- Adding and deleting anchor points
- Using the Reshape tool
- Using the Smooth tool
- Cutting paths
- Joining paths

Manipulating Existing Points

After you draw a path, you might want to change the shape or style of the points, adjusting the curve of the path or making a corner point a smooth point. Several tools enable you to modify a path by changing, adding, or deleting points.

The Direct Selection Tool

Perhaps the simplest form of editing a path is to use the white arrow, or Direct Selection tool. By selecting only one anchor point, you can reposition it. By selecting a path and then dragging on a control point, you can change the shape of the curve (see Figure 7.1).

FIGURE 7.1

Editing a path's curve by dragging the control point with the Direct Selection tool.

The P key is the keyboard shortcut for the Pen tool. Pressing Shift+P cycles repeatedly through the Pen tool, the Add Anchor Point tool, the Delete Anchor Point tool, and the Convert Direction Point tool.

The Add Anchor Point Tool

Simple in concept, the Add Anchor Point tool—which looks just like the Pen tool with a little + (plus) next to it—enables you to put additional anchor points on an existing path (see Figure 7.2). The new point takes on the attributes of the path that you click (see Figure 7.3). If you add a point to a straight path, the new anchor point is a straight anchor point, and clicking a curved path results in a new smooth anchor point.

FIGURE 7.2

Selecting the Add Anchor Point tool.

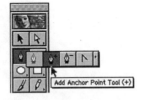

FIGURE 7.3

A point added to a straight path and a curved one.

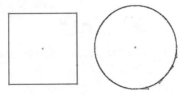

The Delete Anchor Point Tool

The Delete Anchor Point tool, shown in Figure 7.4, simply deletes existing points. It also looks just like the Pen tool, except that it has a - (minus) next to it. If you click an anchor point with the Delete Anchor Point tool, the point is removed, and Illustrator automatically joins the preceding anchor point with the next point on the path (see Figure 7.5).

FIGURE 7.4

Selecting the Delete Anchor Point tool.

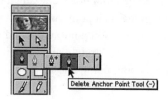

FIGURE 7.5

A square before (left) and after (right) using the Delete Anchor Point tool to delete the lower-right point.

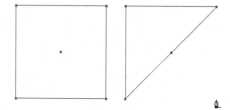

Illustrator 8 has enhanced the functionality of the Pen tool in that you no longer have to select the Add Anchor Point or Delete Anchor Point tools; instead, simply moving your mouse cursor over a path automatically activates the Add Anchor Point tool, and moving your mouse cursor over an existing anchor point activates the Delete Anchor Point tool.

The Convert Direction Point Tool

What do you do when you already have an anchor point, but you need to change it from one type of point to another? You use the Convert Direction Point tool. You can easily access the last tool from the pen tool quartet, the Convert Direction Point tool, shown in Figure 7.6, by pressing (Command+Option)[Control+Alt] when the Direct Selection tool is active or by pressing just the (Option)[Alt] key when any of the Pen tools is active. Notice the cursor changes to an inverted "V" shape (see Figure 7.7).

FIGURE 7.6

Selecting the Convert Direction Point tool.

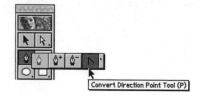

7

FIGURE 7.7

The inverted "V" shape, indicating that the Convert Direction Point tool is in use.

This tool works in the same way that the Pen tool does; clicking a point converts it to a straight anchor point. Pressing and dragging on a point makes that point a smooth anchor point. To make a smooth point into a combination point, press and drag on a control point (see Figure 7.8). If you want to convert a straight anchor point to a combination point, you must first make the point a smooth point, and then press and drag on the control point.

FIGURE 7.8

Creating a combination point with the Convert Direction Point tool.

Editing Paths

Illustrator offers several tools for controlling and editing paths. The newest, the Reshape tool, modifies the shape of a curve without requiring you to select a control point. The Knife and Scissors tools cut paths, whereas the Join and Average commands connect paths together.

The Smooth Tool

Sometimes a path is not exactly to your liking, and you just want to smooth it out a bit. Well, the Smooth tool is just the tool for you then (see Figure 7.9). To use it, simply click and drag over any portion of a path. In fact, it works just like the Pencil tool you learned about in the preceding hour, except that it smoothes the parts of the path that you drag over. Paths need not be selected before you use the Smooth tool.

Of course, double-clicking on the Smooth tool in the Toolbox allows you to change the Fidelity and Smoothness settings. See Hour 8, "The Paintbrush Tool," for more information about these settings.

FIGURE 7.9

The Smooth tool.

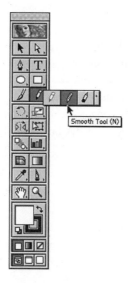

The Erase Tool

What's a pencil without an eraser? That's right, the antithesis of the Pencil tool is the eraser, and Illustrator's Erase tool is a wonderful feature (see Figure 7.10). With the Erase tool selected, you can simply draw over any section or part of a path, and that part magically disappears. While you are dragging with the Erase tool, pressing the (Option)[Alt] key activates the Smooth tool. Let go of the key, and the Erase tool returns.

FIGURE 7.10

The Erase tool.

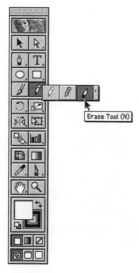

7

The Reshape Tool

One of the new features of Illustrator is the Reshape tool (see Figure 7.11). By simply clicking and dragging a path, you can reshape a curved path without having to select a control point. Even more important, the Reshape tool can edit multiple control points at the same time. In Figure 7.12, the first star is the original. The second star has been scaled, but notice that it was stretched at only one point in the object. The third star was scaled with the Reshape tool. Notice how the scale has been applied evenly throughout the selected points. In contrast, the Direction Selection tool can edit only one control point at a time.

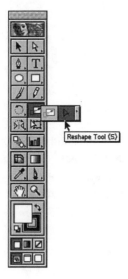

FIGURE 7.11

Selecting Illustrator's new Reshape tool.

FIGURE 7.12

Scaling with the Reshape tool.

The Reshape tool can also quickly add points to a path to increase the editability of the path. When you move the Reshape tool over a part of the path where no point exists, the cursor changes to indicate that a point can go there (see Figure 7.13). Simply clicking or pressing and dragging places the point.

FIGURE 7.13

Notice the change in the cursor as it approaches the line.

The Scissors Tool

Sometimes editing a path calls for splitting it in two. The Scissors tool, shown in Figure 7.14, is used to sever an individual path. With the Scissors tool selected, you can click anywhere on any path, and Illustrator severs the path where you clicked. A path need not even be selected when using the Scissors tool, so be careful where you click when using it.

FIGURE 7.14

The Scissors tool.

Using the Scissors tool can be quite a pain because you have to click exactly on the path you want to cut. Also, in most cases, you are using the Scissors tool to cut a line and join it to another, which just means more editing. If all the clicking and joining frustrates you (as it does me), then stick around for Hour 13, "Transformations," where you'll learn about some cool path editing commands. You'll never use the Scissors tool again....

The Knife Tool

Based on the same premise as the Scissors tool, the Knife tool is used to sever objects (see Figure 7.15). The similarities end there, however. To use the Knife tool, drag it over an object, and the object is sliced where you dragged, just as if you had cut it with a knife, leaving you two (or more) filled objects (see Figure 7.16).

An important point to remember here is that the Knife tool cuts through all objects that cross its path, even unselected ones. So dragging the Knife tool over a group of items slices all the items (see Figure 7.17). This great feature has lots of uses, but sometimes you want to cut through only one selected object without cutting what is underneath. To do so, hold down the Shift key before pressing and dragging, and Illustrator slices only the selected object (see Figure 7.18). Holding the Shift key also constrains the Knife tool to slice in straight lines only.

7

FIGURE 7.15

Selecting the Knife tool.

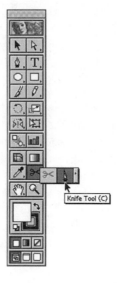

FIGURE 7.16

Slicing an object with the Knife tool.

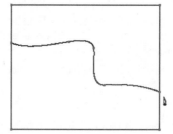

FIGURE 7.17

The Knife tool slices all objects it crosses, even those layered underneath.

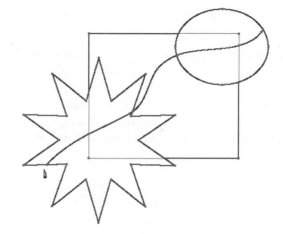

FIGURE 7.18

Using the Shift key, you can slice just selected objects.

 After you start dragging with the Shift key pressed, you can release the Shift key and draw freely, and Illustrator still slices only the selected object. You can also slice multiple objects in straight lines by first pressing and dragging with the Knife tool and then pressing the Shift key.

The Join and Average Commands

Alas, at some point, you will want to connect one path with another. Say you have a square, for example, but only three sides have lines between the points. You need to connect the last two points to complete the square. Connecting is easy with the Join command, which you find by choosing Object➥Path➥Join. Join does one of three things:

- Closes an open path if the entire path is selected (see Figure 7.19).

FIGURE 7.19

Quickly closing an open path with the Join command.

 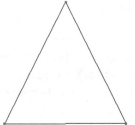

7

- Connects two separate points with a line, be it the endpoints of a single path or the endpoints of two different paths (see Figure 7.20).

FIGURE 7.20

Connecting the dots. You can clean up the resulting path with the Delete Anchor Point tool.

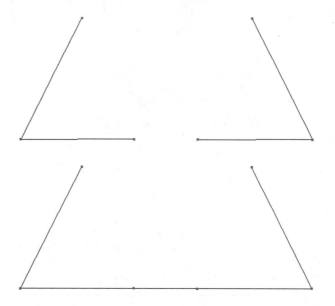

- Connects two overlapping points by combining them into one point (see Figure 7.21).

FIGURE 7.21

When you're joining two overlapping points, Illustrator asks if you want to make the new combined point a smooth or corner anchor point.

The Average command is also found in the Path submenu. Basically, you can use Average to align selected endpoints of a path or paths. When you have two or more points selected, using Average aligns them either vertically, horizontally, or both (see Figure 7.22).

FIGURE 7.22

From left to right, original lines with the left endpoints selected, and then averaged horizontally, vertically, and both.

Summary

You now know the different ways you can edit Bézier paths in Illustrator. In this hour, you learned how to modify paths by cutting them with the Scissors and Knife tools, by using the Smooth and Erase tools, and also by joining and averaging them. In the next hour, you'll learn all about a cousin of the Pencil tool: the Paintbrush tool.

Workshop

The Workshop contains quiz questions to help you solidify your understanding of the material covered in this hour and exercises to provide you with experience using what you have learned. You can find the answers to the quiz questions at the end of the hour.

Quiz

1. One of the capabilities of the Reshape tool is
    a. Editing multiple control points
    b. Scaling the shape
    c. Doing a triple-toe loop jump

2. If you have the Pen tool selected, which keyboard shortcut activates the Convert Direction Point tool?
    a. (Option)[Alt]
    b. (Option+Shift)[Alt+Shift]
    c. (Command+Option)[Control+Alt]

3. The Scissors tool can cut a line even if it is not selected.
    a. True
    b. False

7

4. While you're using the Knife tool, which modifier key do you use to slice only selected objects?

    a. (Command)[Control]

    b. Shift

    c. (Option)[Alt]

5. If you want to align several selected anchor points, you use which function?

    a. Join

    b. Average

    c. Align

Exercises

1. Draw a long path with the Pencil tool. Now smooth parts of it using the Smooth tool. Then switch to the Erase tool, and practice removing chunks from the middle of the path.

2. Practice using the Average function to position points precisely in no time.

3. Draw several overlapping shapes and, using the Knife tool, practice slicing just certain objects without damaging others (remember the Shift key).

Answers to Quiz Questions

1. a

2. a

3. a

4. b

5. b

Hour 8

The Paintbrush Tool

Now it's time to put a little pizzazz and a little spunk into your drawings. The Paintbrush tool (see Figure 8.1) in Illustrator 8 is all new and completely revised, allowing for some really cool drawing possibilities. Actually, this tool is made up of four different kinds of brushes. These brushes are called "live" brushes because you can edit them even after you've drawn them, and Illustrator recalculates and redraws them as necessary.

In this hour, you will learn about the following:

- The Brushes palette
- The Calligraphic brush
- The Scatter brush
- The Art brush
- The Pattern brush

FIGURE 8.1

The Paintbrush tool.

The Brushes Palette

Before you learn about the different kinds of brushes themselves, you first need to meet the Paintbrush tool's partner-in-crime, the Brushes palette.

Remember as a child when you played with the Play-Doh Fun Factory? You would squeeze the Play-Doh through one end, and on the other end, you could put different shapes and sizes of attachments that would determine in what shape the Play-Doh came out. Well, the Paintbrush tool is like the Play-Doh factory, and the Brushes palette is your set of attachments; the only difference here is your hands don't smell like Play-Doh.

Open the Brushes palette now, and take a look at what it has to offer. You open this palette by choosing Show Brushes from the Window menu (see Figure 8.2). Illustrator has a default collection of brushes that are already loaded into the Brushes palette (see Figure 8.3). You can easily tell which brush is selected by the double outline, as evident in Figure 8.3, where the Leaf brush is selected.

Illustrator comes with many preset brushes. To load other Brush palettes, choose Window➡Brush Libraries, and choose from the list of other brush sets.

While you are looking at the Brushes palette, take note of the two icons on the bottom right of the palette. (Two others icons to the left are grayed out, totaling four, and I'll get to those in a little bit.) They are the New Brush and the Delete Brush icons. You can create a new brush by clicking on the New Brush icon, and you can duplicate an existing brush by dragging an existing brush shape onto the New Brush icon. You can delete brushes either by selecting them and clicking on the Delete Brush icon, or you can drag selected brush shapes directly on top of the Delete Brush icon and let go of the mouse button. Illustrator then asks you to verify that you want to delete the brush shape.

FIGURE 8.2

Opening the Brushes palette.

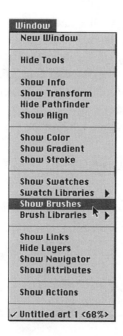

FIGURE 8.3

The Brushes palette. Notice the double outline, indicating that the Leaf brush is selected.

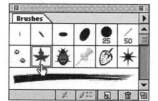

Drawing with the Paintbrush Tool

I can tell that you're already itching to use the Paintbrush tool, so take the time now to draw a couple of items before visiting the four kinds of brushes Illustrator has to offer. Drawing with the Paintbrush tool is easy. Just select the Paintbrush tool, press the mouse button, and drag. Let go of the mouse button as you complete each stroke in your drawing.

When you're using the Paintbrush tool, several options can change the way the paintbrush works. Double-click the Paintbrush tool in the Toolbox, and Illustrator presents you with the Paintbrush Tool Preferences dialog box (see Figure 8.4). The Fidelity and Smoothness options affect how smooth and clean your paintbrush strokes appear. Of course, drawing with the mouse is difficult, so Illustrator smoothes your paths as you draw them. Lower Fidelity and Smoothness settings result in more ragged strokes, and higher settings result in smoother, less jerky strokes. Note the two other options here: Fill New Brush Strokes, which determines whether you want your paintbrush strokes to have a Fill attribute (covered later in Hour 10, "Fills"), and Keep Selected, which tells Illustrator whether you want a paintbrush stroke to stay selected immediately after you draw it (you learned all about selections in Hour 4, "Working with Selections").

FIGURE 8.4

The different options available with the Paintbrush tool.

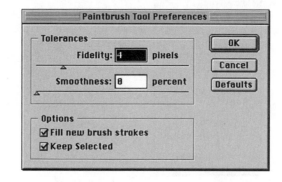

Now take a look at each of the four kinds of brushes the Paintbrush tool has.

The Calligraphic Brush

A calligraphy pen has an angled tip, or "nib," which, when used to draw or write, creates a tapered line that gets thicker or thinner, depending on the angle and direction of the stroke (see Figure 8.5). The Calligraphic brush simulates this effect. Illustrator has many options for controlling the Calligraphic brush, and they're worth a look.

FIGURE 8.5

A stroke drawn with the Calligraphic brush.

Here's how to get started:

1. If the Brushes palette isn't already open, open it by choosing Show Brushes from the Window menu.

2. In the upper-right corner of the Brushes palette is a little triangle facing right. By clicking and holding the mouse button down on it, you are presented with the Brushes palette pop-up menu. At the bottom of the menu are four options: Show Calligraphic Brushes, Show Scatter Brushes, Show Art Brushes, and Show Pattern

Brushes. A check mark next to each one means those kinds of brushes are visible
in the Brushes palette (see Figure 8.6). Hide all brushes except for the Calligraphic
ones for now. You should see only the Calligraphic brushes in the palette now (see
Figure 8.7).

FIGURE 8.6

Viewing the Brushes palette pop-up menu.

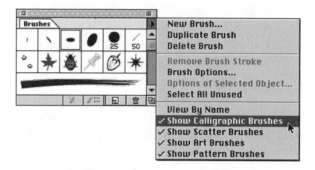

FIGURE 8.7

The Brushes palette with only the Calligraphic brushes visible.

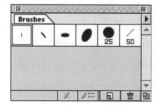

3. Double-click on any of the Calligraphic brushes in the Brushes palette to bring up
   the Calligraphic Brush Options dialog box (see Figure 8.8).

FIGURE 8.8

The Calligraphic Brush Options dialog box.

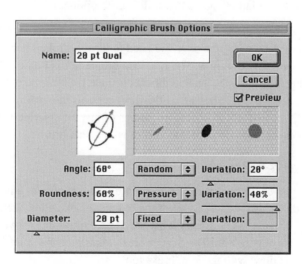

In the Calligraphic Brush Options dialog box, you can specify exactly how the tip of the brush should function. Let me go through each of the options with you:

- At the top of the box, you can specify a name for the brush.

- Directly underneath the name is a white box with a picture of an ellipse with an arrow going through it, and two black dots on either side. This is the Brush Shape Editor. Simply click and drag on the arrow to rotate the brush shape and adjust its angle. Click and drag inward or outward on the black dots to adjust the roundness of the brush shape.

- To the immediate right of the Brush Shape Editor is a window that shows you a preview of what your brush shape looks like. Notice the three shapes. The outer two are grayed out, and the center one is black. If you have variations set (which I'll get to in a minute), the gray shapes illustrate the minimum and maximum values for the brush shape.

- The next three options are numerical values that you can enter for the brush shape: Angle, Roundness, and Diameter. These values are automatically adjusted when you edit the brush shape by using the Brush Shape Editor you just learned about. Each of these options can also have three attributes:

    Fixed—The number you have specified remains constant.

    Random—Illustrator randomly changes the setting.

    Pressure—Uses information collected from a pressure-sensitive tablet to calculate how the brush changes as you draw.

  For each of these attributes, you can specify how much of a variation is allowed by using the Variation sliders that follow each option.

Before going on to the next kind of brush, I'd like to introduce you to two other icons at the bottom of the Brushes palette. You need to have a stroke selected, so if you haven't already drawn one, do so now. The first icon on the left is Remove Brush Stroke. Clicking this icon removes the Paintbrush attribute from the path and turns it back into an ordinary Bézier path. The one on the right controls the options of the selected object. In this way, you can edit the brush properties of just the selected stroke, without having it affect any other strokes in your document that use that brush.

The Scatter Brush

Imagine if you could dip your paintbrush into a bucket of cute little ladybugs, and when you painted, each stroke left a trail of the red and black cuties. Well, wake up and smell the flowers because that's exactly what the Scatter brush does—well, not with *real* ladybugs, silly (see Figure 8.9). The Scatter brush takes predefined art and distributes it along the stroke you draw with the Paintbrush tool.

FIGURE 8.9

A stroke drawn with the Scatter brush.

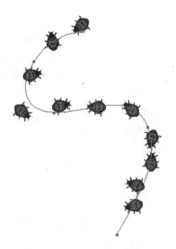

Follow these steps to use the Scatter brush:

1. If the Brushes palette isn't already open, open it by choosing Show Brushes from the Window menu.

2. In the preceding exercise, remember that you hid all brushes except for the Calligraphic ones. Show the Scatter brushes by selecting Show Scatter Brushes from the Brushes palette pop-up menu. You should now see the previous Calligraphic brushes and the Scatter brushes below them (see Figure 8.10).

FIGURE 8.10

The Brushes palette with both the Calligraphic and Scatter brushes visible.

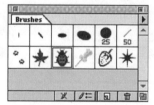

3. Double-click on any of the Scatter brushes in the Brushes palette to open the Scatter Brush Options dialog box (see Figure 8.11).

In the Scatter Brush Options dialog box, you can specify exactly how the tip of the brush should function. Let me go through each of the options with you:

- At the top of the box, you can specify a name for the brush.

- Directly underneath are four options in which you can enter numerical values to specify the Size of the art when it's drawn on the path; the Spacing between the art as it appears on the stroke; the Scatter, which defines how far from the path the art can stray; and finally, the Rotation, which specifies the rotation of each individual piece of art on the path. You can set the Rotation to be relative to the page or to the actual path itself. For each of these four settings, you can specify Fixed values, Random, or Pressure, just as you could in the Calligraphic brushes, as I mentioned earlier in this hour. The Pressure option works only if you are using a pressure-sensitive tablet such as a Wacom tablet.

- The final option for the Scatter brush is Colorization. This option allows you to make color changes to the art that appears on your painted strokes. Choosing None keeps the color consistent with the original color defined with the brush you have selected. To use the Hue Shift option, click on the Eyedropper box, and click to choose a color from the art that appears in the box to the right. This procedure works on colored images only, not black-and-white images. Clicking on the Tips button can help you see how the color changes are applied.

FIGURE 8.11

The Scatter Brush Options dialog box.

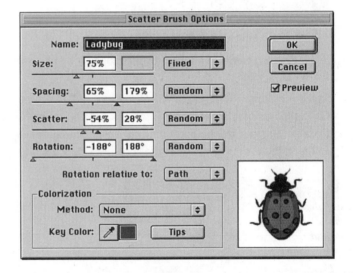

To create a Scatter brush of your own, simply drag your art into the Brushes palette. When Illustrator asks you which kind of brush you want to create, select Scatter Brush and click OK. After you name your new Scatter brush and make any necessary adjustments, click OK and it will appear in the Brushes palette with the other brushes.

The Art Brush

The Art brush differs from the Scatter brush in that the Art brush stretches a single piece of predefined art along a stroke, whereas the Scatter brush litters the stroke with many copies of the art (see Figure 8.12).

FIGURE 8.12

A stroke drawn with the Art brush.

8

You can use the Art brush as follows:

1. If the Brushes palette isn't already open, open it by choosing Show Brushes from the Window menu.

2. As you did in the preceding exercise, you need to show the Art brushes, which you hid earlier. Select Show Art Brushes from the Brushes palette pop-up menu, and scroll down to the bottom of the palette. You should now see the Art brushes (see Figure 8.13).

FIGURE 8.13

Viewing the Art brushes in the Brushes palette.

3. Double-click on any of the Art brushes in the Brushes palette to open the Art Brush Options dialog box (see Figure 8.14).

In the Art Brush Options dialog box, you can specify exactly how the tip of the brush should function. Let me go through each of the options with you:

- At the top of the box, you can specify a name for the brush.

- Directly underneath the name is a white box with the art in it. Notice that an arrow goes through the art. This arrow indicates the direction the art is drawn on the stroke; you can edit it by clicking on any of the arrows that appear to the right of the white box.

- Below the Direction option is the Size option, in which you can specify what size the art appears on the painted stroke. If you click on the Proportional button, the art appears in proportion with the length the stroke is painted. You can also specify whether the art should be flipped along or across the painted stroke.

- The final option for the Art brush is Colorization. This option allows you to make color changes to the art that appears on your painted strokes. Choosing None keeps the color consistent with the original color defined with the brush you have selected. To use the Hue Shift option, click on the Eyedropper box, and click to choose a color from the art that appears in the white box above. Clicking on the Tips button can help you see how the color changes are applied.

FIGURE 8.14

The Art Brush Options dialog box.

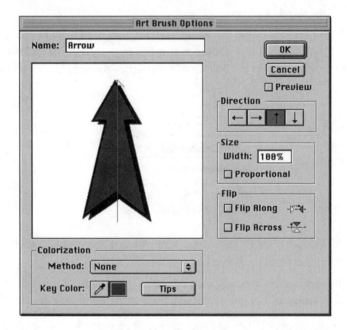

To create an Art brush of your own, simply drag your art into the Brushes palette. When Illustrator asks you which kind of brush you want to create, select Art Brush and click OK. After you name your new Art brush and make any necessary adjustments, click OK and it will appear in the Brushes palette with the other brushes.

The Pattern Brush

You have to give Adobe credit. Just when you think Adobe has given you every kind of brush you could possibly dream of, it throws in one more. The Pattern brush takes patterns and applies them across a painted stroke. What makes this different from any brush you've encountered previously is that you can define patterns with different attributes for corners and ends (see Figure 8.15). Patterns are covered in detail in Hour 10, so I'll just touch on the subject here.

FIGURE 8.15

A stroke drawn with the Pattern brush. Notice how the corners line up perfectly.

8

To use the Pattern brush, just follow these steps:

1. If the Brushes palette isn't already open, open it by choosing Show Brushes from the Window menu.

2. Select Show Pattern Brushes from the Brushes palette pop-up menu, and scroll down to the bottom of the palette. You should now see the Pattern brushes (see Figure 8.16).

FIGURE 8.16

Viewing the Pattern brushes in the Brushes palette.

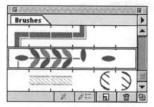

3. Double-click on any of the Pattern brushes in the Brushes palette to open the Pattern Brush Options dialog box (see Figure 8.17).

In the Pattern Brush Options dialog box, you can specify exactly how the tip of the brush should function. As before, let me go through each of the options with you:

- At the top of the box, you can specify a name for the brush.

- Directly underneath the name are five boxes, each representing a different tile of the pattern: Side, Outer Corner, Inner Corner, Start, and End. You do not need to define all five parts, and Illustrator uses the parts only when necessary. With a tile section selected, choose a pattern from the list that appears directly under the tiles.

- As with the previous brushes, you can also specify Size and Spacing, as well as specify if the pattern should be flipped along or across.

- With the Pattern brush, you can decide how Illustrator fits the pattern to the path. Obviously, not every pattern will fit every path length perfectly. If you select Stretch to Fit, Illustrator stretches the pattern tiles to make the pattern fit seamlessly across the entire painted stroke. If you select Add Space to Fit, Illustrator does not adjust the size of the pattern tiles, but spaces them evenly across the painted stroke. Finally, the Approximate Path option adjusts the size of the path itself to fit the size of the pattern tiles.

- The final option for the Pattern brush is Colorization. This option allows you to make color changes to the art that appears on your painted strokes. Choosing None keeps the color consistent with the original defined with the brush you have selected. To use the Hue Shift option, click the Eyedropper box, and click to choose a color from the art that appears in the white box above. Clicking on the Tips button can help you see how the color changes are applied.

FIGURE 8.17

The Pattern Brush Options dialog box.

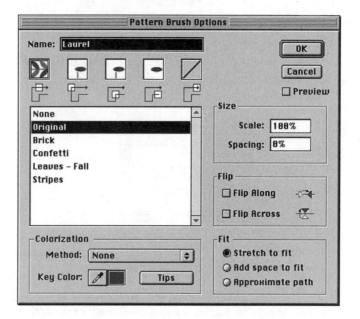

To create a Pattern brush of your own, simply drag your art into the Brushes palette. When Illustrator asks you which kind of brush you want to create, select Pattern Brush and click OK. After you name your new Pattern brush and make any necessary adjustments, click OK and it will appear in the Brushes palette with the other brushes. For detailed information on creating pattern tiles, see Hour 10.

In closing, if you find it hard to tell what type each brush is just by looking at the Brushes palette, you can opt to view the brushes by name. Choose View by Name from the Brushes palette pop-up menu. Notice that on the far right of each line is an icon that indicates what kind of brush each one is (see Figure 8.18).

FIGURE 8.18

When viewing your brushes by name, you can quickly tell what kind of brush each one is from the icon that appears to the right of each name.

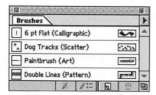

8

You can apply a paintbrush stroke to any shape that you learned to draw earlier this hour. Try applying Art or Scatter brushes to spirals and stars for really interesting effects. To remove a paintbrush stroke from these shapes, just click on the Remove Brush button.

Summary

Isn't the Paintbrush tool cool? This hour, you learned how to use the Paintbrush tool to create all different kinds of art. Besides learning how to use the Calligraphic, Scatter, Art, and Pattern brushes, you also now know how to create and edit the brush shapes and brush art themselves. Now that you have a great understanding of how to draw all kinds of shapes in Illustrator, in the next hour, you'll begin learning how to color them.

Workshop

The Workshop contains quiz questions to help you solidify your understanding of the material covered in this hour and exercises to provide you with experience using what you have learned. You can find the answers to the quiz questions at the end of the hour.

Quiz

1. How many brush types are available in the Paintbrush tool?

    a. 3

    b. 4

    c. 5

2. What affects the smoothness of a painted stroke?

    a. Spacing

    b. Colorization

    c. Fidelity

3. You can't change the brush options of one path without affecting all other paths with the same brush attribute.

    a. True

    b. False

4. The Brush Shape Editor is used with which type of brush?

    a. Art

    b. Pattern

    c. Calligraphic

Exercises

1. Using the Paintbrush tool, draw several strokes. Now using the Selection tool, change the paths to use different kinds of brushes.

2. Remember that brushes are live, meaning that if you change the path itself, the artwork will reconfigure to the path. Try using the Pen tool to edit the same paths you drew in the preceding exercise, and watch what happens.

3. Create your own brushes by dragging artwork right into the Brushes palette.

Answers to Quiz Questions

1. b

2. c

3. b

4. c

Hour 9

Coloring Objects

Now you're ready to add some color. Illustrator has lots of options when it comes to coloring objects. Besides solid colors, Illustrator can fill objects with gradients and patterns—all customizable. Illustrator also has support for custom colors such as Pantone, TRUMATCH, and even Web-specific colors (for use on the World Wide Web). Throughout this hour, you'll learn about each of these colors in detail, including the following:

- The Color palette
- The Swatches palette
- The Eyedropper tool
- The Paint Bucket tool

Fill and Stroke

In Illustrator, each object has two attributes: a fill and a stroke (see Figure 9.1). As you'll soon see, Illustrator has several kinds of fills and strokes. You can give a fill and a stroke to just about any object (with the exception of a mask), even one that is an open path (see Figure 9.2).

FIGURE 9.1

Each object has a fill and a stroke.

FIGURE 9.2

Illustrator fills an open path by using the two open points as a boundary.

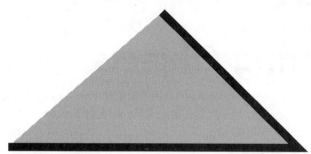

At the bottom of the Toolbox are the Fill and Stroke indicators (see Figure 9.3). They are very similar to Photoshop's Foreground and Background color indicators. The box to the upper left is the Fill indicator, and the one to the lower right is the Stroke indicator. You can click either one to make it active, or you can press X to toggle between them. When the Fill box is selected, any changes you make in the Color palette are applied to the fill of a selected object, and the same is true for the Stroke.

FIGURE 9.3

Illustrator's Fill and Stroke indicators.

You can find two more icons there: in the upper right, a curved arrow, and in the lower left, a pair of little boxes. Clicking on the arrow swaps the fill and stroke, meaning if the fill is currently white and the stroke is black, clicking the arrows makes the fill black and the stroke white. Clicking the little boxes sets the fill and stroke to Illustrator's default setting (as does pressing D), which is a white fill and black stroke. Note that this does not affect the weight (thickness) of the stroke.

The Fill and Stroke indicators also appear in the Color palette, which I'll discuss next.

9

When you're changing the color of the fill or stroke, any object that is selected while you make the change will take on the new color attributes. If no object is selected, the next object you create will take on the new color attributes you just set.

The Color Palette

Illustrator's Color palette, shown in Figure 9.4, consists of the Fill and Stroke indicators, a color slider (or sliders) with percentage boxes, and a color bar, which, depending on what colors are selected, is either a color spectrum or a grayscale/tint ramp. If all you see is the color bar, select Show Options from the palette menu (see Figure 9.5).

FIGURE 9.4

Illustrator's Color palette.

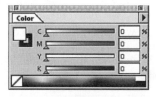

FIGURE 9.5

Selecting Show Options in the Color palette.

NEW TERM   Illustrator works with any of four different *color models*: CMYK, Grayscale, RGB, and HSB. To quickly cycle through each of the color models, hold down the Shift key, and click on the color bar in the Color palette (see Figure 9.6).

FIGURE 9.6

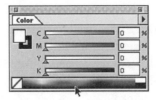

*Shift+clicking the
color bar in the Color
palette cycles through
each of Illustrator's
four color models.*

Selecting a Color

To select a color, either click anywhere in the color spectrum or tint ramp, or adjust the
sliders manually by clicking on the little triangles and dragging them to the left and right.
You can also enter percentages manually by clicking in the field, entering a number, and
pressing the Tab key to advance to the next field, or pressing Shift+Tab to go back to the
previous field.

After you put the "focus" into the Color palette, you can quickly move
through all the fields by pressing the Tab key. If you have other palettes
docked to it as well, such as the Gradient or Stroke palette, you can cycle
through those fields as well. To put Illustrator's focus into the last used
palette, press (Command+~)[Control+~].

Illustrator's slider bars are very intuitive and change color as you drag to
approximate other colors. You can also hold down the Shift key while dragging any one slider, and all sliders move proportionately, making it easy to
get lighter or darker shades of colors.

Color Models

I mentioned that Illustrator supports four different color models. Illustrator also enables
you to have colors from different color models within the same document (see the following note). You need to keep this point in mind as you work on each project. Some
jobs may require that you work in CMYK, others in RGB, and so on. To ensure that your
finished artwork looks as you intended it to, make sure you are using the right color
model from the beginning. Switching between color models after a job is in progress or
finished may result in color shifts and changes.

Although Illustrator allows you to have a document containing colors from different color models, that doesn't mean you should do it. In fact, using different color models can be very bad. If you are working on a job that will be printed, use only the CMYK or Grayscale color model. If you are doing multimedia work, use RGB or HSB. Using different color models within the same document can make for inconsistent color shifts and can become a production nightmare.

CMYK

The CMYK color model (cyan, magenta, yellow, and black) is the standard for most of today's offset printing and is also known as four-color process. If your color artwork will be printed on paper, you're probably going to create it in CMYK. To select a CMYK color from the Color palette, either Shift+click to cycle through the color models until CMYK shows up, or choose CMYK from the palette menu (see Figure 9.7).

FIGURE 9.7

Choosing the CMYK color model.

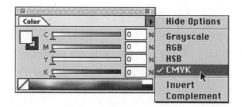

Grayscale

For black-and-white work, use Grayscale, which supports 256 levels of gray. In this mode, the Color palette has a grayscale ramp to choose different percentages (see Figure 9.8).

FIGURE 9.8

The grayscale ramp in the Color palette.

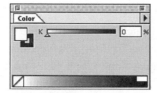

RGB

The RGB color model (red, green, and blue) is the standard used for today's televisions and computer monitors. If you are designing work for multimedia applications or for the

World Wide Web, use the RGB Color palette. RGB colors have a much wider range, or gamut, and have more colors that are brighter than CMYK. For more information on Web colors, see Hour 23, "Web Graphics."

HSB

The HSB color model (hue, saturation, and brightness) is not as widely used and is based on the human perception of color. The Hue value determines which color you get, whereas Saturation determines how intense that color is, and Brightness determines how light or dark it is. In most cases, though, if you are using HSB colors, you will eventually have to convert them to RGB or CMYK for output.

Custom Colors

NEW TERM   Though not a color model, another kind of color is supported within Illustrator: *custom colors*. A custom color is a predefined color that you can either create or choose from a list such as PANTONE, FOCOLTONE, TOYO, or TRUMATCH. Custom colors are also called *spot colors*. They are standard colors that have been designated to ensure color accuracy.

The Pantone system, for example, was created so that when a designer wanted to print red, he or she could specify a Pantone number, which a printer could match exactly by using a red ink, instead of producing the color with a combination of cyan, magenta, yellow, and black inks. Custom colors act the same way as grayscale does. You can specify a tint of a custom color, and the Color palette looks identical.

Loading Custom Color Palettes

Included with Illustrator are several useful custom color libraries. They include DIC-COLOR, FOCOLTONE, PANTONE (coated, process, and uncoated), TOYO, and TRU-MATCH, plus system palettes for both Macintosh and Windows for multimedia work. Illustrator also has a wonderful color-safe Web palette for use when you're creating art for the World Wide Web.

To load any of these palettes, choose Swatch Libraries from the Window menu (see Figure 9.9), and choose one of the libraries. But say you went through all the trouble of creating your own custom colors in one document, and you want to use them in another one. At that point, you select Other Library from the submenu (see Figure 9.10), after which Illustrator asks you to locate another Illustrator file and imports its custom colors.

Figure 9.9

Choosing a custom color library.

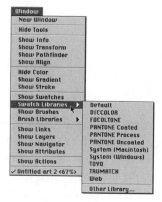

Figure 9.10

Importing custom colors from another Illustrator file.

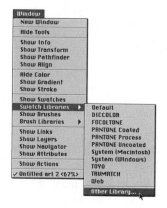

The Swatches Palette

NEW TERM   Imagine if every time you wanted to apply a color, you had to enter the percentages of that color in the Color palette. Besides being a pain, it would also be a big waste of time. To save time and trouble, use the Swatches palette instead. A *swatch* is a color that you define. It can be a process color, a spot color, or even a gradient or pattern, as you'll soon see. After you define a swatch, you can apply it to any object. You can also edit and modify an existing swatch.

Now take a look at the Swatches palette (see Figure 9.11). If the palette is not already open, choose Show Swatches from the Window menu.

FIGURE 9.11

The Swatches palette.

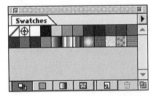

First, notice the little "chicklet" icons across the bottom of the palette. From the left, the first one is Show All Swatches. The next three are for Color, Gradient, and Pattern swatches, respectively. At first glance, the palette may look too messy, and it may be difficult to determine what's what. By clicking the Color, Gradient, or Pattern icon, you can choose to view only those swatches, making it easier to choose a swatch (see Figure 9.12).

FIGURE 9.12

The chicklet icons on the bottom of the Swatches palette. Notice that only the Gradient swatches are shown.

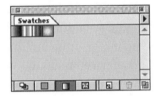

Next are the New Swatch and Trash icons. Clicking the New Swatch icon creates a new swatch with whatever color is currently selected. (Selected swatches have a white border.) Clicking the Trash icon deletes any selected swatch. To select a swatch, simply click it. You can select several contiguous swatches by holding down the Shift key, or you can select noncontiguous swatches by holding the (Command)[Control] key when selecting the swatches (see Figure 9.13).

FIGURE 9.13

Selecting multiple swatches with the (Command)[Control] key.

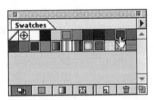

> Illustrator has drag-and-drop capabilities. You can delete swatches by dragging them into the Trash icon, and you can also create a duplicate swatch by dragging an existing swatch on top of the New Swatch icon. You can drag colors between the Fill and Stroke indicators, the Color palette, and even between custom color and Swatches palettes.

Double-clicking a swatch brings up the Swatch Options dialog box (see Figure 9.14). You can then edit the name of the swatch, determine whether it should be a spot or process color, and choose which color model to use. You also should see a box marked Non-Global. With this box checked, each object you color with this swatch is independent. However, by unchecking this box and making the swatch Global, you can edit the swatch at any time, and all objects colored with that swatch will update to reflect those changes.

FIGURE 9.14

The Swatch Options dialog box.

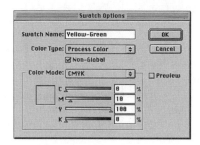

If you want to change the values of an existing swatch, follow these steps:

1. Select the swatch you want to modify.

2. In the Color palette, edit the color.

3. When you're done editing the color, press and hold the mouse button on the color swatch in the Color palette.

4. While still pressing the mouse, hold down the (Option)[Alt] key, and drag the color swatch (either the one in the Color palette or the one in the Toolbox) on top of the swatch you want to edit in the Swatches palette.

Notice that some swatches have a small dot in the lower-right corner. This dot indicates that the swatch is a spot color. You can also change the order of the swatches simply by dragging and moving them around.

Viewing the Swatches Palette

Illustrator also gives you three ways to view the Swatches palette: Small Swatch, Large Swatch, or Name (see Figure 9.15). To choose a viewing mode, select a choice from the palette menu. You can also select the functions I mentioned earlier, such as Duplicate Swatch and Delete Swatch, as well as sort the swatches by kind or name (see Figure 9.16). When you view swatches by name, an icon on the far right of the swatch name indicates whether the swatch is spot or process.

FIGURE 9.15

The three viewing modes of the Swatches palette.

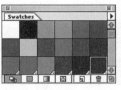

FIGURE 9.16

Sorting the swatches through the palette menu.

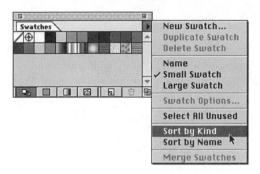

 Remember that a keyboard shortcut is available for the None attribute. To quickly fill an object or stroke it with None, press the slash (/) key. Whether the fill or stroke of the selected object is changed to None depends on the focus of the Fill and Stroke icons on the Toolbox.

 After you put the focus into the Swatches palette (Command+Option) [Control+Alt] or (Command+~)[Control+~], if you last used the Swatches palette, you can type the first few letters of a color or the numbers of a Pantone color, and Illustrator jumps to that swatch. Press Enter to bring the focus back into your artwork.

The Eyedropper Tool

The Eyedropper tool, as shown in Figure 9.17, is used to sample colors and attributes for use in applying those colors and attributes to other objects. Say you have a shape with one color, for example, and you want it to be the color of another shape. Without deselecting your shape, you can switch to the Eyedropper tool and click the other object. This operation colors your selected object the same as the one you clicked on.

FIGURE 9.17

The Eyedropper tool.

You can also press and hold down the mouse while using the Eyedropper tool, and then drag anywhere to sample the pixel color of anything on your screen (in real-time, I might add—watching the colors zip through the Fill indicator is cool).

To control exactly which attributes the Eyedropper (and Paint Bucket) picks up, double-click the Eyedropper tool in the Toolbox. Illustrator presents you with a comprehensive dialog box in which you can specify settings for picking up strokes and fills, and even font and text attributes (see Figure 9.18). To see all the attributes, use the scrollbars to scroll down, and click on the little triangles to access each section.

FIGURE 9.18

Specifying options for the Eyedropper and Paint Bucket tools.

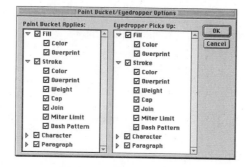

The Paint Bucket Tool

Working in tandem with the Eyedropper tool, the Paint Bucket tool, as shown in Figure 9.19, applies colors and attributes to unselected objects. You just click an object, and Illustrator fills that object with whatever colors and attributes are selected.

FIGURE 9.19

The Paint Bucket tool.

If you press the (Option)[Alt] key with the Paint Bucket tool selected, it toggles to the Eyedropper tool, and vice versa. With this simple operation, you can quickly sample a color and apply it to other objects.

Summary

What a colorful hour! You learned all about the different kinds of colors Illustrator uses, and you learned how to create and edit swatches of colors. You also learned about two new palettes: the Swatches palette and the Color palette. Next hour, you'll learn what you can do with all these wonderful colors.

Workshop

The Workshop contains quiz questions to help you solidify your understanding of the material covered in this hour and exercises to provide you with experience using what you have learned. You can find the answers to the quiz questions at the end of the hour.

Quiz

1. Which is not an attribute of a shape in Illustrator?

   a. Fill

   b. Stroke

   c. Color

2. What is the keyboard shortcut for setting colors to the default white fill and black stroke?

   a. (Command+D)[Control+D]

   b. D

   c. W

3. Which of these color models is not supported in Illustrator.

   a. CMYK

   b. CIE LAB

   c. HSB

4. To modify an existing swatch, you drag a new color onto the existing swatch while holding which key?

   a. S

   b. (Command)[Control]

   c. (Option)[Alt]

5. The Eyedropper tool can sample what point size a font is.

   a. True

   b. False

Exercises

1. Select all three view options for the Swatches palette, and see which one is most comfortable for you. Then get used to using the "chicklet" icons on the bottom of the palette to view only certain kinds of swatches.

2. With no objects selected, practice using the Eyedropper to sample attributes and colors, and then press the (Option)[Alt] key to toggle to the Paint Bucket tool so you can quickly apply those attributes to other objects, without having to select them.

Term Review

Color model—A specific defined color space, such as CMYK, RGB, or HSB.

Custom color—A color defined in Illustrator that separates to its own plate. *See* Spot color.

Spot color—A specified color that is independent of any other colors in a job and separates to its own plate.

Swatch—Illustrator's metaphor for a defined color, pattern, or gradient.

Answers to Quiz Questions

1. c
2. b
3. b
4. c
5. a

HOUR 10

Fills

As I mentioned before, a vector object in Illustrator has two attributes: a fill and a stroke. This hour focuses on the fill attribute. Remember how, when you were little, you used crayons on coloring books, and you were so careful not to "go out of the lines"? Well, that's what a fill in Illustrator is—coloring an object, up to the boundary of the path. The good thing about Illustrator is that it never draws out of the lines—it's perfect every time—and you don't have to worry about sharpening the crayon.

In this hour, you'll learn about the following:

- Applying a fill to an object
- Making gradient fills
- Working with the Gradient Mesh tool
- Making pattern fills
- Using the Expand command

Solid Color Fills

A solid color fill is rather simple. Using the same crayon example as earlier, a solid color fill is akin to using one particular crayon for the interior of the object. In the preceding hour, you learned how to define new colors in Illustrator, as well as how to apply them to objects.

The two other kinds of fills in Illustrator are gradients and patterns. In this hour, you'll learn how to define and apply these kinds of fills.

Gradients

NEW TERM *Gradients* are a powerful feature in Illustrator, enabling you to specify a fill of different colors blending with each other. Illustrator can create a gradient between just 2 colors or up to 32 colors. Gradients can be used to achieve cool shading effects or to add dimension to objects, and they are also a great design element (see Figure 10.1).

FIGURE 10.1

Gradients used for shading and adding dimension.

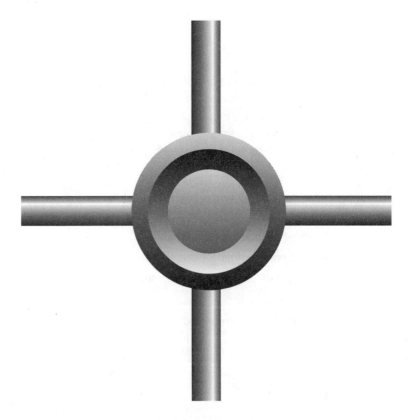

The Gradient Palette

You can apply a gradient by simply selecting a gradient swatch from the Swatches palette. To create or edit a gradient, however, you need to open the Gradient palette (F9). There you will find a gradient swatch, an option to make the gradient Linear or Radial, fields for Angle and Location, and a gradient slider (see Figure 10.2).

FIGURE 10.2

The Gradient palette.

Defining a Gradient

You create a gradient much the same way you create a color. First, you define the gradient, and then you click the New Swatch icon in the Swatches palette. After you create the new swatch, you should double-click it and give it a name. Illustrator just calls it "Unnamed gradient," and after you have 15 unnamed gradients in your Swatches palette, you just might forget which one is which.

NEW TERM Notice that underneath the gradient slider are icons that look like little houses. They are *color stops* indicating the points at which a color is used in the gradient. To create a new color stop, click anywhere underneath the gradient slider. When a new house appears, you can drag it to the left or right. You can also drag any color from the Swatches or Color palette onto the gradient slider to create a color stop in that color. To change an existing color stop, either drag a new color directly on top of it, or click the icon to select it and change the color in the Color or Swatches palette.

Also, notice that little diamond-shaped icons appear on top of the gradient slider. They indicate the location of the midpoint of the gradation. In other words, wherever the diamond is, that's the place where 50 percent of each color appears (see Figure 10.3). You can drag the midpoint indicator left or right to adjust where the midpoint should be.

FIGURE 10.3

Notice the color stops and location point indicators.

Now you're ready to define a gradient:

1. Open the Gradient palette (F9), the Color palette (F6), and the Swatches palette (F5).

2. In the Gradient palette, click the gradient swatch (it's the large square in the upper left of the palette). Notice that the gradient slider below becomes active, and the color stops and midpoint indicators become visible.

3. Click a color stop. Now a color stop is visible underneath the color swatch in the Color palette.

4. Using the sliders in the Color palette, or using the spectrum at the bottom of the Color palette, select a color for the selected color stop. Alternatively, you can drag a color from the Swatches palette directly onto the color stop in the Gradient palette.

5. Create a new color stop. Click anywhere directly underneath the gradient slider in the Gradient palette. Notice that another color stop appears. Apply a color to it the same way you did in step 4. Alternatively, you can drag a color from the Swatches palette directly onto the gradient slider. When you let go of the mouse, a color stop of the color you dragged appears.

6. Delete a color stop. To do so, you need at least three color stops in order to delete one (a minimum of two color stops is required). Click and drag downward on the color stop you want to delete. When the color stop disappears, release the mouse.

7. Make your final adjustments by moving the color stops and the midpoint indicators.

8. After your gradient is complete, click the mouse on the gradient swatch, and drag it into the Swatches palette, where it appears highlighted with a white outline.

9. Double-click the new swatch, and give it an appropriate name. Then click OK.

Editing a Gradient

To edit an existing gradient, modify the gradient in the Gradient palette, and then drag the gradient swatch on top of the swatch you want to update while holding down the (Option)[Alt] key.

You can change the angle of the gradient in the Angle field of the Gradient palette. The angle does not affect the object in any way; it affects only the gradient that fills the object. In Figure 10.1, for example, 3D effects were achieved just by flipping the gradient 180 degrees.

Using the Gradient Tool

The Gradient tool is used to control the direction and placement of a gradient in an object or over several objects (see Figure 10.4). After you fill an object with a gradient, select the Gradient tool (G), and with the object still selected, click and drag across the object in the direction you want the gradient to go. The place where you begin dragging is the position where the gradient starts, and the place where you let go is the position where the gradient ends. If you stopped dragging before the end of the object, Illustrator continues to fill the object with the color at the end of the gradient. This tool is perfect for specifying where the center of a radial blend should be when you're making 3D spheres (see Figure 10.5).

FIGURE 10.4

The Gradient tool.

FIGURE 10.5

Using the Gradient tool, you can make realistic-looking 3D spheres.

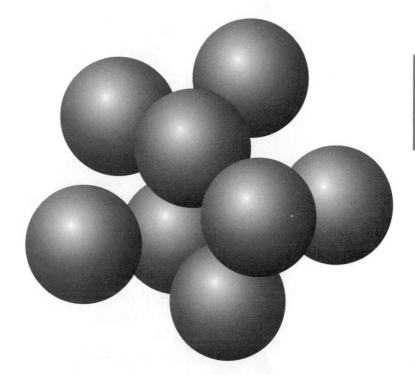

10

The Gradient Mesh Tool

Gradients are pretty cool, but all colors in a gradient fill work in a predictable way, and they all must be in the same direction. Going back to something I mentioned in Hour 1, "Getting to Know Illustrator," one of the advantages of working with raster paint programs is the ability to create blended painterly effects. Illustrator 8 addresses that exact issue with the new and exciting Gradient Mesh tool (see Figure 10.6). Why do I say it's exciting? Because you've never seen anything like it (see Figure 10.7).

FIGURE 10.6

The Gradient Mesh tool.

FIGURE 10.7

An object with a fill created using the Gradient Mesh tool.

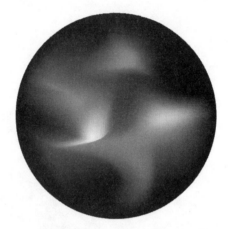

To use the Gradient Mesh tool, you start with any filled shape. You then apply "grids" to the shape, each grid representing a different gradient. The grid is made up of anchor and control points that function the same way as they do in a vector path. Each gradient is defined by the position of the anchor and control points of its grid (see Figure 10.8). Using this tool may sound difficult, but as soon as you try it, you'll understand—which brings you to the next step-by-step.

FIGURE 10.8

The object selected, with the mesh "grids" visible.

1. Draw a shape. Start with a rectangle to make your job easier.

2. Press the U key to select the Gradient Mesh tool. Without pressing the mouse button, move the cursor into the rectangle, and then move it out. Notice how the cursor changes to indicate where you can use the tool (see Figure 10.9).

3. With the cursor inside the rectangle, click once. A mesh "grid" then appears (see Figure 10.10).

FIGURE 10.9

The cursor on the right indicates that Illustrator is ready to add a mesh to the object. The cursor on the left indicates that you cannot place a mesh at the current spot.

10

FIGURE 10.10

After you click inside the shape, a mesh is applied to the shape.

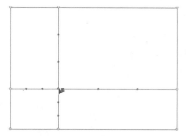

4. Apply a color to this mesh. Go ahead and select a red color from the Swatches palette, or create your own color in the Color palette. The color then appears in the mesh (see Figure 10.11). Right away, you can tell how the Gradient Mesh is unique. Notice how the center, or highest concentration of color, is the place where the anchor point is located, where you clicked. More important, notice how the gradient stretches and fades out based on the control handles and the grid.

FIGURE 10.11

The first color, applied to the mesh.

5. Edit the mesh to your liking. Grab a control or an anchor point, and drag it to a different location. See how the Gradient now follows the new path (see Figure 10.12).

6. Add another grid. To do so, find an open area in the same shape and click. Another mesh grid is then added to the shape (see Figure 10.13).

FIGURE 10.12

Note how the gradient follows the shape of the mesh.

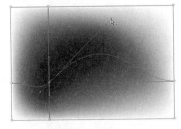

FIGURE 10.13

The rectangle with another mesh added.

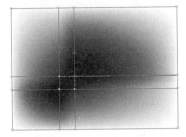

7. Select a new color for the new grid you just made. You can add as many grids as you like, with each grid representing a different color as well.

8. Delete any singular grid by pressing and holding the (Option)[Alt] key while clicking on the center anchor point of the mesh grid.

You can create a mesh gradient in yet another way. With an object selected, you can choose Object➡Create Gradient Mesh (see Figure 10.14). Illustrator prompts you with a dialog box asking how many rows and columns you want in the mesh and how intense the highlight should be, as well as whether the gradient should face inward or outward (see Figure 10.15).

FIGURE 10.14

Selecting the Create Gradient Mesh option from the Object menu.

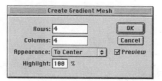

FIGURE 10.15

The Create Gradient Mesh dialog box.

10

If you want to add or delete anchor points in your mesh, you can use the Pen tool as you would on any Illustrator path. You cannot delete anchor points that are part of the original mesh. You can delete only the anchor points you added using the Add Anchor Point tool.

I would like to make just a few comments about the Gradient Mesh tool before moving on. The Gradient Mesh tool takes advantage of certain new technologies, mainly PostScript 3 (see Hour 22, "Printing"). The Gradient Mesh tool also requires computer power, as each mesh that you add slows down the system as well as the screen draw.

Patterns

Patterns can be real timesavers. A pattern is a defined piece of art created in Illustrator that, as a Fill attribute, is repeated over and over again, much like wallpaper (see Figure 10.16).

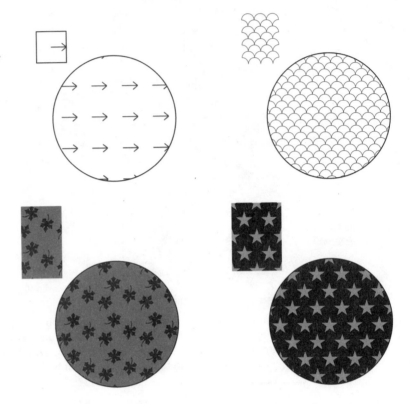

FIGURE 10.16

Several pattern tiles and what they look like when used to fill an object.

Defining a Pattern

Defining a pattern is a little different from defining gradients or colors. Instead of clicking the New Swatch icon, you drag your objects directly into the Swatches palette to define the pattern. Again, after you create the swatch, you need to give it a unique name so that you can find and edit it quickly.

When you're creating a pattern design, remember that your object will be repeated over and over again, so be careful how you set it up. If you need extra space around your art, create a box with a fill and stroke of None, and send it to the back of your artwork. Then select your art along with the background box and define the pattern. Illustrator treats that empty box as the boundary for the pattern tile (see Figure 10.17).

FIGURE 10.17

The patterns with their bounding boxes (top) and the way they appear in a filled object (bottom).

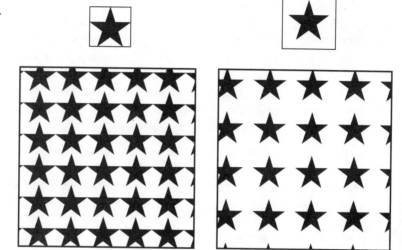

10

A pattern tile cannot contain another pattern or a gradient. If you want to have a gradient effect or use a pattern within your pattern, use the Expand command to convert the gradient or pattern into individual filled objects. The Expand command is covered later in this hour.

To edit a pattern, drag the new artwork on top of the swatch you want to change while pressing the (Option)[Alt] key. Also, if you lose the artwork for your pattern, don't worry. When you drag a pattern swatch out of the Swatches palette and onto the page, the objects that make up the pattern are placed onto the page as new objects, just as if you had drawn them there.

To move the pattern around within the object, select the object with the Selection tool, and then click and drag the object while holding down the tilde (~) key. When you let go, only the pattern is repositioned; the object does not move.

Using the Expand Command

NEW TERM Gradients in Illustrator first appeared in version 5 for Macintosh. In versions prior to that, you were able to achieve a gradient look by blending objects into each other. Basically, the Blend tool created many objects, or *steps*, each with a color slightly different than the next. This effect gave the appearance of a gradation. Of course, gradients are more intuitive and are easier to edit, but if you need to bring your artwork, which was created in version 8 with gradations, into version 3.2, you will lose the gradient information, as it is not supported in version 3.2.

In these circumstances, as well as others, you need to convert an object filled with a gradient into separate objects that create a blend. To make this conversion, select the filled object and choose Expand Fill from the Object menu (see Figure 10.18). When expanding the gradient, you can specify how many steps Illustrator breaks it into.

FIGURE 10.18

Choosing Expand Fill.

You can also expand an object filled with a pattern. By doing so, the fill that until now has been uneditable turns into editable objects and ceases being a patterned fill. The shape also becomes a mask that blocks out parts of the pattern tiles that should not be visible (see Figure 10.19). See Hour 12, "Compound Paths and Masks," for more information on masks.

FIGURE 10.19

From the top, a pattern and gradient as viewed in Preview mode, the same pattern and gradient viewed in Artwork mode, and on the bottom, the same pattern and gradient viewed in Artwork mode after being expanded.

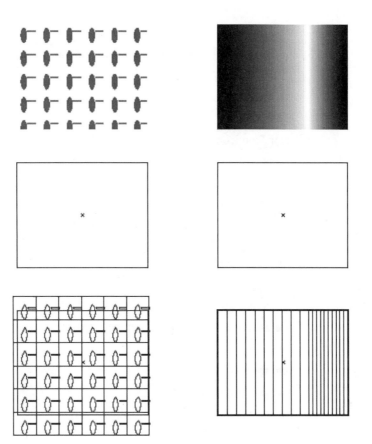

10

Summary

Are you all filled up? In this hour, you learned how to fill your shapes not only with flat, solid colors but also with interesting multicolor gradients and patterns. As if the totally rad Gradient Mesh tool was not enough, you also learned how to use the Expand feature to convert your gradients and patterns into editable objects. In the next hour, I'll discuss the Stroke attribute.

Workshop

The Workshop contains quiz questions to help you solidify your understanding of the material covered in this hour and exercises to provide you with experience using what you have learned. You can find the answers to the quiz questions at the end of the hour.

Quiz

1. The diamond-shaped icon above the gradient slider is called the

    a. Color Stop

    b. Midpoint indicator

    c. Swatch

2. The Color Stop icons look like

    a. diamonds

    b. squares

    c. little houses

3. The Gradient Mesh tool can simulate what kinds of effects that were previously found only in raster paint programs?

    a. Gaussian blurs

    b. Transparent images

    c. Painterly effects

4. To define a pattern, you drag your artwork where?

    a. into the Swatches palette

    b. into the Pattern palette

    c. into the Color palette

5. The Expand command is used for gradients only.

    a. True

    b. False

Exercises

1. Create a shape and fill it with a gradient. Using the Gradient tool, practice changing the angle and adjusting the start and endpoints for the gradient. Remember that you can start or end a gradient anywhere on the page; it need not fit within the shape. Illustrator takes care of the rest.

2. Create a shape and make multiple multicolored mesh grids. Then practice removing them one by one.

3. Create a pattern and make several different versions, each with different bounding box settings. Observe how each pattern falls differently within your shape.

Term Review

Color stop—The point in a gradient where a new color is introduced.

Gradient—A fill that contains two or more colors that blend into each other.

Steps—Individual parts of a blend. Each step is a slightly different color, giving the illusion of a smooth transition.

Answers to Quiz Questions

1. b
2. c
3. c
4. a
5. b

10

HOUR 11

Strokes

A stroke is the line around an object. You can give an object's stroke a different color than its fill. You also have several stroke options, which actually make for some very interesting and useful implementations, to be covered later in this hour.

Throughout this hour, you will learn about the following:

- The Stroke palette
- Stroke weights, miters, and caps
- Dashed lines
- Layered strokes

The Stroke Palette

The Stroke palette (F10) can be set either to show only the stroke weight or all the stroke attributes including Miter Limit, Line Caps and Joins, and Dashed Lines (see Figure 11.1). You can choose either setting by selecting Show Options from the palette menu.

FIGURE 11.1

Viewing the entire Stroke palette.

Weight and Miter Limit

NEW TERM　The most-used option in the Stroke palette is the *Stroke Weight*. It determines how thick or thin the stroke is. Illustrator's default is 1 point. For hairline rules, most people use .25 point. You can enter any amount from 0 to 1000 points. You can even enter numbers in different measurements (such as 2.5 in.), and Illustrator converts them to points for you.

The *Miter Limit* option determines how far the stroke sticks out on a sharp corner. A thick line, for example, needs more room to complete a sharp point than a thin one does (see Figure 11.2).

FIGURE 11.2

From the left, a 2-point stroke with a miter limit of 2, a 20-point stroke with a miter limit of 2, and a 20-point stroke with a miter limit of 4.

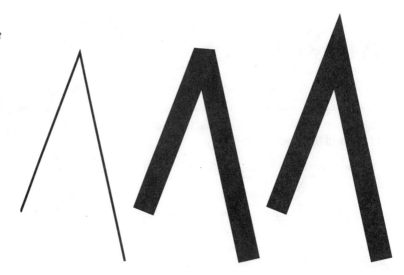

Line Caps and Joins

NEW TERM　*Line caps* determine the ends of a stroked path. This setting in the Stroke palette is used only for open-ended paths. By choosing different caps, you can make the ends either flat or rounded or have the stroke width enclose the end of the path as well (see Figure 11.3).

Line joins control how the stroke appears at each corner on the path. You can choose Mitered, Round, or Beveled joins (see Figure 11.4).

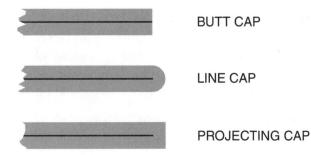

FIGURE 11.3

The three types of line caps. Notice how the bottom two actually protrude one-half the stroke weight from the actual anchor point.

BUTT CAP

LINE CAP

PROJECTING CAP

FIGURE 11.4

A star with (from left) mitered, round, and beveled joins.

11

Dashed Lines

NEW TERM The last option in the Stroke palette, Dashed Lines, can be one of the most powerful. Here, you can specify dashed or dotted lines. Depending on what settings you have set for weight, line caps, and joins, you can create a *stitched line*, a *skip line*, or almost anything. You control the *dash* and *gap* (the space between each dash) by entering numbers into the Dash and Gap fields at the bottom of the palette. If you're just using one sequence, you can enter just the first two fields. Alternatively, you can enter up to three different Dash and Gap settings to achieve complex dash patterns (see Figure 11.5).

FIGURE 11.5

A variety of strokes with different Dash and Gap settings. The last stroke uses round caps to achieve the dotted line effect.

(1, 6, 6, 1)

(2, 10, 10, 10)

(2, 8,8)

(12, 2)

(4, 2, 4, 20)

(1, 6 – Round Cap)

Creating Special Effects with Layered Strokes

Using strokes with different settings and layering them on top of each other, you can achieve some interesting results. How interesting, you ask? Well, how about railroad tracks? or maybe a nice highway? With some imagination and forethought, you can apply the power of strokes to more and more functions. The possibilities are endless!

Everybody's Doing the Locomotion

Follow these steps to create railroad tracks:

1. With the Pencil tool, draw a nice squiggly line with a fill of None and a stroke of Black (see Figure 11.6).

FIGURE 11.6

Start with a nice curved line.

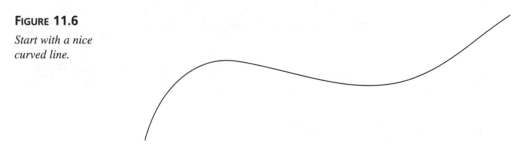

2. Give the line a Stroke Weight of 20 points and a Miter Limit of 4 (see Figure 11.7).

FIGURE 11.7

I've been workin' on the railroad....

3. Press (Command+C)[Control+C] to copy the path, and then press (Command+F)[Control+F] to paste the path directly in front of the existing path. (You won't see a change onscreen, but it's there.)

4. Give this path a fill of None and a stroke of White.

5. Change the Stroke Weight to 14 points. You should now see a double line (see Figure 11.8). Because the white line is narrower, you see 3 points of the bottom line on either side (20 minus 14).

FIGURE 11.8

In reality, you're see-ing a white line block-ing out the middle of a thicker black stroke.

6. Press (Command+C)[Control+C], and then press (Command+F)[Control+F] to create another copy of the path.

7. Give the path a fill of None and a stroke of Black.

8. Change the Weight to 26 points, and give the stroke a Dash of 2 points and a Gap of 10 points (see Figure 11.9).

FIGURE 11.9

The completed train tracks.

Look at that! You created train tracks from just three paths. For an even more amazing effect, switch to Artwork mode by pressing (Command+Y)[Control+Y] to see only one thin line.

Life in the Illustrator Fast Lane

Think that exercise is cool? Well, my good friend Ted Alspach of Illustrator fame put together something even cooler: a four-lane freeway, made up entirely of strokes. Just follow these steps:

1. Draw a path with the Pen tool that looks like the one shown. You can make your path longer if you'd like; I've created a path that's fairly short so it looks good in the sample figures.

2. Change the paint style (Fill=None; Stroke=300 pt., C=100, M=10, Y=90, K=18). This path is the grass border of the highway.

3. Copy by pressing (Command+C)[Control+C] and Paste in Front by pressing (Command+F)[Control+F]. Change the paint style (Stroke=240 pt., K=80). This step creates the dark asphalt edge of the highway.

4. Paste in Front (Command+F)[Control+F]. Change the paint style (Stroke=165 pt., white). This step creates the white line along the outside edge of the highway.

5. Paste in Front (Command+F)[Control+F]. Change the paint style (Stroke=160 pt., K=40). This path is the main road.

6. Paste in Front (Command+F)[Control+F]. Change the paint style (Stroke=85 pt., white, Dash=12, Gap=20). Though they don't look like it right now, you just created the dashed lines.

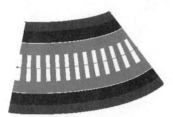

7. Paste in Front (Command+F)[Control+F]. Change the paint style (Stroke=80 pt., K=40). This step creates the passing lane.

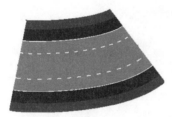

11

8. Paste in Front (Command+F)[Control+F]. Change the paint style (Stroke=8 pt., M=10, Y=100). This step creates the double yellow line.

9. Paste in Front (Command+F)[Control+F]. Change the paint style (Stroke=3 pt., K=40). This path separates the double yellow lines.

You now should see an intricate four-lane freeway.

Offset Path and Outline Path

For outlining and special effects, Offset Path is a great function. Offset Path creates an object that perfectly outlines, or traces, a selected path at an offset that you specify. To use it, select one or more objects, and choose Object➡Path➡Offset Path (see Figure 11.10). The Offset Path dialog box then appears (see Figure 11.11). Enter an amount to offset (you can use positive or negative numbers) and click OK. Note that Offset Path always makes a copy of your selection and does not affect the original (see Figure 11.12).

FIGURE 11.10

Choosing Offset Path from the Object menu.

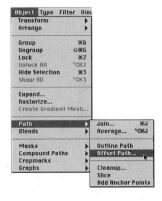

FIGURE 11.11

You can select one of three Join options: Round, Bevel, and Miter.

11

You might notice that the Offset Path command produces what look like extra lines in each object (see Figure 11.12). To "clean up" these lines, use the Pathfinder Unite function (it's the first button on the upper left of the Pathfinder palette). Running this function right after you use Offset Path is best because your selection is still active. (You can find more details on the Unite and Pathfinder commands in Hour 13, "Transformations.")

FIGURE 11.12

The result of using Offset Path.

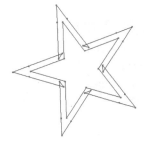

Outline Path is another great feature that converts strokes into filled objects (see Figure 11.13). Found in the same location as the Offset Path command, the Outline Path works by taking the stroke width and creating a filled shape the size of the stroke width (see Figure 11.14). This feature can be a real timesaver in a production environment; it also allows workarounds such as filling an outlined stroke with a gradient (a gradient cannot be applied to a stroke).

FIGURE 11.13

On the left, a stroked path. On the right, the path converted to an outline.

FIGURE 11.14

With the same images viewed in Artwork mode, you can see how the stroke has been outlined.

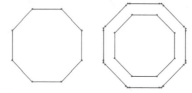

Unfortunately, Outline Path does not use dash information when converting a path to an outline. When you use this option, the path (actually the object) becomes solid.

Summary

Before you even got started using the Stroke palette in this hour, you learned that strokes are a good thing (at least in Illustrator they are). You also learned all about stroke weight and how different joins and caps can make a stroke appear differently. After you looked at dashed lines, you even made an entire illustration out of nothing but strokes.

Workshop

The Workshop contains quiz questions to help you solidify your understanding of the material covered in this hour and exercises to provide you with experience using what you have learned. You can find the answers to the quiz questions at the end of the hour.

Quiz

1. Stroke weight is
   a. A heart condition
   b. The thickness of a line
   c. Another term for how long a line is

2. The miter limit defines
   a. How far a line sticks out at a sharp corner
   b. How long you can park in New York City
   c. How thick a line is

3. How many strokes can you layer on top of each other?
   a. As many as you'd like
   b. 255
   c. 11

4. Illustrator offers three Join options for strokes. The first is Miter, the second is Round, and the third is
   a. Square
   b. Oval
   c. Bevel

5. In Artwork mode, you cannot see the thickness or dash information of a stroke.
   a. True
   b. False

Exercises

1. Draw a line and give it a thick stroke. Experiment with different line caps, and see how they differ from each other.

2. Try using the layering techniques discussed here to create complex line designs using only strokes.

3. Draw a line with sharp changes in direction (such as the letter "v" or "w"). Observe the differences in line joins, and experiment with different miter limits.

11

Term Review

Cap—The stroke attribute used at the endpoints of a stroke.

Dash—The part of a stroke that is visible.

Gap—The part of a stroke that is transparent.

Miter—The extrusion of the stroke weight at a sharp change in direction.

Skip line—A dashed line in which the dash and gap are not consistent.

Stitched line—A steady dashed line, giving the appearance of a sewn stitch.

Stroke weight—The thickness of a line (path).

Answers to Quiz Questions

1. b
2. a
3. a
4. c
5. a

HOUR 12

Compound Paths and Masks

Until now, you have dealt with single objects in Illustrator: a square, a circle, a star, even a set of waves. Now, you can begin to use several objects together. I am not referring to the kinds of groups covered in Hour 4, "Working with Selections." Instead, each of the concepts covered here uses more than one object to create what looks like just one object, such as the following:

- Compound paths
- Masking objects
- Masking placed images

Compound Paths

NEW TERM What exactly is a *compound path*? Well, simply, a compound path is one that is made up of two or more paths. So, you're probably wondering, how is that different from a group? A group is just a bunch of objects all thrown together, but each object is separate by itself. In a compound path, all the paths included are considered to be one path. You can't fill each shape with a different color; the entire compound path can have only one fill and stroke attribute.

So what are compound paths used for? They are used for making objects with holes "cut out" of them, such as the letter "O" (see Figure 12.1).

FIGURE 12.1

In a compound path (left), you can see through the letter "O," but if the "O" is two paths, just a black circle with a white one on top, you can't see what is behind the "O."

Now you're ready to create your own compound path:

1. Draw a nice-sized rectangle, and give it a fill of gray or any color besides black.
2. Draw a circle within the rectangle, and give it a fill of black (see Figure 12.2).

FIGURE 12.2

A gray rectangle with a black circle inside.

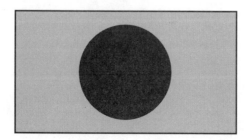

3. Draw another circle within the first circle, and give it a fill of white.

4. Select both circles.

5. Press (Command+8)[Control+8], or choose Object➡Compound Paths➡Make (see Figure 12.3).

FIGURE 12.3

Choosing Make Compound Paths.

You should now be able to see "through" the smaller circle, allowing the background color to show through (see Figure 12.4). You can release a compound path by pressing (Command+Option+8)[Control+Alt+8] or by choosing Object➡Compound Paths➡Release.

FIGURE 12.4

When you combine the two circles to make a compound path, the inner circle becomes the hollow part of the outer circle.

12

So, now you know how to create a compound path, but you are probably still wondering how this works.

It's All in the Direction

The most significant aspect of a compound path is the capability to change the direction of a path within the compound path. All shapes travel in one direction, either clockwise or counterclockwise (see Figure 12.5). In a compound path, paths can run both clockwise and counterclockwise.

FIGURE 12.5

The arrows indicate the direction of each path in the shape.

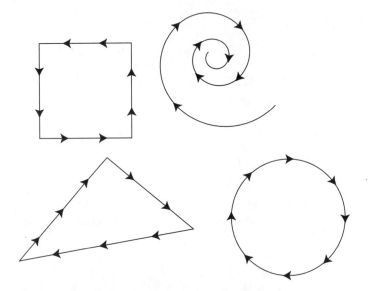

Look at the "O" again. Notice that the direction of the inner path is going in the opposite direction of the outer path (see Figure 12.6). How does this give the "O" a hollow center? Well, imagine that you have a pair of scissors, and you have to cut out the letter "O." How can you cut it out using only one cut, not two? You have to cut around the outside of the "O," and then slice through the "O" and cut out the inside (see Figure 12.7). Notice that when you're cutting the inside, you're going in the opposite direction than you were when you were cutting the outside. Although you can't see where the slice is, in reality, that's what Illustrator is doing.

FIGURE 12.6

The inner path goes clockwise, whereas the outer path goes counterclockwise.

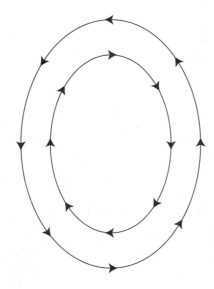

FIGURE 12.7

As you trace around the shape, the direction changes as you move to the inside.

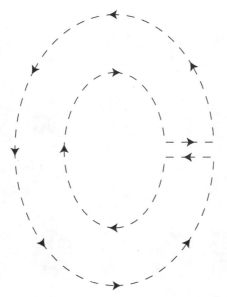

12

Sometimes you might need to change the direction of a path in a compound path (especially when you have more than two paths) to make the path hollow. In the Attributes palette, which you open by pressing (Command+Shift+I)[Control+Shift+I], are the Reverse Path Direction buttons (see Figure 12.8). They are active only when a compound path is selected. Click either button to reverse the path to make a shape hollow.

FIGURE **12.8**

The Reverse Path Direction buttons in the Attributes palette.

Masks

NEW TERM | Just like a physical mask covers part of your face, a *mask* in Illustrator covers part of your artwork. Say you have a photo of your graduating class, and you want to show only the part with you and your best friend, who is standing next to you. By drawing a square and making it a mask, you can make only the parts of the photo that are behind the square visible. The rest of the photo does not show.

For this next exercise, I created a beautiful illustration, which I've called Shapes, that contains many circles and squares (see Figure 12.9). You can either duplicate this file or create one of your own. (If you create your own file, make sure that you group all the objects when you are done.)

FIGURE **12.9**

My shapes.

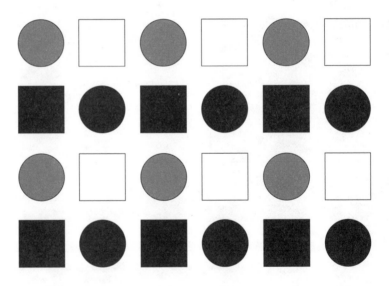

You can get started by following these steps:

1. With the document open, draw a new object, about half the size of the entire artwork in Figure 12.9. I've chosen to use a star (see Figure 12.10). Notice that the star blocks out a good portion of the artwork because it appears in front. A mask must always be in front of the artwork.

FIGURE 12.10

The star will be the mask.

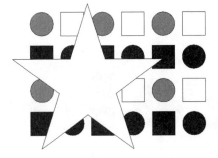

2. Select everything by pressing (Command+A)[Control+A] (see Figure 12.11).

FIGURE 12.11

Everything is selected.

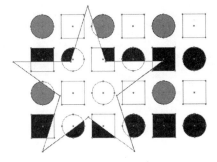

3. Choose Object➡Masks➡Make (see Figure 12.12). Deselect all by pressing (Command+Shift+A)[Control+Shift+A].

FIGURE 12.12

Making the mask.

You just created a mask! Now you can see only the artwork that is within the mask, and the rest is hidden (see Figure 12.13).

FIGURE 12.13

The masked artwork.

Don't worry; the rest of the artwork is still there. In fact, one of the greatest aspects of Illustrator's Mask feature is that you can move the artwork within the mask. Try doing that now:

1. Choose the Selection tool (black arrow).

2. Click one of the circles or squares. Because the artwork is grouped, it all becomes selected—except for the mask, of course.

3. Move the artwork about an inch to the left.

Of course, you can even edit the artwork, and the mask will still be in effect. To remove the mask, select it and choose Object➡Masks➡Release (see Figure 12.14). So, a mask is just like a window behind which you can place different images and move them around for quick and easy editing and positioning. Masking is also great with placed images and with type, which you'll learn about later (Hour 16, "Working with Raster Images," and Hour 14, "Adding Text").

FIGURE 12.14

Releasing a mask.

After you position your mask perfectly, you can lock the mask by choosing Object➧Masks➧Lock. When you lock a mask, the artwork and the mask move together as one unit. Of course, you can unlock it at any time if you need to reposition the artwork.

Summary

This hour covered two important concepts: compound paths, which basically enable you to cut holes through the middle of objects, and what a mask is and how you can use masks to control what parts of an image or what parts of objects are visible.

Workshop

The Workshop contains quiz questions to help you solidify your understanding of the material covered in this hour and exercises to provide you with experience using what you have learned. You can find the answers to the quiz questions at the end of the hour.

Quiz

1. Compound paths are used for

    a. Cutting "holes" out of objects

    b. Walking in the right direction

    c. Blocking parts of a selection

2. Path direction refers to

    a. Listening to your parents

    b. Whether a path goes clockwise or counterclockwise

    c. Combining two objects to create a compound object

12

3. A mask is good for

   a. Mardi Gras

   b. Showing only portions of a photograph

   c. Permanently deleting sections of your artwork

4. If you have a photo, and you draw a small box over it and make the small box a mask

   a. You will see only the part of the photo behind the small box

   b. You will see the whole photo except for the part behind the small box

   c. You will see the entire photo within the small box

5. You might lock a mask because

   a. You don't want someone to steal it

   b. You don't want to delete it accidentally

   c. You don't want the artwork to shift accidentally within the mask

Exercises

1. Practice making compound paths with two, three, and four objects. Now try reversing different paths. Remember to use the Direct Selection tool to select each individual path in your compound path so that you can reverse its direction.

2. Make a mask and experiment moving the mask itself. Then try moving just the artwork without moving the mask. See what happens when you move the artwork away from the mask completely and then move it back again. Switching between Preview and Artwork modes may be easier as you try this exercise.

3. Practice locking and unlocking your mask to allow for easy editing.

Answers to Quiz Questions

1. a

2. b

3. b

4. a

5. c

Hour 13

Transformations

One of the biggest advantages computers give you in terms of creating art is the capability to edit or transform art. I remember when I used to draw squares for a layout and send out for several copies of them to save time when doing layout. Now I can create numerous duplicates of art in nanoseconds. By scaling, rotating, and reflecting existing art, you not only cut production times in half, but you create better, more accurate art as well (see Figure 13.1).

In this hour, you'll learn about the following:

- Scaling and rotating
- The Free Transform tool
- The Align palette
- The Blend tool
- The Pathfinder palette

The Transformation Tools

Illustrator has five basic transformation functions: Move, Rotate, Scale, Reflect, and Shear. Illustrator also has a feature called Transform Each that enables you to apply several different transformations to several different objects—all in one step. You also can use the Transform palette, which makes for quick and precise transformations.

Before beginning, I want to point out one particular keyboard shortcut that is a real time-saver—especially when it comes to transformations. Pressing the (Command)[Control] key at any time activates the most recent selection tool you've used. If, for example, you last used the black arrow, pressing the (Command)[Control] key while using any of Illustrator's other tools temporarily activates the black arrow.

When it comes to transformations, you are always selecting objects and making minor changes to the art, and having to switch back and forth between the transformation tools and the selection tools is a pain. With the (Command)[Control] key, the selection tool is always just a keystroke away. By the way, pressing (Command+Tab)[Control+Tab] toggles between the black and white arrow.

Moving Objects

Although not necessarily a transformation in that the actual object is changed, moving an image is considered a transformation because the coordinates of the object are being changed.

To demonstrate, press F8 to open the Info palette (see Figure 13.1). Now select the Rectangle tool (press M), and move your mouse around the screen. The Info palette has four fields: X, Y, W, and H. Notice the X and Y numbers change as you move the mouse. They are the coordinates of your cursor, and they represent the starting point of your rectangle (either the center point or the upper-left point, depending on which rectangle tool you are using). After you begin drawing the rectangle, the W and H (width and height) coordinates become active, giving you real-time feedback as to the size of your object.

FIGURE 13.1

Illustrator's Info palette: In this example, the measurements are shown in inches, as per my setting in Preferences.

You already learned one way to move an object: by clicking and dragging on a selection. Illustrator also lets you move things more precisely. If you click and drag a selection and then hold down the Shift key, you are only able to drag your selection along a constrained axis, in increments of 45 degrees.

Want to get even more precise? After you make your selection, you can use your keyboard's arrows (up, down, left, and right) to "nudge" your selection, one increment at a time. You can control how much each nudge is in General Preferences (see Figure 13.2) by quickly pressing (Command+K)[Control+K].

FIGURE 13.2

The value in the Cursor Key field determines how much a "nudge" is.

But you say you need even more precision? After all, you are dealing with a computer, right? To move a selection numerically, make your selection and then double-click the Selection tool in the Toolbox (the black arrow). In the resulting dialog box, you can specify an exact amount to four decimal places (see Figure 13.3). In this dialog box, you can also create a copy. It even sports a Preview button that enables you to view the results of the move before clicking OK.

FIGURE 13.3

Double-clicking the black arrow brings up the Move dialog box.

13

There's yet another way to move something: Illustrator's Transform palette, which I'll get to soon in the section called "The Transform Palette."

Rotate, Scale, Reflect, and Shear

The four transformation tools—Rotate, Scale, Reflect, and Shear—are all very similar. As you should know by now, before making any transformations, you must first make a selection. Otherwise, Illustrator has no idea what it is you want to transform. A rectangle works best for demonstration purposes.

Rotate

NEW TERM When you select the *Rotate* tool (R), notice that a different symbol appears at the center of your selection (see Figure 13.4). This spot is your origin point. With the Rotate tool, your origin point is the rotation point, which means your selection revolves around that point. To rotate the object, simply click and drag clockwise or counterclockwise (see Figure 13.5). Clicking the outer portion of a selection makes it easier to control the transformation. Holding the Shift key while dragging constrains your rotation to increments of 45 degrees.

FIGURE 13.4

Besides the usual selection points, when performing a transformation, Illustrator indicates the origin point.

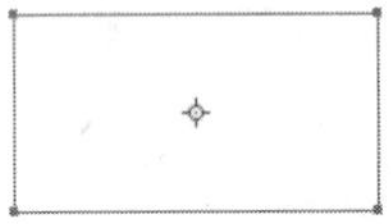

FIGURE 13.5

Notice the object rotates around the origin point.

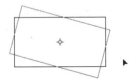

You can move the origin point to better control your transformations by clicking and dragging it. Go ahead, try it! Drag the origin point to the lower-left corner of the rectangle (see Figure 13.6). Notice that the origin point takes advantage of Snap to Point, which makes aligning images a lot easier. Now click and drag from the opposite side of the rectangle, and notice how the object rotates from the lower-left corner (see Figure 13.7).

FIGURE 13.6

Repositioning the origin point.

FIGURE 13.7

The object being rotated around the newly placed origin point.

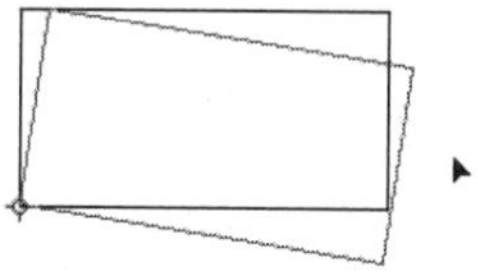

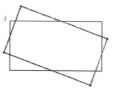

Besides being able to freely rotate a selection, you can also precisely rotate an object numerically. To do so, double-click the Rotate tool. This operation brings up the Rotate dialog box. After specifying a rotation angle, you can click OK to rotate your selection, or you can click Copy, which rotates a duplicate of your selection, and leave the original selection untouched (see Figure 13.8).

FIGURE 13.8

Clicking Copy transforms a duplicate while leaving the original untouched.

Double-clicking the Rotate tool always rotates the selection numerically from the center, but what if you want to rotate a selection numerically from a different origin point? After you select the Rotate tool, hold down the (Option)[Alt] key and click where you want the origin point to be. The Rotate dialog box appears, and the origin point is located where you clicked.

When you're using the Rotate dialog box, if the object you are rotating is filled with a pattern, you have the option to rotate the object without rotating the pattern, to rotate the pattern and the object simultaneously, or to rotate just the pattern (see Figure 13.9). Without using the dialog box, you can rotate just the pattern fill if you press and hold the tilde key (~) while dragging to rotate. The tilde key shortcut works with any of the transformation tools, including Move.

13

FIGURE 13.9

*From left to right, the
original object, the
object rotated without
the fill, the object and
the fill rotated together,
and the fill rotated
without the object.*

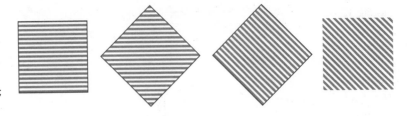

Scale

NEW TERM Probably the most frequently used transformation tool, the *Scale* tool (S) is used
to resize selected objects, making them larger or smaller (see Figure 13.10). Just
like the Rotate tool, the Scale tool also uses an origin point to determine which point to
scale from.

FIGURE 13.10

Illustrator's Scale tool.

To use the Scale tool, drag inward toward the origin point to reduce the size of the
object. Drag outward from the origin point to enlarge the object. You can move the origin
point by pressing and dragging it or just clicking to create a new origin point. If you hold
down the Shift key as you drag, the object scales proportionally.

To scale items from the center, numerically, double-click the Scale tool to bring up the
Scale dialog box (see Figure 13.11). Although Scale Stroke Weight appears in General
Preferences (see Hour 2, "Customizing Illustrator"), it appears here again, in case you
want to make an exception (see Figure 13.12).

FIGURE 13.11

The Scale dialog box.

FIGURE 13.12

The box on the left has been reduced with Scale Stroke Weight off. The box on the right has Scale Stroke Weight turned on. It appears to be an optical illusion, but the stroke has remained the same in the first example and been scaled proportionally in the second.

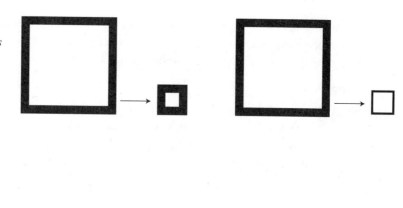

As with the Rotate tool, if you want to scale a selection numerically, but from a specified origin point, select the Scale tool and (Option+click)[Alt+click] the place where you want the origin point to be.

Reflect

NEW TERM   The *Reflect* tool (O) is also known as the Mirror tool (see Figure 13.13). Working in the same way as the Rotate and Scale tools, the Reflect tool flips a selection horizontally or vertically. This tool is most useful for creating symmetrical artwork. After you create half of your art, simply flip a copy of it to complete the image (see Figure 13.14).

FIGURE 13.13

Illustrator's Reflect tool.

FIGURE 13.14

By using the Reflect tool, you can create a perfect image in half the time.

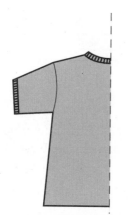

As with the other transformation tools, holding the Shift key constrains movement to 45-degree increments, and double-clicking the Reflect tool or (Option+clicking)[Alt+clicking] in the document brings up the Reflect dialog box.

Shear

NEW TERM The last of the transformation tools, the *Shear* tool (O), as shown in Figure 13.15, is used to skew objects (see Figure 13.16). Again, this transformation tool is like the others when it comes to specifying an origin point and using the Shift key. Of course, double-clicking the Shear tool brings up the Shear dialog box, and (Option+clicking)[Alt+clicking] in your document defines an origin point and enables you to specify a shear numerically.

FIGURE 13.15

Illustrator's Shear tool.

FIGURE 13.16

A square that has been sheared. Notice that by shearing a copy of the star, you can create a cast shadow.

The Free Transform Tool

Sometimes you might want to apply several different transformations to an object, which is exactly why Illustrator has the Free Transform tool (see Figure 13.17). The Free Transform tool can move, rotate, scale, and skew—all while never deselecting the object. Try it out now to see how it works:

FIGURE 13.17

The Free Transform tool.

1. Draw a rectangle, and then select the Free Transform tool.

2. Without pressing the mouse button, move the mouse around so the cursor is outside the rectangle. The cursor looks like bent arrows, indicating the Rotate function (see Figure 13.18).

FIGURE 13.18

The bent arrows, indicating the rotate function.

3. Move the cursor over one of the handles, and the cursor changes to an arrow, indicating the Scale function (see Figure 13.19).

FIGURE 13.19

The cursor, indicating the Scale function.

4. Move the cursor to the inside of the rectangle, and the cursor again changes, this time to indicate the Move function.

5. Move the cursor to the outside of the box, and then click and drag to rotate the rectangle (see Figure 13.20).

FIGURE 13.20

Rotating the selection.

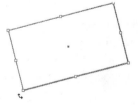

13

6. Click and drag on one of the corner handles to scale your selection. Notice that only the side of the image that you grabbed is scaled.

7. Press and hold the Shift key while dragging, and your selection is scaled while maintaining the aspect ratio.

8. To have the opposite side of the selection scale as well, press and hold the (Option)[Alt] key while dragging.

9. To shear or skew your selection, click and drag on one of the middle handles, and then press the (Command)[Control] key while still dragging.

10. While holding the (Command)[Control] key to shear, you can simultaneously hold the (Option)[Alt] key to skew the opposite side of the selection as well.

11. To move the selection, simply click and drag from the inside of the shape.

You may be wondering why you should ever bother switching between all those other transformation tools when you have the Free Transform tool. Well, for one, the Free Transform tool always uses the center of an object as the origin point, whereas the individual transformation tools allow you to specify an origin point.

Second, because the (Option)[Alt] key is used for a special purpose with the Free Transform tool, you cannot duplicate as you transform (not even with the Move function), as you could with the individual transform tools (see "Makin' Copies!," later in this hour).

Transform Each

The Transform Each function offers two excellent features: the capability to perform Scale, Move, and Rotate transformations simultaneously; and the capability to transform each object in a selection independently of each other. Take a closer look.

First, making multiple transformations is a snap when you use Transform Each. Choose Object ➡Transform➡Transform Each to bring up the Transform Each dialog box. Here, you can specify measurements for scaling, moving, and rotating your selection. A Preview button enables you to view your transformation in real-time. You'll see in a minute how this feature is more powerful than you think.

The second feature I mentioned was the capability to transform multiple objects individually. To demonstrate, I've created a grid of squares (see Figure 13.21). If I select all the squares and use the Rotate tool to rotate my selection 45 degrees, my entire selection rotates as one piece (see Figure 13.22). If I use the Transform Each command with the same selection and specify a 45-degree rotation, however, each square rotates individually (see Figure 13.23).

FIGURE 13.21

Many squares.

FIGURE 13.22

A normal Rotate rotates all objects around the center point of the entire selection.

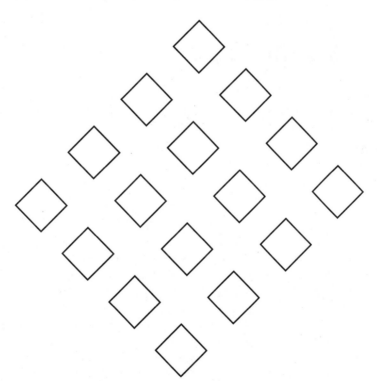

13

FIGURE 13.23

Transform Each rotates each square around its own center.

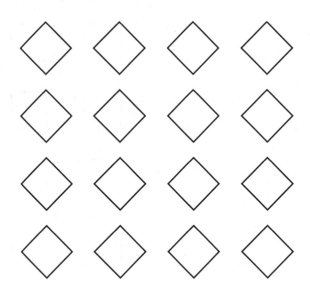

The Random button in the Transform Each dialog box transforms each object a little differently, making for an irregular, almost hand-drawn look (see Figure 13.24).

FIGURE 13.24

Using Transform Each's Random feature.

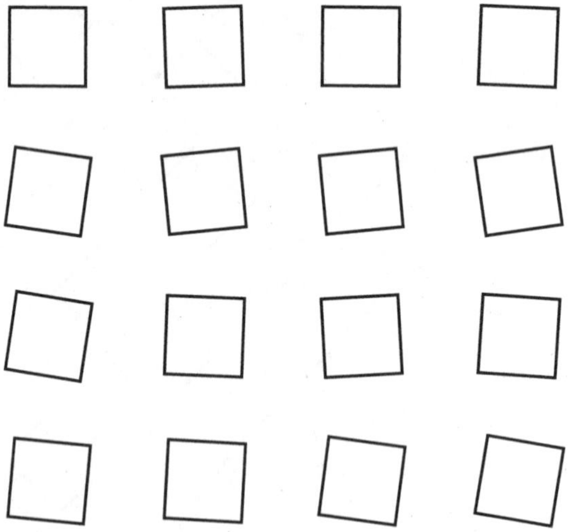

Makin' Copies!

As you've seen, all the transformation dialog boxes include a button to make the transformation on a copy of the object. Holding the (Option)[Alt] button as you drag with any transformation tool does the same thing. If you want to rotate a copy of a selection, just hold down the (Option)[Alt] key after you begin dragging to rotate. Even when you're dragging items with the black or white arrows, holding the (Option)[Alt] key creates a duplicate. Be sure to release the mouse button before you let go of the (Option)[Alt] key.

Do It Again!

Without a doubt, the most powerful transform function in Illustrator is Transform Again. The keyboard command for it is (Command+D)[Control+D]. Learn it. Transform Again applies the last transform that you've done, which is why Sandee Cohen, the famed vector guru, likes to call the function "Do It Again," which also makes it easier to remember (Command+D)[Control+D]. Try these few simple exercises:

1. Draw a rectangle.
2. Using the black arrow, move the rectangle a bit.
3. Press (Command+D)[Control+D]. Notice how Illustrator applies the same Move command to the square again.
4. Rotate the square 20 degrees (see Figure 13.25).

FIGURE 13.25

Rotating the square.

5. Press (Command+D)[Control+D] again. And again. The square rotates another 20 degrees each time (see Figure 13.26).

FIGURE 13.26

Getting dizzy?

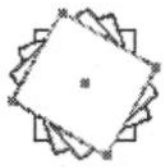

13

6. Select the black arrow again.
7. Create a duplicate of the square by clicking and dragging it and then holding the (Option)[Alt] key (see Figure 13.27).

FIGURE 13.27

Duplicating the square.

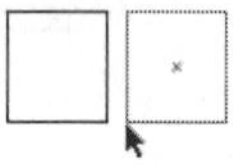

8. Press (Command+D)[Control+D] several times. You just performed a step-and-repeat, creating several squares, each equally distant from the other (see Figure 13.28).

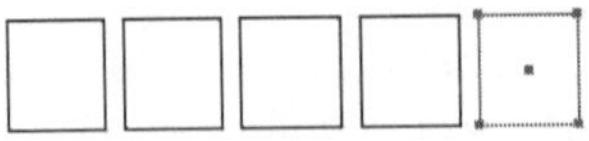

FIGURE 13.28

Many squares.

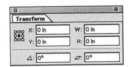

Now go back to the Transform Each function. Remember, using Transform Each, you can apply several transformations in one step. Using the Transform Again function in conjunction with Transform Each gives you a powerful means to apply multiple transformations again and again—quickly.

The Transform Palette

You knew it was coming, didn't you? That's right, another Illustrator palette. Using the Transform palette, you can quickly specify transformations (see Figure 13.29).

FIGURE 13.29

The Transform palette.

First, notice the funny-looking icon on the far left (see Figure 13.30). It is a proxy where you assign an origin point for the selection. Although you can't precisely position the origin point as you could with a transform tool, clicking the little squares lets you quickly specify center, upper-left corner, and so on.

FIGURE 13.30

The Transform proxy for determining the origin point.

You can move objects around in your document by entering the x and y coordinates. To change the width and height of your selected objects, enter new values in the W and H fields. But what if you know only one dimension and want to transform your object proportionally? Say, for example, you want to make your object 3 inches wide. Put 3 inches in the W field and then hold down the (Command)[Control] key and press Enter. Illustrator automatically figures out the correct height, scaling your object proportionally.

This palette also contains fields for rotation and shearing. If you hold down the (Option)[Alt] key when pressing Enter, Illustrator creates a duplicate and leaves the original item untouched.

The Align Palette

NEW TERM Because I'm talking all about moving things around, I thought now might be a good time to introduce you to the Align palette (yet another Illustrator palette to deal with). The Align palette, as shown in Figure 13.31, was at one time a list of commands under the Filter menu. As a palette, however, it is much easier to use and understand. To use it, simply select your objects and click any of the *Align* or *Distribute* buttons. Distribute works by taking the two outermost objects and then evenly spacing the objects that appear between them. To center two objects vertically and horizontally, for example, you click the Horizontal Align Center button and then the Vertical Align Center button (see Figure 13.32).

FIGURE 13.31

The Align palette.

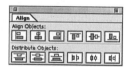

FIGURE 13.32

From left to right, the original objects, after horizontally aligning them, and then after vertically aligning them.

 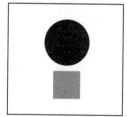 

The Pathfinder Palette

One of the greatest timesaving features in Illustrator, the Pathfinder commands are a set of powerful path-editing functions. In fact, they are so powerful that they have their own palette. You can open the palette by choosing Window➥Show Pathfinder. The Pathfinder commands enable you to perform complex path functions quickly on multiple objects. As I go through them, I'll describe each function, as well as present an example to demonstrate what each command does.

Combine Unite, Intersect, Exclude, Minus Front, Minus Back

The first group of Pathfinder commands is used to make complex shapes out of simple ones. You can quickly create unique art by using Illustrator's basic drawing tools and then modify them by using these Pathfinder commands.

13

Unite

The most commonly used Pathfinder command, Unite simply takes all selected objects and combines them into one object. Unite doesn't just group the objects together; it "glues" them all together, leaving just one large shape, removing all paths that overlap (see Figure 13.33). When you're running the Unite command, the final object is automatically brought to the front. Whatever color attributes (both Fill and Stroke) the front-most object in your selection has become the color attributes of the final, united object.

FIGURE 13.33

The Unite command combines objects.

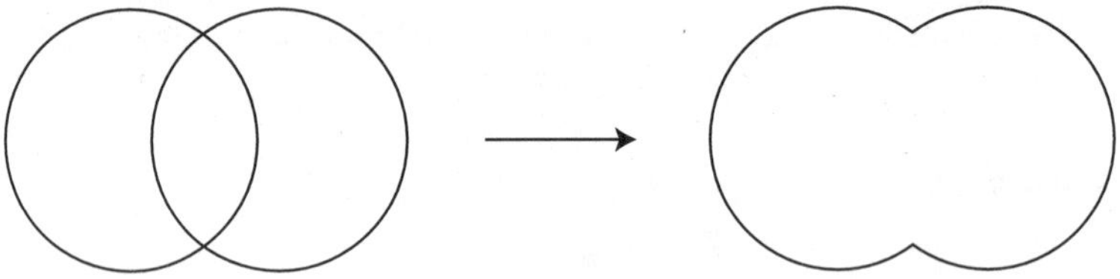

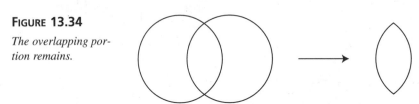

Intersect

The Intersect function is used on two objects that overlap each other. After you choose Intersect, the area in which the objects overlap remains as one combined path, and the rest of each object is deleted (see Figure 13.34). This command doesn't work if you have more than two objects selected.

FIGURE 13.34

The overlapping portion remains.

Exclude

The exact opposite of the Intersect command, Exclude takes two objects that overlap each other and deletes the areas where they overlap (see Figure 13.35). The remaining objects are grouped together. Again, this command doesn't work if you have more than two objects selected.

FIGURE 13.35

Removing the overlapping portion.

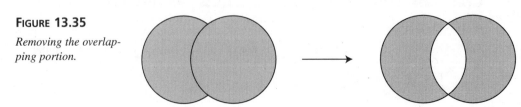

Minus Front

Minus Front takes two objects and subtracts the front-most object from the object behind it (see Figure 13.36). This command is great for cutting little shapes or bits out of larger objects. If the front image fits within the back image, Minus Front creates a compound path for you. It works a lot like a cookie cutter, except that what you end up seeing is what's left of the dough, not the cookie. This command doesn't work if you have more than two objects selected.

FIGURE 13.36

Removing the front object and whatever is behind it.

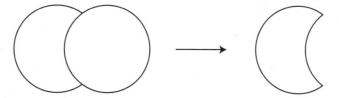

Minus Back

The reverse of Minus Front, Minus Back subtracts part of an image based on the image behind it (see Figure 13.37). Going back to the cookie cutter example, this filter would produce the cookie. This command doesn't work if you have more than two objects selected.

FIGURE 13.37

Removing the rear object and taking whatever is in front of it with it.

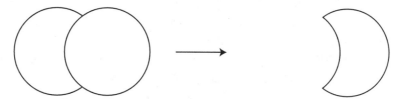

Divide/Trim/Merge/Crop/Outline

The next group of Pathfinder commands—Divide, Trim, Merge, Crop, and Outline—deals with splitting objects into parts or deleting unwanted parts of objects.

Divide

Divide takes any overlapping shapes and cuts them up into separate shapes wherever they overlap (see Figure 13.38). An invaluable tool, Divide enables you to split up objects quickly without once having to use the Scissors tool. Also, using the precision of drawn shapes, you can perform careful slices and divisions without using the clumsy Knife tool.

13

FIGURE 13.38

Divide turns each intersecting part into a separate image.

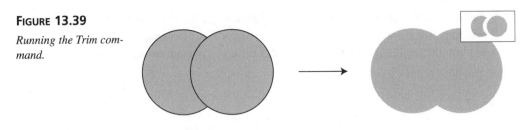

Divide looks at each object and divides each overlap individually, so it makes no difference if you're dividing compound paths, groups, or whatever—they all become individual shapes. After Divide runs, all objects are grouped together. You have to ungroup them if you want to work with each piece separately.

Trim

The Trim command removes the parts of the back object that are behind the front objects. It also removes the stroke (see Figure 13.39).

FIGURE 13.39

Running the Trim command.

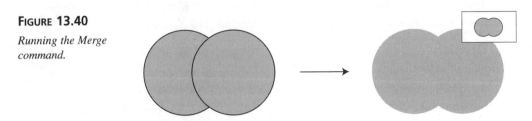

Merge

The Merge command operates differently, depending on the fills of the selected objects. If they're all the same, it's similar to Unite, making them one object. If they're all different, it works like the Trim command, mentioned previously. If some of the objects are filled the same, the like objects are united, and the rest are trimmed (see Figure 13.40).

FIGURE 13.40

Running the Merge command.

Crop

The Crop command removes any parts of selected objects that are not directly underneath the front-most object (see Figure 13.41). The final result of the Crop command is exactly what a mask would do. The only difference is that the Crop command actually deletes the art that is not visible, unlike a mask, which just covers it up. Be careful before you run this command because you cannot retrieve the artwork that is cropped out.

FIGURE 13.41

The Crop command.

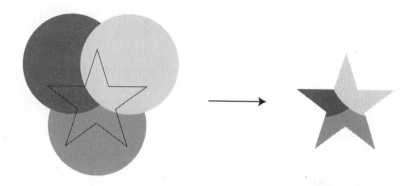

Outline

Choosing the Outline command converts all shapes to outlines (see Figure 13.42) and also divides the lines where they intersect (similar to a Divide command for strokes).

FIGURE 13.42

The Outline command.

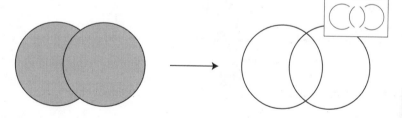

Hard and Soft

You can access the last three Pathfinder commands by choosing Show Options from the Pathfinder palette pop-up menu (see Figure 13.43). The Mix/Trap commands are then visible in the palette.

13

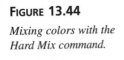

FIGURE 13.43

Choosing Show Options from the Pathfinder palette pop-up menu.

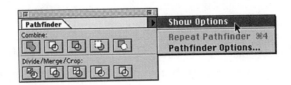

Hard Mix

The Hard Mix command takes overlapping objects and mixes the values of the colors where the shapes overlap (see Figure 13.44).

FIGURE 13.44

Mixing colors with the Hard Mix command.

Soft Mix

The Soft Mix command is identical to the Hard Mix command, except for the fact that you can control how the colors are mixed by specifying a percentage. Although Hard Mix might produce an image that looks transparent, Soft Mix might be used to create an object that appears translucent (see Figure 13.45).

FIGURE 13.45

Creating a translucent effect with the Soft Mix command.

Trap

The Trap command takes selected art and traps it as specified (see Figure 13.46). Many printers require that you provide artwork that is trapped properly. You should speak with your printer and discuss your options. If you need to trap your own artwork, make sure your printer provides you with the settings he or she needs.

FIGURE 13.46

The Pathfinder Trap dialog box.

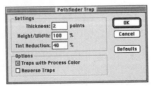

A computer is perfect. When you draw a square of one color and place it right up against another square of another color, you get two squares touching each other, with one color ending where the next one begins.

In the world of printing presses, however, this relationship is not always so easy. A printing press uses a separate "plate" to print each color on your page. Because a printing press is (usually) a large machine, it's nearly impossible for the plate to hit each sheet of paper in the exact same place. What usually happens—in this case, with the squares—is that a slight shift occurs from sheet to sheet, letting a sliver of white, or whatever color the paper is, sneak through between the two squares.

NEW TERM To get around this problem, printers rely on a process called *trapping*. If you slightly extend the colors (called choking and spreading) and have them overprint each other, the squares do not just touch each other, but they actually overlap a bit. Now, if the press shifts a bit, there is enough of an overlap of color that a white sliver doesn't show through. By setting a color to *overprint*, you are instructing the colors to print over each other, achieving the trap.

Because the Trap command makes changes to your artwork, saving a copy of your file before you use it is a good idea. Also, save it for the last step to make for easier editing.

Overprints

Because I'm mentioning traps, I thought I'd also show you how you can specify *overprints* through Illustrator's Attributes palette (see Figure 13.47). After you select an object, you can choose to overprint the fill or the stroke by checking the appropriate box.

FIGURE 13.47

The Attributes palette.

One More Shortcut

Before wrapping things up with the Pathfinder palette, I would just like to point out that (Command+4)[Control+4] performs the last-used Pathfinder command. Many times when you're editing multiple objects, you need to apply Pathfinder commands over and over again, and having to move your mouse repeatedly to position your cursor over the Pathfinder palette is a bit of a pain.

13

The Blend Tool

The Blend tool (see Figure 13.48) is used to create a group of evenly distributed objects that originate from one object and end at the other. As the objects get closer to the ends, they gradually take on the attributes of those objects (see Figure 13.49). If there was one feature that Illustrator users have been asking for all these years, it was that the Blend tool should be "live." When a blend is live, you can make changes to the end shapes even after the blend is created, and the blended objects will automatically update to reflect those changes—without having to re-create the blend. Well, for all those people out there, Adobe has finally done it: Illustrator 8 has live blends.

FIGURE 13.48

The Blend tool.

FIGURE 13.49

A blend.

Try your hand at creating a blend:

1. Start by creating a star at one end of the screen and a circle at the other end (see Figure 13.50).

FIGURE 13.50

Starting with two shapes.

2. Select the Blend tool (W), and click on the circle.
3. Click on the star. You have just created a blend. The line that runs through all the objects is called the spine (see Figure 13.51). Alternatively, you can select both the circle and the star and choose Object➡Blends➡Make.

FIGURE **13.51**

The finished blend. Notice the spine of the blend.

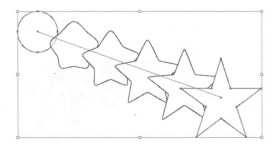

As I discussed earlier, blends are live, which means you can now change the attributes of the objects at either end of the blend, and the blended objects will automatically update, reflecting those changes. Go back to the blend you were just working on to see how this process works:

1. Using the Direct Selection tool, select just the star and fill it black. Notice that the blend automatically updates to create a smooth transition between the white circle and the black star (see Figure 13.52).

FIGURE **13.52**

The updated blend.

2. In the blend you just made, Illustrator has created many more shapes or "steps" between the two shapes to best blend the colors of the shapes. Change some of the options in the blend to get better results. With the star still selected, choose Object➡Blends➡Blend Options.

3. From the pop-up bar, choose Specified Steps and enter a value of 4 (see Figure 13.53). The blend is now updated, and you can better see what the blend really does (see Figure 13.54).

FIGURE **13.53**

Changing the Blend Options.

13

FIGURE 13.54

The updated blend.

4. Look at the blend's spine by selecting any of the end shapes with the selection tool. The spine is the path that the objects follow between the end shapes. You can edit the spine as you would any path in Illustrator—with the Pen tool. Try adding a point to the spine and then moving that point. See how the blend now follows the edited path (see Figure 13.55).

FIGURE 13.55

The updated blend, with the shapes now following the edited path.

Of course, you can still change the options of the blend, and you can continue to change the end objects; the blend will continue to update as you make changes. You can change whether the circle or star is in front by choosing Object➡Blends➡Reverse Front to Back.

Another powerful feature is Replace Spine. You can create a path, or take an existing one, and use that as the spine for your blend. To do so, simply select both the blend and the path you want to use, and choose Object➡Blends➡Replace Spine.

You can remove the blend from the shapes at any time by choosing Object➡ Blends➡ Release.

Summary

This hour was topsy-turvy. You flipped, flopped, turned, moved, rotated, scaled, slanted, and jolted. You also learned about some new palettes, plus some pretty cool features, such as (Command+D)[Control+D] and Transform Each. And if that weren't enough, Pathfinder rules! You learned how the Pathfinder commands slice, dice, mince, chop, and mix together all your favorite vector recipes. After a description of trapping and over-printing, you finished things off with the all-new powerful Blend tool. Hang in there now; the next hour explains how to use text in Illustrator.

Workshop

The Workshop contains quiz questions to help you solidify your understanding of the material covered in this hour and exercises to provide you with experience using what you have learned. You can find the answers to the quiz questions at the end of the hour.

Quiz

1. The point from which a transformation is made is called the

   a. Origin point

   b. Starting point

   c. Transformation point

2. The Free Transform tool functions exactly like the rest of the transformation tools.

   a. True

   b. False

3. If you want to transform many shapes individually at one time, you use the

   a. Free Transform tool

   b. Transform Each command

   c. Candlestick in the library with Colonel Mustard

4. The keyboard shortcut for Transform Again is

   a. (Command+T)[Control+T]

   b. (Command+D)[Control+D]

   c. (Option+D)[Alt+D]

5. In Illustrator, a spine is

   a. The path that a blend follows

   b. The place where all the vertebrae are

   c. The exact center of the page

13

Exercises

1. Use several of the transformation tools, and then try using the Free Transform tool. Get a feel for when the best time is to use it instead of the individual transform tools.

2. Practice using the Pathfinder commands. Try using them, especially the Unite command, to create complex shapes out of simple ones. For example, try creating an outline of a Mickey Mouse head using one large circle and two smaller ones for the ears. Try to do so by using the Unite command.

3. Make a blend between two colors' shapes. Now create a circle, and use the Replace Spine function to make the circle the spine for the blend. Change the number of steps in the blend to better fit the circle.

Term Review

Align—Command used to align objects in respect to each other.

Distribute—Command used to evenly distribute objects throughout a specified area.

Overprinting—In technical terms, forcing one color to print on top of another.

Rotate—The act of making a selection turn on a two-dimensional axis.

Reflect—The act of flipping a selection to create a mirror image.

Scale—The act of resizing a selection.

Shear—The act of skewing a selection, giving the appearance of a slant.

Trapping—The process of spreading or contracting strokes and/or fills so that they slightly overlap each other when printed. This process compensates for movement on a press.

Answers to Quiz Questions

1. a
2. b
3. b
4. b
5. a

Hour 14

Adding Text

Illustrator would be incomplete without text capabilities. Whether you're designing a logo, creating a headline and body copy for an ad, or creating a caption for a technical illustration, Illustrator can handle it. Text alone can also be a powerful way of graphic expression. Illustrator works with type in a variety of ways, and as you go through this hour, you'll learn where and when to use each one.

Topics this hour covers include the following:

- Point text
- Area text
- Text on a path

Before you begin using the Type tool, let me remind you that your Preferences dialog box contains an option on how to select type: Type Area Select (under File➧Preferences➧Type & Auto Tracing). With Type Area Select activated, you can select text by clicking with the Selection or Direct Selection tool anywhere within the type's bounding box. With Type Area Select turned off, you must click the baseline to select the type. If you have trouble selecting type because other objects get in the way, lock or hide those objects first, and then you can select and edit your type easily.

Using the Type Tool

Illustrator has three types of text: point text, area text, and text on a path. To create text in Illustrator, you use one of the many type tools found in the Toolbox (see Figure 14.1).

FIGURE 14.1

A multitude of type tools.

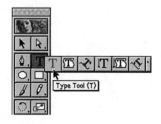

Point Text

NEW TERM The most popular kind of text in Illustrator is point text. Also called headline text, *point text* is defined by a single point, meaning that justification (such as left, right, or centered text) is based on that one point (see Figure 14.2). Creating point text is also very easy: With the Type tool (T) selected, just click a blank area anywhere on the page and start typing.

FIGURE 14.2

Although the points are aligned vertically, the type can be aligned to the right, center, or left of the point.

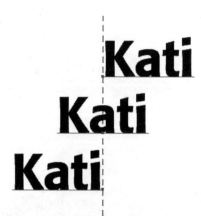

Editing Text

After you create the text, you can edit it by simply using the Text tool to click and drag letters. This action highlights the text (see Figure 14.3), and typing something new replaces the highlighted text. To simply add text to an existing block of type, click where you want the type to begin, and a blinking cursor appears, ready for you to add text.

FIGURE 14.3

The "T" is selected.

Area Text

Area text, also called body text, is defined by a shape—much like QuarkXPress, in which all type must be within a text box or frame (see Figure 14.4).

FIGURE 14.4

Type within a circle.

AS HARRY CHAPIN SANG, "ALL MY LIFE'S A CIRCLE, SUNRISE AND SUNDOWN. THE MOON ROLLS THROUGH THE NIGHTTIME, TILL THE DAYBREAK COMES AROUND. ALL MY LIFE'S A CIRCLE BUT I CAN'T TELL YOU WHY, SEASONS SPINNING ROUND AGAIN THE YEARS KEEP GOIN' BY"

14

You can create area text in several ways:

- With the Area Type tool selected (see Figure 14.5), click an existing path. Any type you enter fills the interior of the path.

FIGURE 14.5

Selecting the Area Type tool from the Toolbox.

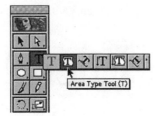

- With the Type tool selected, click and drag diagonally to draw a box (see Figure 14.6). Any type you enter fills the interior of the path.

FIGURE 14.6

Drawing a text box with the Type tool.

- With the Type tool selected, click an existing path. As you drag your cursor over a path, it changes to the Area Type Tool cursor (see Figure 14.7). Any type you enter fills the interior of the path.

FIGURE 14.7

Dragging the Type Tool cursor over a path turns it into the Area Type Tool cursor.

Linking Text Blocks

If you have more type than can fit into the selected shape, a small plus sign in a box appears at the lower right of the shape (see Figure 14.8). The symbol indicates that more text overflows from the shape.

FIGURE **14.8**

*The little plus sign
symbol indicates a text
overflow.*

—— Plus sign

Illustrator enables you to link shapes so that overflow type from the first shape flows into
the next shape. You can do so by selecting the object with the overflowing type, along
with the object you want to link it to. Then choose Type➥Blocks➥Link (see Figure 14.9).

FIGURE **14.9**

Linked text blocks.

Lorem ipsum dolor sit amet, consectetuer adipiscing elit, sed diam nonummy nibh euismod tincidunt ut laoreet dolore magna aliquam erat volutpat. Ut wisi enim ad minim veniam, quis nostrud exerci tation ullamcorper suscipit lobortis nisl ut aliquip ex ea commodo consequat. Duis autem vel eum iriure dolor in hendrerit in vulputate velit esse molestie consequat, vel illum dolore eu feugiat nulla facilisis at vero eros et accumsan et iusto odio dignissim qui blandit

praesent luptatum zzril delenit augue duis dolore te feugait nulla facilisi. Lorem ipsum dolor sit amet, consectetuer adipiscing elit, sed diam nonummy nibh euismod tincidunt ut laoreet dolore magna aliquam erat volutpat. Ut wisi enim ad minim veniam, quis nostrud exerci tation ullamcorper suscipit lobortis nisl ut aliquip ex ea commodo consequat. Duis autem vel eum iriure dolor in hendrerit in vulputate velit esse molestie consequat, vel

illum dolore eu feugiat nulla facilisis at vero eros et accumsan et iusto odio dignissim qui blandit praesent luptatum zzril delenit augue duis dolore te feugait nulla facilisi. Nam liber tempor cum soluta nobis eleifend option congue nihil imperdiet doming id quod mazim placerat facer possim assum. Lorem ipsum dolor sit amet, consectetuer adipiscing elit, sed diam nonummy nibh euismod tincidunt ut laoreet dolore magna aliquam erat volutpat. Ut wisi

Rows and Columns

All this talk about linking text blocks reminds me about a wonderful feature in Illustrator
called Rows and Columns. Although you can't create columns of text within one text
block, you can create several blocks of type and link them. This handy feature makes creating rows and columns of type easy. Here's how to get started:

1. Draw an ordinary box. It should be large enough to contain all the rows or columns
    you want to create.

2. Select Rows & Columns from the Type menu (see Figure 14.10). You are presented
    with the Rows & Columns dialog box (see Figure 14.11).

14

FIGURE 14.10

*Choosing Rows &
Columns from the Type
menu.*

FIGURE 14.11

*The Rows & Columns
dialog box.*

3. Enter the number of rows (horizontal) and columns (vertical) and the gutter (the
   space between each row or column). The height and width are adjusted automatically. If you have the Preview button checked, you can see the rows and columns
   changing in real time as you enter the numbers (see Figure 14.12).

FIGURE 14.12

*The box before and
after the Rows and
Columns feature has
been applied.*

To make life even easier, the Rows and Columns feature even links the boxes for you so that type automatically runs from one to the next (see Figure 14.13). By choosing from the Text Flow icons, you can specify which direction the type should flow (see Figure 14.14). You can also choose to add guides, which is a great timesaving feature in itself, as Illustrator draws guides automatically to help you align objects to your rows and columns.

FIGURE 14.13

After the columns are created, the text is placed in the first box and runs its course through the linked boxes.

Lorem ipsum dolor sit amet, consectetuer adipiscing elit, sed diam nonummy nibh euismod tincidunt ut laoreet dolore magna aliquam erat volutpat. Ut wisi enim ad minim veniam, quis nostrud exerci tation ullamcorper suscipit lobortis nisl ut aliquip ex ea commodo consequat. Duis autem vel eum iriure dolor in hendrerit in vulputate velit esse molestie consequat, vel illum dolore eu feugiat nulla facilisis at vero eros et accumsan et iusto odio dignissim qui blandit praesent luptatum zzril delenit augue duis dolore te feugait nulla facilisi. Lorem ipsum dolor sit amet, consectetuer adipiscing elit, sed diam nonummy nibh euismod tincidunt ut laoreet dolore magna aliquam erat volutpat.

Ut wisi enim ad minim veniam, quis nostrud exerci tation ullamcorper suscipit lobortis nisl ut aliquip ex ea commodo consequat. Duis autem vel eum iriure dolor in hendrerit in vulputate velit esse molestie consequat, vel illum dolore eu feugiat nulla facilisis at vero eros et accumsan et iusto odio dignissim qui blandit praesent luptatum zzril delenit augue duis dolore te feugait nulla facilisi. Nam liber tempor cum soluta nobis eleifend option congue nihil imperdiet doming id quod mazim placerat facer possim assum. Lorem ipsum dolor sit amet, consectetuer adipiscing elit, sed diam nonummy nibh euismod tincidunt ut laoreet dolore magna aliquam erat volutpat. Ut wisi enim ad minim

FIGURE 14.14

These icons specify which way the text should link from box to box.

Now I'll tell you a little secret: You don't have to use Rows and Columns only for text blocks. This feature is great for making quick grids or rows of even-sized boxes, too. Ready for a little bit o' fun?

1. Draw a large square.

2. Select Rows & Columns from the Type menu.

3. For the number of rows, enter 3, and for the number of columns, enter 3. Set the gutter for each to 0.25 inch, and click OK (see Figure 14.15).

14

FIGURE 14.15

*The completed 3×3
grid.*

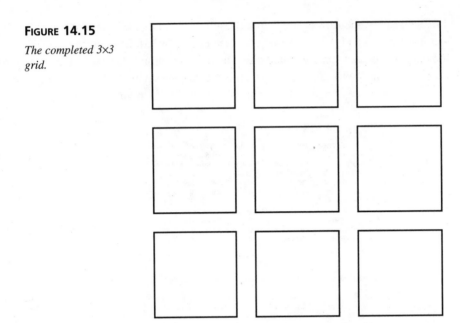

Now you can play tic-tac-toe, design the Ralston logo, or even better, make believe you are on *The Brady Bunch*!

Type on a Path

One of Illustrator's most popular type features is its capability to place text along a path (see Figure 14.16). You can place text along any path in Illustrator, whether it's an open path or a closed one.

To place text on a path, do one of the following:

- With the Path Type tool selected (see Figure 14.17), click any path and begin typing.

FIGURE 14.16

Type on a path.

AS HARRY CHAPIN SANG, "ALL MY LIFE'S A CIRCLE, SUNRISE AND SUNDOWN..."

FIGURE 14.17

Choosing the Path Type tool.

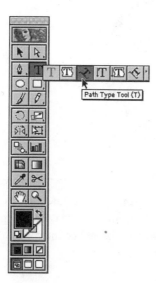

Path Type Tool (T)

14

- With the Type tool or the Area Type tool selected, press and hold the (Option)[Alt] key while clicking any path, and begin typing. Notice that the cursor changes to the Path Type Tool cursor when you press the (Option)[Alt] key (see Figure 14.18).

FIGURE 14.18

With the Type tool selected, the cursor changes to the Path Type Tool cursor when the (Option)[Alt] key is pressed.

Moving Text Along a Path

When text is on a path, you can move its position as well as flip it to the other side of the path. To see how, follow these steps:

1. Select the type or the path by using the Selection tool (the Direct Selection tool or Group Selection tool does not help here). Notice that the path is highlighted as well as the I-beam insertion point for the type.

2. To edit where the type lies on the path, click the I-beam and drag in the direction you want to move the type.

3. To flip the type to the other side of the path, double-click directly on the I-beam, or drag toward the opposite side of the path (see Figure 14.19).

FIGURE 14.19

By double-clicking the I-beam, you can flip the type to the inside of the circle.

Vertical Text

Illustrator also supports vertical text (see Figure 14.20), as well as complicated alphabets such as Kanji (Japanese). The Vertical Type tool, Vertical Area Type tool, and Vertical Path Type tool all work the same as their horizontal counterparts.

Figure 14.20

*Samples of type creat-
ed with the vertical
text tools.*

To see how to work with vertical text, follow these steps:

1. Draw an open path that goes from north to south.

2. Select the Vertical Path Type tool, and click on the path.

3. Type the words `Vertical Text on a Path`.

Summary

Up to this point, you've examined just about all the creation tools in Illustrator. First, you
covered drawing shapes, so now you know how to add text to your illustrations. You also
learned about the three types of text in Illustrator: point text, area text, and text on a path.
Don't go anywhere just yet, though. There's plenty more to learn, and in the next hour,
you'll learn how to work with the text you just learned to create.

Workshop

The Workshop contains quiz questions to help you solidify your understanding of the
material covered in this hour and exercises to provide you with experience using what
you have learned. You can find the answers to the quiz questions at the end of the hour.

14

Quiz

1. Which of these is not a Type tool in Illustrator?

    a. Area Type tool

    b. Straight Type tool

    c. Vertical Path Type tool

2. Area text is also called

    a. Body text

    b. Wide text

    c. Headline text

3. Point text is also called

    a. Small text

    b. Sharp text

    c. Headline text

4. A small plus sign at the bottom of a text block indicates that

    a. There is additional text

    b. The text in the block is the truth

    c. Something is wrong with your screen

5. The Rows and Columns feature can be used only to create text blocks.

    a. True

    b. False

Exercises

1. Draw three shapes, and link two of them. Add text so that the text flows from one shape to the next. Now unlink the two shapes, and link the first shape to the third.

2. Create a path and flow text along the path. Now practice moving the text around on the path, as well as flipping the text from the inside of the path to the outside.

3. Practice editing, copying, and pasting text by highlighting it with the Type tool.

Term Review

Area text—Type in Illustrator that is defined by a closed shape. Usually used for running body copy.

Point text—Type in Illustrator that is defined by a single point. Usually used for headlines and logos.

Answers to Quiz Questions

1. b
2. a
3. c
4. a
5. b

14

Hour 15

Advanced Typography

In the preceding hour, you learned all about creating text in Illustrator. You learned about the three kinds of text, and you learned how to move the text around. But there's a lot more to text than just the words themselves. In this hour, you'll learn how to work with the type—or more important, how to make it look good. Of course, that's the goal with anything you do, and Illustrator has the tools to make text look great.

In this hour, you'll learn all about the following:

- The Character palette
- Fonts
- The Paragraph palette
- The Tab palette
- The MM Design palette
- Multiple master fonts

The Character Palette

You control your type (and believe me, type needs lots of controlling) by using Illustrator's Character palette (see Figure 15.1). To open the Character palette, use the (Command+T)[Control+T] keyboard shortcut, or select Character from the Type menu. In the Character palette, you specify fonts, point size, leading, and kerning. The Character palette is the central location for editing type style—how your type looks.

FIGURE 15.1

The Character palette, in all its glory, with the Multilingual Options section open.

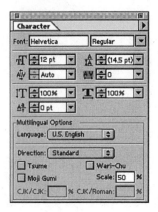

To edit text, you must select it. To do so, you can either use the Selection tool to select the entire text block, or you can select characters individually by

- Clicking and dragging text with the Type tool
- Clicking in the text with the Type tool and pressing the left or right arrow key on the keyboard while holding down the Shift key

Font

NEW TERM A *font* is a style of type, usually grouped in families such as Helvetica or Times. Many different fonts are available, and a font is basically the personality of your type. Loud text such as "SALE!" might be in a fat bold font, and more delicate words, such as "Love," might be in a script italic font (see Figure 15.2).

FIGURE 15.2

Type in different fonts.

After you choose a font, you also specify what style you want, such as roman (normal), italic, bold, and so on.

Size

New Term Type is traditionally measured in *points*. You can specify your type to be any size from 0.1 point (really small) up to 1296 points (really large). You can quickly enlarge or reduce your type in two-point increments by pressing (Command+Shift+>) [Control+Shift+>] or (Command+Shift+<)[Control+Shift+<], respectively. This method works regardless of how you selected the type (with the arrow or the Text tool).

> If you need even bigger type, you can simply convert your text to outlines (you learn about them later in this hour). Once your type is a path, you can scale to virtually any size by using the Scale tool.

Leading

New Term *Leading* (pronounced *ledding*) is the amount of space between each baseline in a paragraph of type. Leading is also measured in points. If the leading size and the point size are the same, your text has solid leading. A lot of space between each baseline is called open leading, whereas very little space is called tight leading (see Figure 15.3). Leading is important in determining readability. Typically, the wider your block of text, the more leading you need.

Figure 15.3

Text with open leading (left) and tight leading (right).

AS HARRY CHAPIN

SANG, "ALL MY LIFE'S

A CIRCLE, SUNRISE

AND SUNDOWN. THE

MOON ROLLS

THROUGH THE

NIGHTTIME, TILL THE

DAYBREAK COMES

AROUND...

AS HARRY CHAPIN
SANG, "ALL MY LIFE'S
A CIRCLE, SUNRISE
AND SUNDOWN. THE
MOON ROLLS
THROUGH THE
NIGHTTIME, TILL THE
DAYBREAK COMES
AROUND...

The keyboard shortcuts for increasing and decreasing leading are (Option+down arrow)[Alt+down arrow] and (Option+up arrow)[Alt+up arrow], respectively.

Kerning and Tracking

NEW TERM *Kerning* is the space between letters. *Tracking* is the amount of letterspacing applied globally across many letters. Negative numbers mean your kerning or tracking is tight, and the letters are closer to one another. Positive numbers mean your kerning or tracking is loose, and the letters are farther apart from each other (see Figure 15.4).

FIGURE 15.4

The top word has tight tracking, whereas the bottom type has loose tracking.

KATI
K A T I

The keyboard shortcuts for tightening and loosening kerning or tracking are (Option+left arrow)[Alt+left arrow] and (Option+right arrow)[Alt+right arrow], respectively. If you have more than one letter selected, Illustrator automatically applies tracking. Otherwise, invoking the keyboard shortcut applies kerning.

Horizontal and Vertical Scale

Using horizontal and vertical scale, you can adjust the width and height of selected text (see Figure 15.5). Adjusting the text this way can result in type that looks squashed and distorted in unsightful ways. For true horizontal and vertical scaling, try to use multiple master typefaces, which are covered later in this hour.

FIGURE 15.5

From the left, the original letter, scaled vertically 50%, and then scaled horizontally 50%.

a a a

Baseline Shift

All type is aligned to a baseline. You can select type and shift the baseline for that selection (see Figure 15.6). Shifting type is useful for creating superscripts or subscripts and also for creating type effects. In Illustrator, however, one of the most useful applications for baseline shift occurs when you have type on a path (see Figure 15.7). You can use baseline shift to move the type off the path, and you can give the path a stroke. (Make sure you use the Direct Selection tool; otherwise, the type gets a stroke, too.)

FIGURE 15.6

The "T" has a positive baseline shift.

FIGURE 15.7

By using baseline shift to move up the type, you can create a colored stroke by using the same path the type is on.

The keyboard shortcuts for raising and lowering baseline shift are (Option+Shift+up arrow)[Alt+Shift+up arrow] and (Option+Shift+down arrow)[Alt+Shift+down arrow], respectively.

I saw you sit up straight in your chair just now. Admit it, you thought that what you saw in Figure 15.7 was pretty cool. Why don't you try it now?

1. Press L to select the Ellipse tool, and draw a circle.

2. Switch to the Text tool by pressing the T key.

3. While holding down the (Option)[Alt] key, click on the path of the circle at the top.

4. When you see a blinking cursor where you clicked, Illustrator is waiting for you to type something. Type `Baseline Shift` (or any words that may come to mind).

5. With the cursor still blinking, press (Command+A)[Control+A] to select all your type.

6. Press (Command+Shift+C)[Control+Shift+C] to center the text on the path. (I'll cover centering in detail later in the hour, so don't worry.)

7. Increase the type size by pressing (Command+Shift+>)[Control+Shift+>] repeatedly until you achieve the size you want.

8. Press (Option+Shift+up arrow)[Alt+Shift+up arrow] repeatedly until the type is as far from the baseline as you like.

9. Press (Command+Shift+A)[Control+Shift+A] to deselect everything, and then press the A key to select the Direct Selection tool.

10. To make this process easier, switch to Artwork mode by pressing (Command+Y) [Control+Y]. You should now be able to see the path. Using the Direct Selection tool, click on the path to select it.

11. If the Stroke palette is not already open, press the F10 key to open it, and enter a weight for the stroke. I used 2 points.

12. Switch back to Preview mode by pressing (Command+Y)[Control+Y]. You now have the stroked path and the type on the path, all within one object.

The Paragraph Palette

On the Paragraph palette, you specify justification, indents, word and letter spacing, as well as options such as auto-hyphenation and hanging punctuation (see Figure 15.8).

FIGURE 15.8

The Paragraph palette.

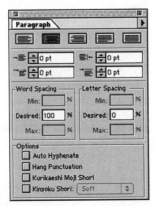

Justification

NEW TERM *Justification* is a fancy word for paragraph *alignment* (see Figure 15.9).

FIGURE 15.9

Paragraph alignment.

FLUSH LEFT	FLUSH RIGHT	CENTERED	JUSTIFIED	FORCED JUSTIFIED
Lorem ipsum dolor sit amet, consectetuer adipiscing elit, sed diam nonummy nibh euismod tincidunt ut laoreet dolore magna aliquam erat volutpat. Ut wisi enim ad minim veniam, quis nostrud exerci tation ullamcorper suscipit lobortis nisl ut aliquip ex ea commodo consequat. Duis autem vel eum iriure dolor in hendrerit in vulputate velit esse molestie consequat, vel illum dolore eu feugiat nulla	Lorem ipsum dolor sit amet, consectetuer adipiscing elit, sed diam nonummy nibh euismod tincidunt ut laoreet dolore magna aliquam erat volutpat. Ut wisi enim ad minim veniam, quis nostrud exerci tation ullamcorper suscipit lobortis nisl ut aliquip ex ea commodo consequat. Duis autem vel eum iriure dolor in hendrerit in vulputate velit esse molestie consequat, vel illum dolore eu feugiat nulla	Lorem ipsum dolor sit amet, consectetuer adipiscing elit, sed diam nonummy nibh euismod tincidunt ut laoreet dolore magna aliquam erat volutpat. Ut wisi enim ad minim veniam, quis nostrud exerci tation ullamcorper suscipit lobortis nisl ut aliquip ex ea commodo consequat. Duis autem vel eum iriure dolor in hendrerit in vulputate velit esse molestie consequat, vel illum dolore eu feugiat nulla	Lorem ipsum dolor sit amet, consectetuer adipiscing elit, sed diam nonummy nibh euismod tincidunt ut laoreet dolore magna aliquam erat volutpat. Ut wisi enim ad minim veniam, quis nostrud exerci tation ullamcorper suscipit lobortis nisl ut aliquip ex ea commodo consequat. Duis autem vel eum iriure dolor in hendrerit in vulputate velit esse molestie consequat, vel illum dolore eu feugiat nulla	Lorem ipsum dolor sit amet, consectetuer adipiscing elit, sed diam nonummy nibh euismod tincidunt ut laoreet dolore magna aliquam erat volutpat. Ut wisi enim ad minim veniam, quis nostrud exerci tation ullamcorper suscipit lobortis nisl ut aliquip ex ea commodo consequat. Duis autem vel eum iriure dolor in hendrerit in vulputate velit esse molestie consequat, vel illum dolore eu feugiat nulla

You can align a paragraph of type in five different ways in Illustrator:

- Align left—(Command+Shift+L)[Control+Shift+L]
- Align right—(Command+Shift+R)[Control+Shift+R]
- Centered—(Command+Shift+C)[Control+Shift+C]
- Justify full lines—(Command+Shift+J)[Control+Shift+J]
- Justify all lines (flush left and right)—(Command+Shift+F)[Control+Shift+F]

You can select these options quickly by clicking the icons found at the top of the Paragraph palette (see Figure 15.10).

FIGURE 15.10

The justification icons in the Paragraph palette.

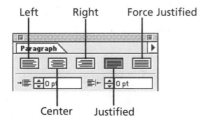

Left   Right   Force Justified

Center   Justified

 Certain characters do not show up on your screen when you type them, such as a space, a soft or hard return, a tab, and so forth. Some page layout programs—QuarkXPress, for example—have an option called Show Invisibles, which allows you to see these characters as symbols. (They don't print, of course; you can just see them onscreen.) Illustrator can also show these characters. Simply select Show Hidden Characters from the Type menu. To hide the characters, simply select the menu item again.

Indents

The three different *indent* settings on the Paragraph palette are Left Indent, First Line Indent, and Right Indent. The left and right indents affect the entire paragraph of type, whereas the first line indent affects just the first line of the paragraph.

Illustrator also includes a setting for space before each paragraph. Sometimes you might want to add a little bit of extra space before each paragraph to increase readability, as well as make it easier to identify where a paragraph ends and the next one begins (see Figure 15.11).

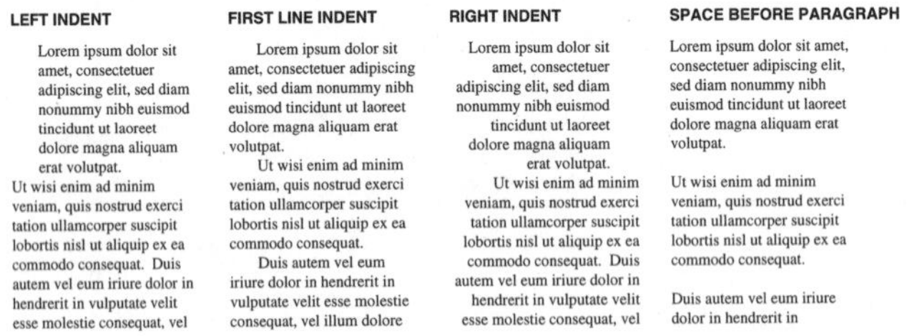

FIGURE 15.11

The different paragraph settings.

LEFT INDENT

Lorem ipsum dolor sit amet, consectetuer adipiscing elit, sed diam nonummy nibh euismod tincidunt ut laoreet dolore magna aliquam erat volutpat.
Ut wisi enim ad minim veniam, quis nostrud exerci tation ullamcorper suscipit lobortis nisl ut aliquip ex ea commodo consequat. Duis autem vel eum iriure dolor in hendrerit in vulputate velit esse molestie consequat, vel

FIRST LINE INDENT

Lorem ipsum dolor sit amet, consectetuer adipiscing elit, sed diam nonummy nibh euismod tincidunt ut laoreet dolore magna aliquam erat volutpat.
Ut wisi enim ad minim veniam, quis nostrud exerci tation ullamcorper suscipit lobortis nisl ut aliquip ex ea commodo consequat.
Duis autem vel eum iriure dolor in hendrerit in vulputate velit esse molestie consequat, vel illum dolore

RIGHT INDENT

Lorem ipsum dolor sit amet, consectetuer adipiscing elit, sed diam nonummy nibh euismod tincidunt ut laoreet dolore magna aliquam erat volutpat.
Ut wisi enim ad minim veniam, quis nostrud exerci tation ullamcorper suscipit lobortis nisl ut aliquip ex ea commodo consequat. Duis autem vel eum iriure dolor in hendrerit in vulputate velit esse molestie consequat, vel

SPACE BEFORE PARAGRAPH

Lorem ipsum dolor sit amet, consectetuer adipiscing elit, sed diam nonummy nibh euismod tincidunt ut laoreet dolore magna aliquam erat volutpat.

Ut wisi enim ad minim veniam, quis nostrud exerci tation ullamcorper suscipit lobortis nisl ut aliquip ex ea commodo consequat.

Duis autem vel eum iriure dolor in hendrerit in

Word and Letter Spacing

Word and Letter Spacing settings in the Paragraph palette let you control spacing between words and letters when justified type is used. These settings control when words become hyphenated, or forced to another line, by specifying how far Illustrator can stretch the spacing between words and letters.

The Tab Palette

To create tabs in a paragraph, open the Tab Ruler by choosing it from the Type menu (see Figure 15.12). It's a floating palette, so you can position it anywhere on the page (see Figure 15.13). To add a tab, click the ruler where you want the tab to appear. After you click, a highlighted tab arrow appears. You can now make the tab a right, center, left, or decimal tab by clicking the icons in the upper-left corner of the Tab palette (see Figure 15.14). To delete a tab, drag it off the palette (see Figure 15.15), and to change the measurement system quickly, Shift+click in the upper portion of the palette.

FIGURE 15.12

Choosing the Tab Ruler from the Type menu.

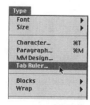

FIGURE 15.13

The Tab palette.

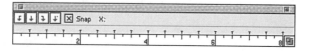

FIGURE 15.14

Clicking these icons defines the type of tab.

FIGURE 15.15

Deleting a tab.

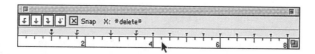

The MM Design Palette

Illustrator has full support for multiple master typefaces. Developed by Adobe, a multiple master typeface contains a variable width or weight or even serif axis (see Figure 15.16). By controlling the axis, you can modify the typeface to fit your exact specifications. The MM Design palette (found under the Type menu) lets you modify multiple master typefaces in real-time right in Illustrator (see Figure 15.17). Simply drag the sliders to edit the typeface. You need to have a multiple master font and have it selected to use this feature.

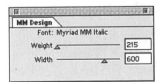

Converting Text to Outlines

One of the most powerful text features in Illustrator is the capability to convert type into
fully editable Bézier paths. If you choose Create Outlines from the Type menu (you need
to have type selected with the Selection tool when you do this), as shown in Figure
15.18, Illustrator turns the type into Bézier paths. You can then edit each letter by using
the techniques you learned in previous hours (see Figure 15.19).

FIGURE 15.18

Choosing Create Outlines from the Type menu (Command+Shift+O) [Control+Shift+O].

15

FIGURE 15.19

Editing type that was converted to outlines.

You can even use the type as a mask. In fact, do so right now by following these steps:

1. Start by creating some art that you want to appear inside the type. I've decided to create a row of evenly spaced horizontal lines (see Figure 15.20). To do the same, select the Pen tool, click once, and then while holding down the Shift key click again to the right or left of the first point. I've given the lines a weight of 8 points.

FIGURE 15.20

A row of evenly spaced horizontal lines.

2. Switch to the Direct Selection tool and, while holding the (Option)[Alt] key, click anywhere in the middle of the line. The line is now selected.

3. Hold the Shift and (Option)[Alt] keys, and click and drag the line down a bit. You have just created a copy of the line (see Figure 15.21).

FIGURE **15.21**

*Using the
(Option)[Alt] drag
function to create a
duplicate.*

4. Press (Command+D)[Control+D] several times to repeat the transformation you just made in step 3. You should now have a row of lines.

5. Because you're going to be using the lines as one unit, group them all together. After selecting them all, press (Command+G)[Control+G] to create the group.

6. Using the Type tool, click away from the lines, and type a word. Make the type large, as it will be easier to see during the following steps.

7. Convert the outlines into paths by pressing (Command+Shift+O) [Control+Shift+O].

8. A mask must be a single shape, so to use the word as a mask, you must make the word a compound path. With all the letters selected, choose Object➥Compound Paths➥Make, or press (Command+8)[Control+8].

9. Position the type over the lines (see Figure 15.22). Remember, you can just press and hold the (Command)[Control] key to access the Selection tool to move the word.

FIGURE **15.22**

*Positioning the word
over the lines.*

10. Select both the word and the lines by pressing (Command+A)[Control+A] to select all.

11. Press (Command+7)[Control+7], or choose Object➥Masks➥Make to create the mask. The words will now mask the lines you created (see Figure 15.23).

15

FIGURE 15.23

*The final masked
word.*

You might want to convert type to outlines for two other reasons. One is that certain filters don't work on type. To run those filters, you need to convert your type to outlines first. Another reason is if you are sending your file out to another person or to a service bureau that might not have your font. Converting the type to outlines assures that it will print perfectly. When you create a logo, converting any type to outlines is always a good idea. This way, whenever you use it, you don't have to worry about fonts.

After text is converted to outlines, it cannot be turned back into text again, so you can't fix any typos. Saving a version of your file before you convert your text to outlines might be a good idea, in case you need to edit the text.

Change Case

This situation happens all the time: You type something in all caps and you need it in lowercase, or vice versa. With this handy little feature, your hands are spared a few more moments from that repetitive strain injury. Simply highlight the type with the Type tool, and choose Change Case from the Type menu (see Figure 15.24). In the resulting dialog box, you can then choose how you want to change your type (see Figure 15.25).

FIGURE 15.24

Choosing Change Case from the Type menu.

FIGURE 15.25

The Change Case dialog box.

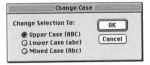

Find Font and Find/Change

You just finished an entire job, and a representative for your client calls to say his bosses loved it, but could you just change one little thing? They want all instances of the word *Fred* to be changed to *Frederick*, or maybe they want to switch one typeface for another. After you hang up the phone and slam your head into the monitor, go to the Type menu and select Find Font (see Figure 15.26). In the Find Font dialog box, you can easily change one font to another throughout the document (see Figure 15.27). As far as changing the actual text, select Find/Change from the Type menu, and in the Find/Change dialog box (see Figure 15.28), type the word you are looking for and what it should be changed to. These functions work the same as they would in any word processing program. All happy now?

FIGURE 15.26

Selecting Find Font from the Type menu.

15

FIGURE 15.27

The Find Font dialog box.

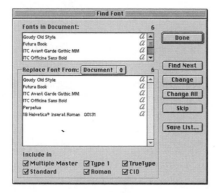

FIGURE 15.28

The Find/Change dialog box.

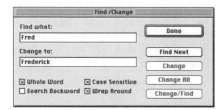

Smart Punctuation

If you want to make your type look as if it were set by an expert typographer, use Smart Punctuation (see Figure 15.29). It replaces regular quotation marks with the curly kind (see Figure 15.30) and inserts ligatures (on the Macintosh), em and en dashes, ellipses, and expert fractions in your document.

FIGURE 15.29

Found in the Type menu, the Smart Punctuation feature lets you make changes to selected text or an entire document.

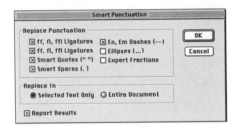

FIGURE 15.30

From left to right, plain quotes and curly quotes.

Check Spelling

Illustrator also has a built-in spell checker. You can find the Check Spelling function in the Type menu (see Figure 15.31). This spell checker, shown in Figure 15.32, works just like any spell checker you would find in any word processor. It allows you to change or skip words as well as add words to the dictionary.

FIGURE 15.31

Choosing Check Spelling from the Type menu.

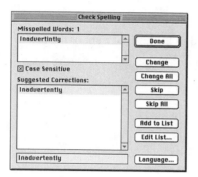

FIGURE 15.32

Illustrator's Check Spelling dialog box.

15

Summary

Fonts, points, leading, kerning, indents, justification: You learned all about these fancy words along with a lot of other cool stuff this hour. You learned how to use multiple master fonts as well as how to adjust word and letter spacing. The Change Case feature will save you many hours of extra typing, and you really felt the power of Illustrator when you converted type to outlines and edited the Bézier paths. By the way, converting type to paths and analyzing how the anchor points are set up is a good way to learn more about Bézier paths.

Workshop

The Workshop contains quiz questions to help you solidify your understanding of the material covered in this hour and exercises to provide you with experience using what you have learned. You can find the answers to the quiz questions at the end of the hour.

Quiz

1. "Leading" refers to

   a. Taking a few steps off first base

   b. The amount of space between baselines of type

   c. The amount of space between letters

2. "Tracking" refers to

   a. The amount of letterspacing applied across several letters

   b. Finding your FedEx package

   c. The distance a paragraph is moved inward from the left and right edges of a text block

3. "Justified" type means

    a. The type is aligned to the left and right of the text block

    b. The measurement system used for measuring type

    c. The paragraph has an indent

4. To delete a tab setting, you

    a. Press the Delete key

    b. Shift+click the tab

    c. Drag it off the Tab palette

5. "Multiple Master" refers to

    a. A dog with more than one owner

    b. A font technology developed by Adobe

    c. A special version of Illustrator

Exercises

1. Create several lines of Area Type, and practice using the keyboard shortcuts to adjust the point size, leading, kerning, and tracking.

2. Experiment using the Baseline Shift feature to create superscripts or subscripts as found in Trademarks™ or H_2O.

3. Create some large text in several typefaces, and convert the text to outlines. Using the Direct Selection tool, examine the paths, looking at the placement of the anchor points and the control handles. Switch to Artwork mode for easier viewing. This exercise is a good way to learn how Bézier paths work.

Term Review

Alignment—The alignment of the text in a paragraph—left, right, centered, or justified.

Fonts—Type styles of different varieties, such as Times, Helvetica, and Symbol.

Indents—The distance a paragraph is moved inward from the left and right edges of a text block.

Justification—The alignment of text to the left and right edges of a text block.

Kerning—The process of adding or removing space between a pair of letters, or the space itself.

Leading—The distance from baseline to baseline in lines of type (pronounced *ledding*).

Multiple Master—A font technology developed by Adobe Systems that gives a font the capability to be scaled on either a weight, width, or serif axis.

15

Points—Measurement system used for measuring type. There are 72 points in one inch, and there are 12 points in a pica, which makes 6 picas in one inch.

Answers to Quiz Questions

1. b
2. a
3. a
4. c
5. b

HOUR 16

Working with Raster Images

Way back in Hour 1, "Getting to Know Illustrator," I discussed the differences between vector and raster images. To quickly review, vector images are mathematically defined (Bézier) shapes that can be scaled to virtually any size without any loss in detail. Raster images are defined by individual pixels, which combine to create an image. Raster images, however, are bound by the resolution in which they were created, and scaling a raster image can produce jaggy or unclear results (see Figure 16.1).

FIGURE 16.1

Both have been enlarged 300 percent. Notice how the raster image becomes jaggy, whereas the vector image remains smooth.

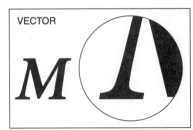 

Although Illustrator is a vector program, it does have support for raster art. In this hour, you'll learn about the following:

- Placing raster images
- Linking and embedding
- Using the Links palette
- Working with raster art in Illustrator

A Pixel for Your Thoughts

NEW TERM You can get a raster image into Illustrator in basically two ways. The first way is to *place* the image. This command takes an existing raster image and places it into your document. The second way is to convert a vector object into a raster object by using Illustrator's Rasterize command. There is a really a third way—opening a raster file directly—but I'll get to that later in the hour.

Placing an Image

If you've used a page layout program, such as PageMaker or QuarkXPress, you're familiar with the Place command. Place lets you import an image right into your Illustrator document. The image could have been created in another application, or it could have been exported from Illustrator in a raster format (see Hour 20, "Saving/Exporting Files").

To place a raster image, choose Place from the File menu (see Figure 16.2). The Place dialog box then asks you to find the file you want to place. After you select the file, click Place. The image then appears in the center of your screen (see Figure 16.3).

FIGURE 16.2

Choosing Place from the File menu.

FIGURE 16.3

The placed EPS file.

16

Notice that the image has a box with an "x" through it that shows the image is selected. Note that the "x" appears only on linked EPS images. All other placed images, whether linked or embedded, have just a box surrounding the image. You can view placed images only when in Preview mode. When you are in Artwork mode, you see only the surrounding box, not the image. However, in the View section of the Document Setup dialog box, a Show Images in Artwork option enables you to see a low-resolution black-and-white preview of placed images when in Artwork mode.

The Rasterize Command

You can rasterize any object in Illustrator right inside Illustrator by using the Rasterize command. Essentially, you are instructing Illustrator to convert a vector object into a raster. When an image is rasterized, it becomes an embedded image (see "Linked and Embedded Images," later in this hour). Follow these steps to rasterize an image:

1. Select one or more objects.
2. Choose Rasterize from the Object menu (see Figure 16.4).

FIGURE 16.4

The Rasterize dialog box.

3. Choose a color model. You can select either RGB, CMYK, Grayscale, or Bitmap.

4. Choose a resolution. When Illustrator converts your selection to pixels, it needs to know how many pixels to create. For screen and Web art, choose 72ppi. If your art will be printed on an imagesetter, you need higher resolution—closer to 300dpi for photographic images, 600 or more for bitmap and line art.

5. Choose whether you want antialiasing or a mask. Both of these features are described in detail later in this hour.

Everyone knows that you can use the Rasterize command on vector objects, but did you know that you can also apply the Rasterize command to raster art? This capability is most useful for converting color images to grayscale (select Grayscale from the Color Model pop-up menu) or for converting grayscale images into color (some Photoshop-compatible filters work only on RGB images).

Antialiasing

One of the biggest advantages of vector art is the smooth lines you get when you print the file. Today's high-end imagesetters print at resolutions upwards of 2500dpi, and you are used to seeing the clean sharp edges in logos, type, and illustrations. Onscreen, however, things can appear jaggy because a monitor's resolution is only 72dpi.

When your final art is printed, the images will be ultra sharp, but what if your images won't be printed? What if you are designing for the Web or for a multimedia presentation, and the final art will be viewed onscreen? Do you have to live with jaggy art in these situations? That's where antialiasing comes in.

Antialiasing is the process of slightly blurring the edges of an image to give it a softer, smoother edge onscreen (see the following Just a Minute). Almost all images on the Web use antialiasing to give a clean and smooth appearance.

You may notice that when you're in Preview mode, all art appears antialiased. When you switch to Artwork mode, the art is not antialiased. This antialiasing appears only onscreen; however, when you print the file, you still get the sharp lines you are used to. This is a great feature that Adobe has added.

When you use the Rasterize command to convert a vector object to raster, and the final image will appear onscreen at 72dpi, antialias the object to give it that smooth appearance. To do so, simply check the Anti-Alias check box in the Rasterize dialog box.

Creating a Mask

A raster image always has a rectangular-shaped bounding box that defines the area of the image. Although vector files can have irregularly shaped edges, a raster requires a clipping path to achieve a nonrectangular edge. When you rasterize an object in Illustrator, you have the option to create a mask for the image. This way, you can place the rasterized image on a colored background without the white background box filling in around the rasterized art (see Figure 16.5).

FIGURE 16.5

The raster image on the left has no mask, whereas the raster image on the right was created by using the Create Mask option.

To create a mask for an object at the time you rasterize it, simply check the Create Mask button in the Rasterize dialog box.

Opening an Image

I mentioned earlier that you can bring a raster image into Illustrator in a third way. Besides placing a file or using the Rasterize command, you can also use the Open command to directly open a raster image, which creates a new document with the raster image in it. Remember, however, that when you open a raster file, it automatically becomes embedded in the Illustrator document, and you cannot link it.

Illustrator also sports a powerful EPS parser. You therefore can open just about any vector EPS (Encapsulated PostScript) file and edit it as if it were an Illustrator document. You can save a QuarkXPress page as an EPS, for example, and then open the file (not place it) and edit the document. Note, however, that editing text may be difficult because of the way the text is imported.

The EPS format, unlike any other, can support both raster and vector art—even within the same document. The parser in Illustrator can convert only vector EPS images (or the vector parts within an EPS) into editable art. Any art that is in raster format remains in raster form and can be edited only as a raster image.

Linked and Embedded Images

As if things weren't already complicated enough, Illustrator handles raster images in two ways. A raster image can either be linked or embedded in an Illustrator document. Except for certain file formats, Illustrator links placed images by default.

NEW TERM   A *linked file* resides outside your Illustrator file, and Illustrator notes the location of that file, whether on your hard drive, on a Zip disk, or on a file server. The image in your document is simply a preview of that raster file. At print time, Illustrator goes to the original file and uses the high-resolution information to print the image where it belongs in the illustration. You cannot print your file without that original raster image.

NEW TERM   An *embedded raster* is actually part of your Illustrator document. After you embed a raster file, you no longer need the original raster file because the entire image is contained within your Illustrator document. Of course, this also means that your file size increases (if the file is a high-resolution one, your Illustrator file could become extremely large).

If you decide not to link a file when you place it, uncheck Link when you import it (see Figure 16.6). The image is then embedded.

FIGURE 16.6

Unchecking the Link box in the Place dialog box.

If you have a linked image in a document, and then you delete or remove the linked image from its place on your disk, Illustrator can't access the image anymore. The next time you open the file, Illustrator alerts you and asks you where the image file currently is. If you can't find it, Illustrator opens the document without the image in place.

The Links Palette

If you have several placed images in your document, keeping track of all the images may become difficult. Along comes the all-new Links palette to the rescue. The Links palette stores information for every placed image in each Illustrator document. To open the Links palette, choose Show Links from the Window menu (see Figure 16.7). Take a closer look at the Links palette now to see what it has to offer.

FIGURE 16.7

Opening the Links palette.

16

The Links palette contains an entry for each raster image in your document. As you will soon see, you can choose to show only certain kinds of images, such as embedded or linked images within the palette at any time, or you can choose to show all images. The palette lists each image name, along with a thumbnail preview of that image (see Figure 16.8).

FIGURE 16.8

This Links palette contains four images. Notice the thumbnail preview icon followed by the image name.

Along the bottom of the palette are the following four buttons, starting from the left:

- The Replace Link button allows you to swap one image for another. After you highlight an image in the Links palette (see Figure 16.9), click on the Replace Link button, and Illustrator prompts you to locate a new image. The new image then replaces the old one, as well as takes on any transformations you may have made to the old one, such as scaling or rotating. This feature is extremely useful when you are replacing low-resolution "placement" images with high-resolution ones for final print.

FIGURE 16.9

Here, the image "Building Photo" is highlighted.

- The Go To Link button makes your highlighted image the active selection in your Illustrator document.
- The Update Link button brings your selected image up to date with the latest version. For instance, if you have placed a photo that you have created in Photoshop, and then you make changes to the original photo in Photoshop, the old version is still in Illustrator. Using the Update Link function brings the latest saved version into Illustrator and ensures that the placed image in your document is current.
- The Edit Original button opens the application in which the placed image was created to allow for editing in that application.

To find out detailed information about a placed image, simply double-click on the image name in the Links palette. Doing so brings up the Link Information window, detailing specifics such as Name, Location, Kind, and even Transform information (see Figure 16.10).

FIGURE 16.10

The Link Information window for "Building Photo."

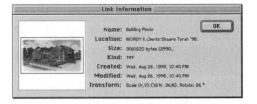

You can access several more options in the Links palette by using the Links palette pop-up menu. You access this menu by pressing and holding the mouse on the little black triangle in the upper-right corner of the Links palette (see Figure 16.11). Here, you can choose to embed a highlighted image or choose to view only modified or embedded images. If you choose Palette Options from the pop-up menu, you can specify what size the thumbnail previews should appear in the Links palette, if any at all (see Figure 16.12).

FIGURE 16.11

The Links palette pop-up menu.

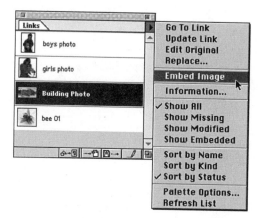

16

FIGURE 16.12

Choosing a thumbnail size.

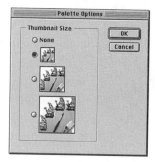

File Formats

Illustrator supports a wide range of image formats. Depending on which platform you are using, Macintosh or Windows, you can open and place an array of different file formats. Some are specific to one particular program, and others are specific to either the Macintosh or Windows platform, such as PICT and BMP.

Some formats, however, can be used on either the Macintosh or Windows platform. These formats include native Illustrator files, Acrobat PDF, TIFF, and EPS formats. PDF files can be viewed on any platform (even the World Wide Web) with the Acrobat Reader program.

Color Management

NEW TERM   Illustrator sports a robust *color management* system. You can edit the color settings in Illustrator by choosing Color Settings from the File menu (see Figure
16.13). You can fine-tune your options within the Color Settings dialog box (see Figure
16.14).

FIGURE 16.13

*Choosing Color
Settings from the File
menu.*

FIGURE 16.14

*The Color Settings
dialog box.*

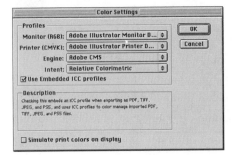

A color management system strives to keep colors consistent as you work with them—
from scanning, to viewing onscreen, to proofing, to final output. Because each of these
processes uses different color technologies and even different color models, you might
discover a noticeable difference between what you see onscreen and what you actually
get when the job is printed. Technologies such as ColorSync and Kodak Digital Science
compensate for color differences by using color profiles from each device, such as your
scanner, monitor, and printer, and try to make color consistent across the board.

A great feature of Illustrator is the capability to simulate print colors on display. This
option lets you view files just like in Photoshop, when you want to view only certain
color channels. It's also great when you're doing print work, to get a better idea of how
your file is going to print.

Using Raster Art in Illustrator

Placed raster images cannot be edited in Illustrator. You can, however, apply transformations to them, and you can also apply certain filters. You transform raster images just as you would any Illustrator object: select it and apply the transformation (see Hour 13, "Transformations"). This operation applies to all the transformation commands and tools—moving, scaling, rotating, reflecting, and shearing.

16

Colorize 1-Bit TIFFs

NEW TERM   Illustrator can colorize *1-bit* (black-and-white) TIFF images. After placing the image into your document, you can assign one color to the black part of the image by assigning a fill to the image.

Use the Autotrace Tool

One of the reasons that you would place a raster image into Illustrator is to trace it. Tracing a raster image creates a vector object that you can edit and scale without worrying about resolution. Illustrator's Autotrace tool was created with this operation in mind. Try it now:

1. Place a raster image into your Illustrator document.

2. Choose the Autotrace tool from the Toolbox.

3. Click the edge of the image to trace.

The Auto Trace Tolerance and Tracing Gap settings in Preferences determine how close and how smooth the traced object is in reference to the raster image. If you need more detail and accuracy for your tracing, you might look into Adobe Streamline, a software product geared specifically toward converting raster to vector art. For more information on tracing images, see Hour 21, "Working Smart in Illustrator."

Use Photoshop-Compatible Filters

Finally, one of the most exciting things you can do to raster images in Illustrator is apply Photoshop-compatible filters to them. Illustrator ships with several filters, including the entire Gallery Effects library of Photoshop-compatible filters. To use a filter, it, or an alias of the filter, must be present in Illustrator's Plug-ins folder when you launch Illustrator.

Photoshop-compatible filters can only be run on embedded raster images, not linked ones. Also, many Photoshop-compatible filters work only on images that are in RGB color mode. If you have an image that is not RGB, use the Rasterize command to convert to the RGB color standard. Also note that some Photoshop-compatible filters require larger memory requirements.

You can find Photoshop-compatible filters under the Filter menu. They look just like the other filters, but they are grayed out unless you have an embedded raster image selected (see Figure 16.15).

Figure 16.15

Without an embedded raster image selected, all Photoshop-compatible filters are grayed out.

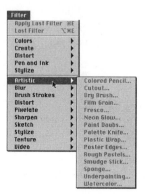

Have fun with the filters, and remember that you can always use the Rasterize command to convert vector art into a raster image, enabling you to apply Photoshop-compatible filters to it.

For more information on Photoshop-compatible filters, check out either *Illustrator Complete* or *Photoshop Complete*, both published by Hayden. These books do a great job of reviewing the filters, their settings, and the results you get.

Summary

In this hour, you learned to live with your pixel friends and proved that raster and vector images can coexist peacefully. You learned about linking and embedding, the Links palette, and also about Illustrator's powerful EPS parser. As if that weren't enough, you traced pixel images and even applied Photoshop-compatible filters to rasters within Illustrator. Next, you get back to the world of vector images and explore all the filters you can apply to vector objects.

Workshop

The Workshop contains quiz questions to help you solidify your understanding of the material covered in this hour and exercises to provide you with experience using what you have learned. You can find the answers to the quiz questions at the end of the hour.

Quiz

1. An "X" crosses through what kind of selected placed image format?

    a. EPS

    b. TIFF

    c. JPEG

2. The Rasterize command works only on vector images.

    a. True

    b. False

3. An image that is contained wholly in the Illustrator document itself is called

    a. Linked

    b. Encapsulated

    c. Embedded

4. In the Links palette, what does the Update Links option do?

    a. Updates the latest stock quotes

    b. Updates modified images

    c. Updates the embedded images

5. You can apply color to the black areas of a 1-bit TIFF image.

    a. True

    b. False

Exercises

1. Place a raster image and apply transformations to it. Then use the Replace Link option in the Links palette to swap the image with another. See how the new image takes on the transformations you applied to the original.

2. Experiment using the different Photoshop-compatible filters on placed images.

Term Review

1-bit—A raster image that contains only black and white pixels.

Color management—Software on a system level, such as Apple's ColorSync or Kodak's Digital Science, that assures consistent color on screens, scanners, printers, and image-setters.

Embedded raster—A raster image that has been included within an Illustrator document.

Linked file—An external raster file that is referenced from within an Illustrator document.

Place—The act of importing an image or art into an Illustrator document.

Answers to Quiz Questions

1. a
2. b
3. c
4. b
5. a

Hour 17

Vector Filters

Illustrator filters, found in the Filter menu (see Figure 17.1), perform a wide variety of tasks, ranging from simple timesavers such as converting all colors to CMYK to more complex functions such as creating intricate borders by using the Path Patterns filter. In this hour, you'll focus on some of these filters, including the following:

- The Adjust Colors filter
- The Object Mosaic filter
- The Roughen filter
- The Twirl filter
- The Zig Zag filter

FIGURE 17.1

The Illustrator Filter menu.

The Filter Menu

The Filter menu actually started out as a place for Illustrator plug-ins, but now that plug-ins can appear anywhere within Illustrator, the Filter menu has become the dumping ground for functions that don't really belong under any other menu. If you have any third-party plug-ins installed, such as KPT Vector Effects or Extensis VectorTools, you'll find them in the Filter menu. So if you have some filters that are not covered in this hour, refer to the documentation that came with those filters. For more information on plug-ins, see Hour 21, "Working Smart in Illustrator."

I've broken down descriptions of the filters as they appear in the Filter menu, and they fall under the following categories: Colors, Create, and Distort. The rest are Photoshop-compatible filters that apply to raster objects only.

Before you begin using these filters, at the top of the Filter menu, you'll notice two commands: Apply Last Filter and Last Filter. You can use them to quickly invoke the last filter you used. The Apply Last Filter option runs the last filter you used, with the settings you used. The Last Filter option opens the dialog box of the last filter you used, enabling you to adjust the settings before running the filter. Remember the keystrokes ((Command+E)[Control+E] and (Command+Option+E)[Control+Alt+E], respectively) for these two commands because sometimes you might want to use a filter repeatedly.

Colors Filters

The Colors filters are production-based filters that you use to fine-tune colors, as well as to address color issues to prepare files for film output (see Figure 17.2).

FIGURE 17.2

The Colors filters.

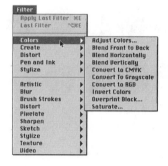

I must point out that these Colors filters do not work on objects filled with gradients or patterns. If you want to adjust gradient or pattern-filled objects with these filters, you have to convert the objects into art by using the Expand function. (Refer to Hour 6, "Drawing Bézier Paths," for detailed information on the Expand command.)

17

Adjust Colors

The Adjust Colors filter lets you tweak the colors of an object or a group of objects (see Figure 17.3). As you do with Photoshop's Levels command, you can adjust colors by changing the CMYK, Grayscale, or RGB values. You can adjust the fill, the stroke, or both simultaneously and preview your results as well (although previewing may slow down performance). You can even click the Convert button to change all selected objects to your current color mode, indicated in the pop-up menu at the top of the Adjust Colors dialog box.

FIGURE 17.3

The Adjust Colors dialog box.

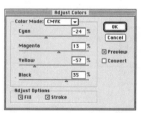

Blending Objects

The Blend Front to Back, Blend Horizontally, and Blend Vertically filters do not affect objects (as the Blend tool does) but do affect the fill color within them. You must have at least three objects selected for these filters to work. Upon running a filter, Illustrator blends the color across the selected objects (see Figure 17.4).

FIGURE 17.4

After you run the Blend Horizontally filter on the row of circles on top, the color is blended evenly across the circles, as shown on bottom.

Switching Between Color Models

The Convert to CMYK, Convert to Grayscale, and Convert to RGB filters speak for themselves. When you use them, any item selected is converted to the color mode chosen. Remember that these filters do not convert gradients or patterns.

Inverting Colors

The Invert Colors filter, identical to the one found in Photoshop, creates an inverted color (negative) for the selected objects.

Overprint Black

NEW TERM In some print jobs, you might need to set the black ink to overprint (as opposed to *knockout*, where the top color prints, but the color behind it does not). For simple jobs that require trapping, overprinting the black ink solves most trapping problems. Instead of having to select each object individually and then choosing the Overprint option in the Attributes palette, simply running the Overprint Black filter saves a lot of time (see Figure 17.5). Refer to Hour 13, "Transformations," for more information on overprinting and trapping.

FIGURE 17.5

The Overprint Black filter's dialog box.

Saturate

Using the Saturate filter can be a lot of fun (see Figure 17.6). By using a simple slider, you can saturate or desaturate the color in an object or a group of objects. This filter is great for creating subtle changes in color, as well as making certain objects more or less vibrant than other objects.

FIGURE 17.6

The Saturate filter's
dialog box.

Create Filters

Basically timesavers, the Create filters let you do in one step what might normally take a
lot more (see Figure 17.7). In this menu, you'll also find the Object Mosaic filter, a powerful filter that you can use to create really interesting effects.

FIGURE 17.7

Illustrator's Create fil-
ter menu.

17

Object Mosaic

Object Mosaic is a powerful filter used to create a vector tile-like mosaic based on a
raster image (see Figure 17.8).

FIGURE 17.8

The image on the left
is the original raster.
The image on the right
is the mosaic created
after running the
Object Mosaic filter.

Follow these steps to use the filter:

1. Select a raster image.

2. Choose Filter➥Create Object➥Mosaic (see Figure 17.9).

FIGURE 17.9

Choosing the Object Mosaic filter.

3. Set your options in the Object Mosaic dialog box. You can choose to delete the raster image after the filter is run (see Figure 17.10).

FIGURE 17.10

Setting the options in the Object Mosaic dialog box.

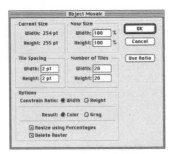

Try different settings to produce different results. Remember, you can also run the Object Mosaic filter on objects rasterized in Illustrator with the Rasterize command. Try using Object Mosaic on rasterized type, as shown here, for some cool effects:

1. Use the Type tool to create some point text. I set my type using the Times font at 72 points (see Figure 17.11).

FIGURE 17.11

Here I typed the word "raster" in 72-point Times Roman.

2. With the type selected, press (Command+Shift+O)[Control+Shift+O] or choose Type➡Create Outlines.

3. Rasterize the type by choosing Object➡Rasterize. Then set your options to RGB, Screen (72dpi), Anti-Alias, and no mask (see Figure 17.12).

FIGURE 17.12

Rasterizing the type.

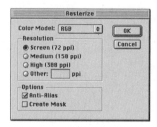

4. With the rasterized type selected, choose Filter➡Create➡Object Mosaic to begin creating the mosaic.

5. In the Object Mosaic dialog box, leave the New Size the same as the Current Size, set the Tile Spacing to 0 for both the Width and Height, set the Number of Tiles to Width 60, click on the Use Ratio button, and the Height will automatically be calculated (16). I've checked the Delete Raster box, which will erase the raster type as soon as the new mosaic is created (see Figure 17.13).

FIGURE 17.13

Setting the options in the Object Mosaic dialog box.

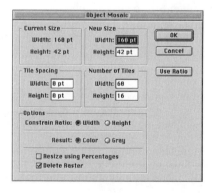

6. Click OK. Illustrator then creates a mosaic based on the raster. The newly created mosaic is made up entirely of vector objects (see Figure 17.14).

17

FIGURE 17.14

The final mosaic.

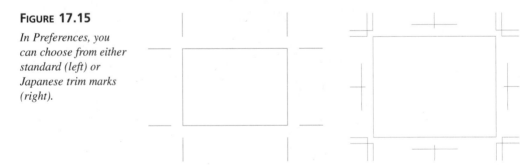

 Another filter, called Photo Crosshatch, converts raster art into vector art. This filter, which utilizes the Ink Pen filter, is covered in Hour 18, "Filters with Style."

Trim Marks

The Trim Marks filter creates a set of trim marks (also known as crop marks) around any selected object. Depending on what option you have set in Preferences, Illustrator creates either standard or Japanese-style trim marks (see Figure 17.15).

Distort Filters

If you like to take reality into other dimensions, Illustrator's Distort filters will be right up your alley (see Figure 17.16). Whether your artwork needs minor tweaking or major funk, these filters comply with the most twisted and demented tasks. Remember that these filters do not work on gradients or patterns, unless you expand them first. (Try it; twirling an expanded gradient is way cool!)

FIGURE 17.15

In Preferences, you can choose from either standard (left) or Japanese trim marks (right).

FIGURE 17.16

*The Distort filters in
the Filter menu.*

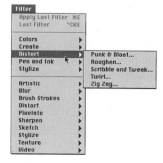

Punk & Bloat

The Punk & Bloat filter, shown in Figure 17.17, does some pretty wild things to art. This filter changes the Bézier curves in a selection to make either sharp points (punk) or round puffy points (bloat), as you can see in Figure 17.18. To use this filter, select the object you want to distort, and choose Filter➡Distort➡Punk & Bloat. Then simply drag the slider to the left and right. If you have the Preview box checked, you can see your results in real time. Click OK when you are done.

17

FIGURE 17.17

*The Punk & Bloat
filter.*

FIGURE 17.18

*The original star is in
the center. To the left is
the "punked" star; to
the right, the "bloat-
ed" one.*

Roughen

Of all the Distort filters, Roughen is probably used the most and has some very practical applications (see Figure 17.19). The Roughen filter makes objects appear rough by adding anchor points and moving them around. If you keep the settings really low, you can make your art look almost hand drawn (see Figure 17.20).

FIGURE 17.19

The Roughen filter.

FIGURE 17.20

The original star (left) and what it looks like after the Roughen filter is used (right).

The Roughen filter is also great for creating torn or crumpled-looking paper. In fact, you can create some crumpled paper right now by following these steps:

1. Using the Rectangle tool, draw a rectangle. Press the D key to set the Fill and Stroke attributes to the default—white Fill, black Stroke. This rectangle is your sheet of paper.

2. With the rectangle selected, choose Filter➡Distort➡Roughen.

3. Use the sliders to change the options. For Size, I used 2%, and for Detail, I used 10/inch. You should set Points to Corner. If you have the Preview box checked, you can see the changes in real time.

4. Click OK, and you've got your crumpled paper. You also can add a drop shadow for a more refined look (see Figure 17.21).

FIGURE 17.21

The final crumpled paper, with drop shadow added.

Scribble and Tweak

The Scribble and Tweak filter, shown in Figure 17.22, is difficult to describe. Based on your settings, Scribble randomly moves anchor points away from the original object, whereas Tweak moves anchor points around on the object, creating interesting distortions, to say the least (see Figure 17.23). To use this filter, select the object you want to distort, and choose Filter➡Distort➡Scribble and Tweak. Then simply drag the sliders to the left and right, and indicate what kinds of points you want the effect to occur to. If you have the Preview box checked, you can see your results in real time. Click OK when you are done.

FIGURE 17.22

The Scribble and Tweak filter dialog box.

17

FIGURE 17.23

From left to right, the original star, scribbled, and tweaked.

Twirl

The Twirl filter is really cool (see Figure 17.24). The filter actually curves the art in a circular motion from the center, as shown in Figure 17.25, based on the number you enter in the Twirl filter dialog box. If you want to twirl an object by eye and watch it change in real time, you can use the Twirl tool, which can be found with the Rotate tool (see Figure 17.26). Click and drag with the tool, and watch your selection spin before your very eyes.

FIGURE 17.24

The Twirl filter dialog box.

From left to right, the original star, twirled 30°, twirled 100°.

FIGURE 17.26

Selecting the Twirl tool from the Toolbox.

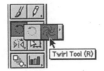

Zig Zag

The Zig Zag filter, shown in Figure 17.27, is another Distort filter that wreaks havoc on anchor points. Playing with the settings on this one can also produce some wild and interesting results (see Figure 17.28). To use this filter, select the object you want to distort, and choose Filter➡Distort➡Zig Zag. Then simply drag the sliders to the left and right, and indicate Smooth or Corner points. If you have the Preview box checked, you can see your results in real time. Click OK when you are done.

FIGURE 17.27

The Zig Zag filter dialog box.

FIGURE 17.28

On the left is the original star; on the right is...well, your guess is as good as mine.

Summary

So many filters! In this hour, you covered a lot of ground learning about some of Illustrator's filters, which enhance your productivity and creativity. Sometimes you just need to use the Roughen filter or even Object Mosaic to add that special touch to your artwork. At this point, you're probably wondering about the rest of the filters found in the Filter menu, such as the Ink Pen. Well, hold on to your chair, because in the next hour you'll dive right in to the rest of these filters.

Workshop

The Workshop contains quiz questions to help you solidify your understanding of the material covered in this hour and exercises to provide you with experience using what you have learned. You can find the answers to the quiz questions at the end of the hour.

17

Quiz

1. Which filter would you use to fine-tune selected colors?

   a. Blend Vertically

   b. Convert to CMYK

   c. Adjust Colors

2. For simple trapping jobs, you can use

   a. The Overprint Black filter

   b. The Saturate Filter

   c. A piece of cheese and a mousetrap

3. The Object Mosaic filter bases vector tile-like mosaics on

   a. Your bathroom floor

   b. Rasterized art

   c. Other vector objects

4. Which filter might you use to create torn or crumpled-looking paper?

   a. Punk & Bloat

   b. Roughen

   c. Zig Zag

Exercises

1. Create or open an illustration. Now select all, and run the Convert to CMYK filter. Then run the Convert to RGB filter. Now run the Convert to Grayscale filter.

2. Practice using the Adjust Colors filter to make changes within your document. Try adjusting just the stroke or the fill instead of the entire object.

3. Draw a flag, and use the Twirl filter to make it look like it's blowing in the wind.

Term Review

Knockout—In trapping, a situation in which only the topmost spot color will print.

Answers to Quiz Questions

1. c
2. a
3. b
4. a, b, and c

HOUR 18

Filters with Style

As everyone knows, style is very important when it comes to working in design. A client always wants a certain style in his or her design or a certain look and feel. The filters in this hour can help you define a style in your work and help you achieve the look you've been searching for. You've seen that Illustrator's vector filters can do some pretty cool stuff, and in this hour, you'll see that they can do some pretty powerful stuff as well.

This hour covers the following:

- The Pen and Ink filter
- The Photo Crosshatch filter
- Arrowheads
- Photoshop-compatible filters

Pen and Ink

Sometimes people don't get the credit they deserve. And sometimes filters don't get the credit they deserve. The Pen and Ink filter fits that description perfectly. A powerful filter, Pen and Ink fills objects with complex stippling and crosshatching effects (see Figure 18.1).

FIGURE 18.1

Some samples of rectangles filled using the Pen and Ink filter.

To fill an object with the Pen and Ink filter, select the object and choose Filter➡ Pen and Ink➡Hatch Effects (see Figure 18.2). You are then presented with the Hatch Effects dialog box (see Figure 18.3), where you can set exactly how you want the effect to look. Note that the Ink Pen filter produces complex fills that can produce large files and can even cause printing problems in some cases.

FIGURE 18.2

Choosing Pen and Ink effects.

FIGURE 18.3

*The Hatch Effects
dialog box.*

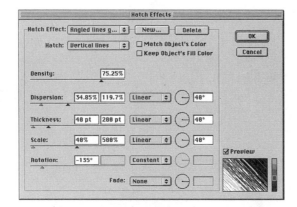

You can even create your own hatches for use in the Pen and Ink filter. To do so, choose
New Hatch from the Pen and Ink submenu (see Figure 18.4). You are presented with a
dialog box in which you can create new hatches (see Figure 18.5).

FIGURE 18.4

*Choosing Pen and
Ink➡New Hatch.*

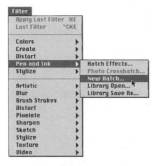

18

FIGURE 18.5

*The New Hatch
dialog box.*

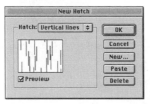

For more in-depth detail on exactly what each setting does in the Ink Pen dialog boxes,
refer to the Adobe Illustrator manual.

The Photo Crosshatch Filter

A variation of the Pen and Ink filter, the Photo Crosshatch filter creates the same cross-hatching effects but does so using a placed raster image as its guideline. It is similar to the Object Mosaic filter you learned about in Hour 17, "Vector Filters," except that instead of creating a mosaic, this filter creates a complex set of layered hatches to define the photo. Of course, after you run the filter, you can delete the raster image, and you are left with the vector effect (see Figure 18.6 through 18.8)

FIGURE 18.6

The image before running the Photo Crosshatch filter.

FIGURE 18.7

The image after running the Photo Crosshatch filter.

FIGURE 18.8

A close-up view of the resulting crosshatching after running the filter.

To use the Photo Crosshatch filter, select a raster image and choose Filter➡Pen and Ink➡Photo Crosshatch. You are presented with the Photo Crosshatch dialog box (see Figure 18.9). Here, you can choose how many hatch layers should be created. Generally, the more layers you have, the more detailed—and more complex—your result will be. For more information regarding the settings for the Photo Crosshatch filter, refer to the Adobe Illustrator manual.

18

FIGURE 18.9

The Photo Crosshatch dialog box.

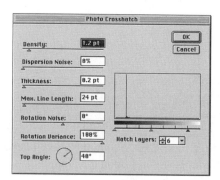

Stylize Filters

You use the Stylize group of filters, shown in Figure 18.10, to add unique and interesting effects and accents to art. Add Arrowheads and Round Corners may not seem so important, but you'll see how you can use them to save precious time when creating artwork.

FIGURE 18.10

The Stylize filters.

Add Arrowheads

Say you're creating a diagram, and you need to create an arrow to point something out in the illustration. No problem. Just draw a line, and use the Add Arrowheads filter (see Figure 18.11). You can apply one of 27 different styles at the beginning, the end, or both ends of the line. The head of the arrow is aligned on the exact same angle as the line, so the arrow is always perfect.

FIGURE 18.11

The Add Arrowheads filter's dialog box.

Drop Shadow

The Drop Shadow filter (see Figure 18.12) is, in my opinion, the most useless filter ever devised. The result of running the filter is simply a duplicate of your object offset from the original. First of all, it's ugly, and second of all, it can be created in a fraction of the time by simply (Option+dragging)[Alt+dragging] the shape (copying it) and then pressing (Command+Shift+[)[Control+Shift+[] (send to back).

FIGURE 18.12

*The Drop Shadow fil-
ter dialog box.*

Round Corners

The Round Corners filter, shown in Figure 18.13, didn't appear to be useful to me at
first. I mean, if I wanted rounded corners, I would use the Rounded Corner Rectangle
tool, right? Then I realized I could apply the Round Corners filter to any shape (see
Figure 18.14). Sometimes the Round Corners filter can be a real timesaver.

FIGURE 18.13

*The Round Corners
dialog box.*

FIGURE 18.14

*The Round Corners fil-
ter gave these road
signs just the touch
they needed.*

18

Photoshop-Compatible Filters

Illustrator ships with many Photoshop-compatible filters, which you can use on any raster image. Refer to Hour 16, "Working with Raster Images," for more information concerning applying these filters.

Summary

In this hour, you learned about some pretty cool filters that can help you in your every-day designs, such as the Add Arrowheads filter and the Round Corners filter. You learned all about the Pen and Ink filter and how it can help you make fills that look more natural, and also the Photo Crosshatch filter, which adds powerful creative tools to your design senses.

Workshop

The Workshop contains quiz questions to help you solidify your understanding of the material covered in this hour and exercises to provide you with experience using what you have learned. You can find the answers to the quiz questions at the end of the hour.

Quiz

1. The Pen and Ink filter creates what kind of effect?

    a. Stippling or crosshatch

    b. Caricature

    c. Charcoal

2. A filter that turns a photo into a vector crosshatch pattern is

    a. Object Mosaic

    b. Photo Crosshatch

    c. Object Crosshatch

3. The Add Arrowheads filter cannot apply arrowheads to both ends of a line at one time.

    a. True

    b. False

4. In this author's opinion, what is the most useless Illustrator vector filter ever devised?

    a. Add Arrowheads

    b. Pen and Ink

    c. Drop Shadow

5. The Round Corners filter works only on rectangles.

    a. True

    b. False

Exercises

1. Try setting some type in Illustrator, and then use the Rasterize command to convert it to a raster image. Then run the Photo Crosshatch filter on it for some interesting results.

2. Fill a shape with a gradient, and then try running the Pen and Ink filter on it. Notice that you can have the stippling effect take on the attributes of the gradient so that the effect gets lighter on one end and darker—or denser—on the other end.

3. Experiment using the Round Corners filter on all sorts of shapes to see how you can make subtle changes to existing artwork.

Answers to Quiz Questions

1. a

2. b

3. b

4. c

5. b

18

HOUR 19

Charts and Graphs

Presenting data in a graphical manner can have enormous impact. I'm referring, of course, to charts or graphs used to convey numerical data in a graphical way, making information easier to understand, as well as making it
more useful (see Figure 19.1).

The advantage of using Illustrator to create graphs over a program such as
Harvard Graphics, which is a dedicated graphing program, is that when you
create a graph in Illustrator, it is made up of Illustrator vector objects. You
therefore can edit the graph just as you would any illustration, giving you
complete control over how your graph looks. If necessary, you can then
export the graph in any of Illustrator's many export formats.

In this hour, you'll learn about the following:

- Creating a graph
- Importing graph data
- Working with graph designs

Figure **19.1**

Using Illustrator's powerful features, you can produce eye-catching charts such as this one.

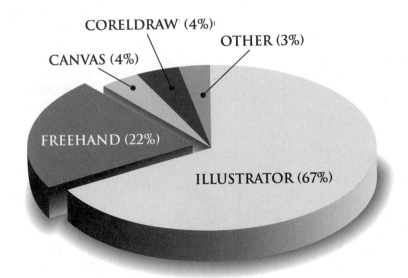

NOTE: THE INFORMATION REPRESENTED IN THIS GRAPH IS
NOT REAL, AND IS MEANT FOR ENTERTAINMENT PURPOSES ONLY

Creating a Graph

Illustrator has several different types of graphs you can use—nine to be exact (see Figure 19.2):

- Column—This type uses vertical bars to compare values.
- Stacked Column—The same as above except that, in this type, values are stacked one upon the other on vertical bars.
- Bar—The same as a Column graph except that bars are horizontal rather than vertical.
- Stacked Bar—The same as a Stacked Column graph except that bars are horizontal, not vertical.
- Line—This type is often used to show trends over a period of time; values are plotted and connected with a line.
- Area—The same as a Line graph except that areas are filled in, indicating totals as well as trends.
- Scatter—This type is similar to a Line graph; points are plotted but not connected with any lines. This type is used to identify patterns and trends.
- Pie—This type of graph is made up of wedges, each wedge representing a portion of the whole.

- Radar—This type of graph is also called a web graph. Radar data is presented in a circular format.

Each of these types of graphs is used to present a different kind of data (see Figure 19.2). If you aren't sure which type you need, don't worry; you can switch between graph types at any time, even after you've entered data.

FIGURE 19.2

The many graph tools in Illustrator.

In Illustrator, you begin making a graph by defining the physical size of the graph. You do so in much the same way you draw a rectangle. Just follow these steps:

1. Select the desired Graph tool.
2. Press and drag to define a rectangle. (Holding down the (Option)[Alt] key while dragging draws out from the center.)

Alternatively, you can just click once with the Graph tool, and Illustrator will prompt you with a dialog box in which you can enter the dimensions of the graph numerically (see Figure 19.3).

FIGURE 19.3

Entering graph dimensions numerically after clicking with the Graph tool.

19

NEW TERM The next step is to give Illustrator the facts—the actual values that will be used to make the graph actually mean something. After it creates the *bounding box* for your graph, Illustrator presents you with the Graph Data palette (see Figure 19.4). If you've ever used Microsoft Excel or Lotus 1-2-3, this palette will look familiar to you. It is filled with rows and columns in which you enter the *graph data*.

FIGURE 19.4

The Graph Data palette.

Importing Graph Data

Across the top of the Graph Data palette are several items. The first is an area where you input your values. Select a cell (cells are the rows of boxes that actually contain the data), and then type your value. Pressing Tab takes you to the next column; pressing Enter takes you to the next row.

You can either enter data manually or import data from programs such as Excel or Lotus (or even from a tab-delimited text file). Notice that in the upper-right corner of the Graph Data palette are six buttons, described here from left to right:

- Import Data—Imports data from an external file.
- Transpose—Switches columns and rows of data, no matter what the graph type is.
- Switch x/y—Swaps the values of the x- and y-axes on a Scatter graph only.
- Cell Style—Sets the parameters for a selected cell (each box in the grid in the Graph Data palette is a cell). You can set the number of decimal places as well as the column width (see Figure 19.5). You can also change the column width manually by grabbing a vertical line and dragging it left or right (see Figure 19.6).
- Revert and Apply—The Revert button sets the data in the graph back to the way it was before you last clicked the Apply button, whereas the Apply button applies your changes to the graph.

FIGURE 19.5

The Cell Style dialog box.

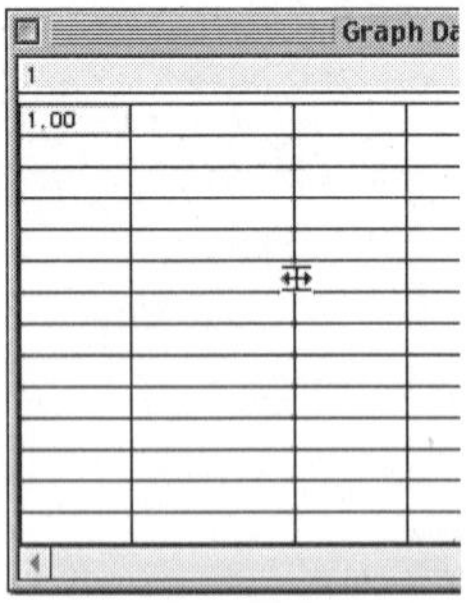

FIGURE 19.6

Adjusting the width of a column manually.

Editing Graph Data

What makes the graph function in Illustrator even more powerful is the capability to update the data in your graph. At any time, you can select the graph and choose Object➧Graphs➧Data. You are presented with the Graph Data palette again, where you can update the numbers. When you click the Apply button in the Graph Data palette, the graph is automatically updated with the new information.

Graph Options

After you create your graph, you can edit it to perfection. Choose Object➧Graphs➧Type, and you are presented with the Graph Type dialog box. You are first presented with Graph Options (see Figure 19.7). Here you can change the type of graph, even though you selected another type earlier from the Toolbox. You can also choose where to place the Value Axis.

FIGURE 19.7

The Graph Type dialog box.

Besides options to add drop shadows or add a legend across the top, you can also set the Column Width and Cluster Width here (see Figure 19.8). These settings control the width and spacing of the bars or columns in a graph. Entering a number greater than 100 causes the columns to overlap and may produce very interesting effects (see Figure 19.9).

19

FIGURE 19.8

Setting the column and cluster width.

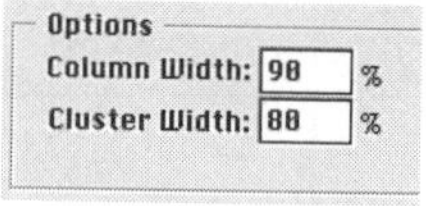

Options

Column Width: 98 %
Cluster Width: 88 %

FIGURE 19.9

Graphs set with different cluster widths.

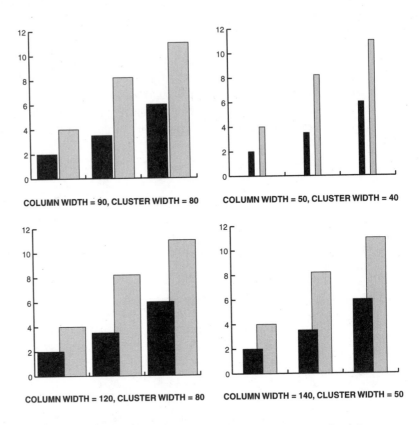

COLUMN WIDTH = 90, CLUSTER WIDTH = 80

COLUMN WIDTH = 50, CLUSTER WIDTH = 40

COLUMN WIDTH = 120, CLUSTER WIDTH = 80

COLUMN WIDTH = 140, CLUSTER WIDTH = 50

In the Graph Type dialog box, you can also specify settings for the Value Axis and Category Axis. Select them from the pop-up menu at the top of the dialog box (see Figure 19.10). In the Value Axis screen (see Figure 19.11), you can set the length of tick marks, which are the lines along the side of the graph that help indicate the position of data (see Figure 19.12).

FIGURE 19.10

Selecting Value Axis from the pop-up menu in the Graph Type dialog box.

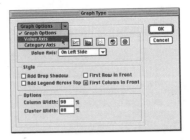

FIGURE 19.11

The Value Axis screen.

FIGURE 19.12

Tick marks.

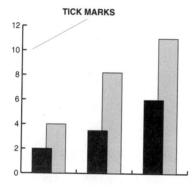

You can also specify the length of the tick marks (see Figure 19.13). Setting them at full length causes the tick marks to be drawn as lines throughout the entire graph. You can also specify these settings for the tick marks for the Category Axis (see Figure 19.14).

FIGURE 19.13

Choosing tick mark specifications.

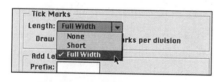

19

FIGURE 19.14

The Category Axis screen.

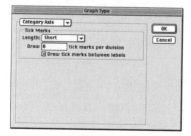

Graph Design

Illustrator includes a feature called Graph Design that enables you to use any vector art to display information in your graphs. Say, for example, you are doing a report on how many shooting stars are seen each year. You would ordinarily make a bar graph, but to add a visual element to your graph, wouldn't it be great if you could use stars instead of boring bars? Here's how to do it:

1. Define the artwork for the bars. To get started, draw a star, and then draw a square with a Fill and Stroke of None and send it behind the star (see Figure 19.15). To define a graph design, you must have a square behind your art to define the boundary of the art.

FIGURE 19.15

Creating the star with a bounding box behind it.

2. With the art and the square selected, choose Object➡Graphs➡Design.

3. Define the graph design by clicking New Design. Then click the Rename button to give your graph design a name. I called mine Star (see Figure 19.16).

FIGURE 19.16

Defining the graph design.

4. Create a graph. Using the Column Graph tool, I dragged a rectangle to create my graph, and when the Graph Data palette opened, I used 350 and 560 for my data (see Figure 19.17).

FIGURE 19.17

The "ordinary" graph.

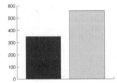

5. With the graph selected, choose Object➥Graphs➥Column.

6. In the Graph Column dialog box, select the star design and choose from the other options listed in the box. I chose a repeating column type so that the star appears for every 100 units, which I've also specified in the box. For fractions (350 and 560 do not represent full stars), I chose to have the stars chopped (see Figure 19.18); the other choice is to have them scaled.

FIGURE 19.18

The Graph Column dialog box.

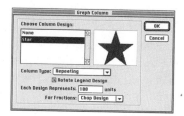

7. Click OK to see the newly designed graph (see Figure 19.19). Remember that you can always go back and tweak the design to get it just how you want it.

FIGURE 19.19

The new graph in all its starry glory.

Ungrouping Your Graph

A graph is actually a group of many objects. You can ungroup a graph at any time, but be aware that when you do, the art loses its reference as a graph, and you no longer can make changes to it through the Graph Data and Graph Type dialog boxes. This process is just like converting type into outlines: After you change it, it becomes a different kind of object. Your best bet is to save a copy of the original graph before ungrouping so that you can go back to it if needed.

Of course, after you ungroup the graph, you have complete and total freedom to do whatever you please with the graph elements. You can color them, run filters on them, and so on. Let your mind roam free, and you can create some really dynamic presentations.

19

Summary

Even though Illustrator is not known for its graphing capabilities, you just learned that Illustrator can really hold its own when it comes to creating great-looking charts. You learned how to import graph data from other applications, and you learned how to take that data and turn it into something that makes sense.

Workshop

The Workshop contains quiz questions to help you solidify your understanding of the material covered in this hour and exercises to provide you with experience using what you learned. You can find the answers to the quiz questions at the end of the hour.

Quiz

1. Illustrator has how many graph types?

   a. 5

   b. 9

   c. 7

2. A tick mark is

   a. A line that indicates a value

   b. A swollen red area on your skin from a bug bite

   c. The length of a column or bar

3. The feature used to create graphs out of vector art is called

   a. VectorGraph

   b. Graph Design

   c. Graph-O-Rama

4. The column width can be greater than 100%.

   a. True

   b. False

5. After you ungroup a graph, you can edit the data.

   a. True

   b. False

Exercises

1. After you enter data into the Graph Data palette, click on the Transpose Row/Column button and the Switch X/Y button to see how they affect the position of the data. Then see how clicking these buttons affects the graph itself.

2. Redo the exercise you did using the star as a graph design, but this time use a different shape such as a circle or spiral.

3. Create a graph using one particular data type. Then switch that same graph to a different graph type, and observe how the data is presented differently.

Term Review

Bounding box—The imaginary box surrounding the area that contains selected items.

Graph data—Numbers indicating relational information or data used to indicate a trend.

Answers to Quiz Questions

1. b
2. a
3. b
4. a
5. b

19

Hour **20**

Saving/Exporting Files

Without a doubt, the most important factor about a computer illustration is the capability to open it and edit it again and again. Compatibility with other software is important as well. You need to have the capability to bring your artwork into other applications, such as a page layout program. Illustrator does all this and more. Illustrator is now completely cross-platform compatible, working identically in both Mac OS and Windows environments.

Everyone knows how important it is to share, and this hour, you'll focus on the following:

- Saving Illustrator documents
- Exporting in PDF format
- Exporting in cross-platform formats

Saving in Illustrator Formats

When you save a document, you can choose from three different format options: Illustrator, Illustrator EPS, and Acrobat PDF. Each of these formats can be opened directly in any version of Illustrator and will retain the most information for future editing.

Native Illustrator

If your work will be done completely in Illustrator, then saving it in Illustrator format is best. The file takes up the smallest amount of disk space, it opens and saves the fastest, and it is always fully editable.

To save a file in Illustrator format, choose Save As from the File menu (see Figure 20.1). After you select a location where your document should be saved, give your file a name, and click the Save button, you are presented with a dialog box in which you can specify what version of Illustrator you want your file saved in (see Figure 20.2). You get these choices for compatibility purposes, but you should keep your file in Illustrator 8 format if possible.

FIGURE 20.1

Choosing Save from the File menu.

FIGURE 20.2

The Illustrator Format dialog box lets you ensure backward compatibility with previous versions.

> Keeping your file in Illustrator 8 format ensures that any features specific to version 8 remain intact in your file. Live blends, for example, are only available in version 8. If you were to save your file in version 6 or 7 format, however, any live blend information in your file would be lost.

Illustrator EPS

NEW TERM If you need to place or import your file as a picture in other programs, then you should use the Illustrator EPS format. *EPS* (Encapsulated PostScript) is a widely supported format. PostScript, which is a printer language created by Adobe, is built into many of today's printers and imagesetters. To print an EPS file, you must have a PostScript printer or a PostScript interpreter.

If you're not sure whether you have a PostScript printer, look for the Adobe PostScript logo (see Figure 20.3). Because PostScript must be licensed from Adobe, PostScript printers tend to be more expensive than those without PostScript. If you paid under $500 for your printer, it probably does not have PostScript. You can use a PostScript interpreter, which is software that runs on your computer and that enables you to print PostScript files to a non-PostScript printer, but these interpreters tend to be very slow. Two such programs are GCI StyleScript (from Infowave) and Freedom of Press (from ColorAge).

FIGURE 20.3

The Adobe PostScript logo.

Because an EPS file will be brought into other programs, you can choose to have a preview file embedded into the EPS. When you place the EPS into another program, the low-resolution preview enables you to see how the file will look.

To save your file in Illustrator EPS format, choose Save As from the File menu and name your file. From the Format pop-up menu, choose Illustrator EPS and click the Save button. Illustrator then presents you with the EPS Format dialog box (see Figure 20.4). Here you can ensure compatibility with previous versions of Illustrator and choose to enclose placed images or fonts within the EPS file, as well as specify previews for viewing on either IBM PC or Macintosh.

20

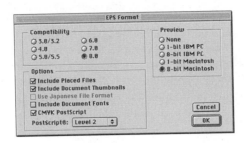

FIGURE 20.4

The EPS Format dialog box gives you control of file settings such as previews.

Acrobat PDF

NEW TERM The *PDF* (Portable Document File) format was developed by Adobe so that you can view documents, in their correct form, on any platform. Using the Adobe *Acrobat Reader*, you can view a PDF file on DOS, Macintosh, Windows, or UNIX. Because PDF uses PostScript technology as its base, you can open and edit a PDF file directly in Illustrator as well.

PDF files are good in several instances. If you're showing artwork to a client and the client has a different system than you, all the client needs is Acrobat Reader to view it. PDF files can also be viewed on the World Wide Web with a Netscape Navigator plug-in called PDFViewer. Both Acrobat Reader and PDFViewer are free and available at http://www.adobe.com. PDF files can also be combined into multipage documents that can aid in making presentations.

To save your file in PDF format, choose Save As from the File menu, and name your file. From the Format pop-up menu, choose Acrobat PDF, as shown in Figure 20.5, and click the Save button. If the PDF file will be viewed on a Windows or DOS machine, make sure you include the file extension .PDF in the name (FILENAME.PDF).

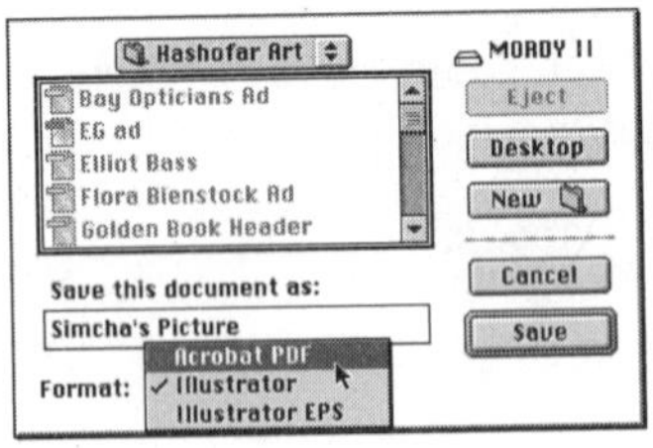

FIGURE 20.5

Choosing Acrobat PDF from the Format pop-up menu in the Save As dialog box.

Exporting to Other File Formats

As I mentioned earlier, Illustrator can export files in many different formats. Some are for placement in other illustration or paint programs, others are for high-end proprietary systems, and still others are for use on the World Wide Web. Some are vector formats, some are bitmap, and some, such as EPS, can support both within the same file. Each format has its strengths and its weaknesses, which are discussed in this hour.

To export a file to any of these formats, choose Export from the File menu (see Figure 20.6), and choose a file format from the Format pop-up menu (see Figure 20.7).

FIGURE 20.6

Choosing Export from the File menu.

FIGURE 20.7

Choices from the Format pop-up menu in the Export dialog box.

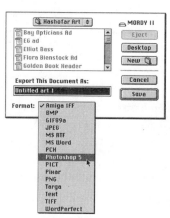

20

Based on what platform you have, all the formats listed here may not be available to you. File export formats that are also available as plug-ins for Illustrator are not listed here. Some are on the Illustrator CD-ROM, and others may be released on Adobe's Web site (such as a FreeHand plug-in that enables you to open Macromedia FreeHand documents in Illustrator).

TIFF

The *TIFF* (Tagged Image File Format) format is a raster format that is supported both on the Macintosh platform and on the Windows platform. The TIFF format is widely supported and can be used in just about any page layout and paint program. Its format also has an option to use the LZW compression scheme, which makes for smaller file sizes without compromising detail.

When you choose to export your file as a TIFF, Illustrator presents you with the TIFF Options dialog box (see Figure 20.8). Here you can choose a resolution for your image as well as select a color model (RGB, CMYK, or Grayscale). If your image is intended to be viewed onscreen, select the Anti-Alias option to ensure your final image has no jaggy edges. You can also choose LZW Compression. Finally, specify a byte order for the platform the file will be used on.

FIGURE 20.8

The TIFF Options dialog box.

Photoshop 5

Many times, you may want to bring Illustrator art into Photoshop. One of the biggest advantages of exporting in Photoshop 5 format is the capability to include Illustrator layer information. When you choose to export as Photoshop 5, you are presented with a dialog box (see Figure 20.9). If you check the Write Layers box, any layers that are in your Illustrator document will carry over into Photoshop, making for easier editing and effects. This feature is also great for Web designers who are creating animations (see Hour 23, "Web Graphics").

FIGURE 20.9

Exporting in Photoshop 5 format.

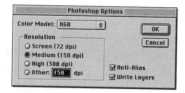

GIF89a, JPEG, and PNG

The GIF89a, JPEG, and PNG formats are primarily used for files that will be viewed on the World Wide Web. These raster formats specialize in compressing information, which makes for small file sizes that can be transmitted quickly over modem phone connections. For more details on these formats, see Hour 23.

PCX

The PCX format is a bitmap that supports up to 24-bit color. It is primarily used on Windows machines and is actually the native format of PC Paintbrush—a paint program popular on the Windows platform. When you export a PCX file, Illustrator prompts you with a dialog box in which you can specify what resolution the file should be (see Figure 20.10).

FIGURE 20.10

The Resolution Options dialog box.

BMP

BMP means bitmap (literally, "bitmap image" means the same thing as "raster image") and is a standard format on Windows and DOS platforms. Besides prompting you to specify what resolution you want the image to be, Illustrator also prompts you with the BMP Options dialog box, where you can indicate Windows or OS/2 compatibility as well as bit depth and compression (see Figure 20.11).

20

FIGURE 20.11

The BMP Options dialog box.

Amiga IFF, Targa, and Pixar

Amiga IFF, TGA (Targa), and Pixar are formats specific to proprietary graphics systems. Whether it's 3D, animation, or full motion video, Illustrator has the capability to export to these programs, giving you the ability to create complex and exact elements in a comfortable environment before bringing them into high-end graphic systems for processing and enhancement.

Summary

Illustrator is not an island. You learned how important it is for your files to be compatible and cross platform. You also learned about a whole lot of file formats and that each one has its strengths and weaknesses. Now you can use Illustrator together with other programs such as QuarkXPress and Photoshop, giving you unlimited creative capabilities in your quest for the ultimate design. You should be fairly comfortable with Illustrator by now as you begin the final stretch—just a few more hours. Hang in there! You're doing great!

Workshop

The Workshop contains quiz questions to help you solidify your understanding of the material covered in this hour and exercises to provide you with experience using what you have learned. You can find the answers to the quiz questions at the end of the hour.

Quiz

1. All printers are PostScript.

    a. True

    b. False

2. PDF stands for

    a. Pretty Darn Funny

    b. Portable Disk Formatter

    c. Portable Document Format

3. The TIFF format uses which compression scheme?

    a. LZW

    b. StuffIt

    c. PKZip

4. Which file format is used for Web graphics?

    a. EPS

    b. TIFF

    c. GIF89a

5. Which format supports Photoshop layers?

    a. PCX

    b. BMP

    c. Photoshop 5

Term Review

Acrobat Reader—The application necessary to view PDF files.

EPS—Encapsulated PostScript. A standard cross-platform image format based on the PostScript printer language. An EPS file can contain vector images, pixel images, or both.

PDF—Portable Document File. Created by Adobe, this format was created to become a standard file format that could be viewed on any computer.

TIFF—Tagged Image File Format. A compression-capable format that is a standard on both Macs and PCs. A TIFF is a raster file.

Answers to Quiz Questions

1. b
2. c
3. a
4. c
5. c

20

Hour **21**

Working Smart in Illustrator

You already know that you can get any particular project done in several different ways. To build a house, for example, you can use wood or bricks. Either way, you'll have a house, but one might be better than the other. The same applies to computer files—especially Illustrator documents. You might have several ways to "build" your document, but you always have a smart way and a not-so-smart way. This chapter guides you in the right direction when you're creating your artwork in Illustrator. A great computer designer knows not only good design techniques but good production techniques as well, such as the following:

- Using actions
- Saving files
- Creating "clean" files
- Tracing images
- Managing placed images

Using Actions

Lifted directly from Photoshop, the Actions palette (see Figure 21.1) allows you to "record" a list of specific functions, which you can have Illustrator "play back" for you at any time. This feature is a great timesaver and can actually help you do your work much faster.

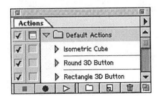

Across the bottom of the palette are six buttons. From the left, they are as follows:

- Stop—Used to stop an action while it is running or to stop an action while it is recording
- Record—Used to begin recording a new action
- Play—Used to activate and run the currently selected action
- Create New Set—Used to—that's right—create a new set or collection of actions
- Create New Action—Used to create a new action
- Trash—Used to delete selected actions from the Actions palette

To the left of each action are two boxes (see Figure 21.2). The leftmost box contains a check mark, indicating that the action is turned on and will run when activated. You can selectively disable, or turn off, any step in an action by clicking on the check mark to remove it. Clicking again brings back the check mark, thereby turning the action step back on.

FIGURE 21.2

Notice how some actions are turned off, whereas others have the dialog option turned on.

The other box is used to toggle the dialog option on and off. When the dialog option is on, any action that is activated pauses at any dialog boxes that it may encounter along the way and waits for your response to them. Turning the dialog option off tells the action to use whatever settings you previously specified for any dialog boxes it may encounter. For example, if you want to print a file differently each time, you turn on a dialog option at a print step in your action so that you can specify a different setting each time.

You can save your actions and send them to friends or coworkers; they can then load the actions into their Actions palettes. Simply use the Actions palette pop-up menu by clicking on the triangle in the upper-right corner of the palette (see Figure 21.3).

FIGURE 21.3

The Actions palette pop-up menu.

Saving Your Documents

If I told you that if you ate a large cheese pizza every day, you would live a long life, you would do it, right? And if I told you that by saving your documents frequently, you can be assured that you will not lose data, you would do that too, right?

Saving your documents is the most important part of working with computers. A computer will crash when you least expect it to (and it most certainly will crash when you expect it to), so save often. You might also want to use the Save As command to save documents as you create them, allowing you the luxury of quickly going back to any stage of your project as it was developed. You can name each document with version numbers, such as Pizza 1.1, Pizza 1.2, and so on, so you can quickly identify when each document was created.

21

Using Intelligent Filenames

Naming your file is more important than most people think. It's very important that you keep your files organized and that you name them so that you can quickly identify what each file is. Macintosh has always allowed long filenames, and now you can create long filenames in Windows 95 and 98, too. Take advantage of it. I remember when I used to name files "Bob's thingy" and "Logo with blue type." That's nice for being creative and all, but in two months when Bob needs his advertisement reprinted, you won't in a million years remember that you called it "thingy."

Also, if you're working in an environment with other designers and share your files with them, naming your files so that other people can quickly identify and find them is even more important. If you have several versions of a logo, for example, you can name the different versions like this: Apple Logo.B&W, Apple Logo.Process, and Apple Logo.Spot. Also, when you finish a job, you might even want to identify it like so: Apple Stationery.Final.

Working with Selections

Illustrator has a few tricks up its sleeve when it comes to making selections. Under the Edit menu, you'll find a Select submenu that contains a few additional commands for making selections (see Figure 21.4). Click an object, for example, and choose Edit➡Select➡Same Fill Color. Illustrator then selects all objects in your document that have the same fill as the one you originally selected. The same applies for Select Same Stroke.

FIGURE 21.4

Using the additional Select commands.

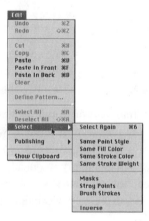

For even more selection tools, see Extensis VectorTools and ILLOM Toolkit in the "Using Third-Party Plug-ins" section, later in this chapter.

Hiding and Locking

You learned that you can hide and lock artwork to make things easier when working on portions of your artwork, but this feature has one small problem. Although you can hide and lock items one at a time, you can only show or unlock all items at once. Therefore, if you want to unlock just one item, you have to unlock everything; then you have to select the items you want to remain locked and lock them again.

To make things a bit easier, try the following:

1. To unlock just one item, unlock everything.
2. Shift+click the item you want to unlock.
3. Select Object➡Lock again.

This shortcut saves you the time of having to reselect everything again.

Keeping Your Documents Clean

You'll never find a mess on my computer. What you will find is an organized group of files. Even more important, each file in itself is "clean" and streamlined.

Allow me to explain. When you create a file, edit it, make revisions, and make revisions again, the file could contain many elements that are not necessary in the final version. Sometimes, for example, you might leave some text loose in the document, such as notes for yourself or maybe a company's address. Or maybe you created a lot of guides. By deleting these elements after a file is complete, you are not only making the file smaller in size (saving precious disk space), but you are also creating a cleaner file that will print faster and have less of a chance of becoming corrupt.

Cleaning Up Individual Paths

Another important part of cleaning your files is deleting unnecessary anchor points. Many times, when you use the Autotrace tool (or even when importing files from Streamline), your Bézier paths contain extraneous anchor points. Of course, the more points in a document, the larger the file size, and the longer it takes to print.

Unfortunately, this is one part of Illustrator that really needs some attention. Macromedia FreeHand has a Simplify function that automatically removes extraneous points on a selected path, and it would be a nice feature for Illustrator to include as well. Some people have FreeHand just for this purpose: They import the art into FreeHand to simplify it and then bring it back into Illustrator to add the finishing touches.

New Term One thing that Illustrator does have is a command called Cleanup (see Figure 21.5), which you can find by selecting Object➡Path➡Cleanup. This handy little janitorial function gladly deletes *stray points* (single anchor points with no paths),

21

unpainted objects, and empty text paths. If only you had this when your mom told you to
clean your room!

FIGURE 21.5

*The Cleanup dialog
box.*

Scanning and Tracing Art

Not everything is created in Illustrator (although I'm sure Adobe would just *love* for that
to happen), and many times you must scan logos and art sketches and then re-create
them in Illustrator. True, you can use the Autotrace tool and even applications such as
Streamline that were made to do this kind of thing, but sometimes the original itself is
not a good copy. The best way to get logos and sketches into clean, good-looking vector
art is to draw them from scratch yourself.

Relax, this process is a lot easier than you might think. Illustrator has the tools to get you
through. Just take this one step at a time.

1. Scan your logo. You should scan your image at 72dpi (you'll only be viewing it
   onscreen) and try to get it as large as possible without blowing out too much detail.

2. Save it in TIFF format. A TIFF does not use a preview for screen viewing but uses
   the actual file so that you get better detail when viewing it in Illustrator—especially when you zoom in close.

3. Open a new document in Illustrator.

4. Place the scanned logo you just saved. Double-click on Layer 1 in the Layers
   palette, and in the Options box, name the layer template and check the Template
   option (see Figure 21.6).

FIGURE 21.6

*Activating the
Template option for the
layer containing the
placed image.*

5. Create a new layer and name it artwork.

6. You can now begin to trace the logo. The first step is to draw guides, which will
   help you as you re-create the logo (see Figure 21.7). Remember that you can turn
   any shape into a guide, so you can use circles or other shapes if necessary.

FIGURE 21.7

Setting up guides to aid in tracing the logo.

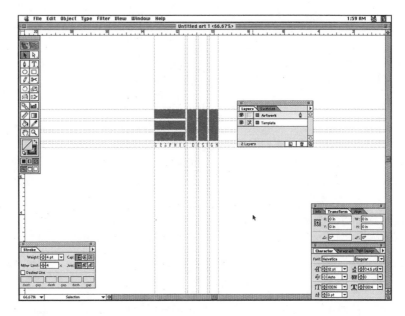

7. See whether you can re-create parts of the logo by using simple shapes, the Rectangle and Ellipse tools, and the Pathfinder filters (see Figure 21.8).

FIGURE 21.8

Using rectangles here greatly reduces the time to re-create the logo.

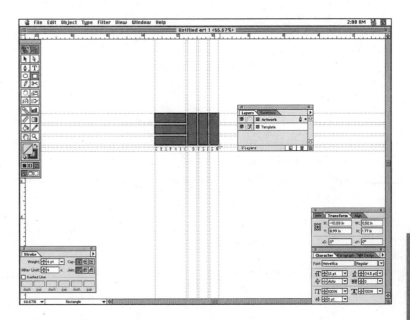

21

8. Complete the rest of the logo using the Pen tool where necessary, and add any necessary fills and colors.

Using Third-Party Plug-ins

NEW TERM Illustrator has tremendous support for *plug-ins*—additions or extensions to Illustrator that add features, tools, and functionality. In fact, many parts of Illustrator are actually plug-ins themselves, such as the Layers palette. Adobe uses these features to make it easy to modify the program and to keep Illustrator's core as clean as possible.

Of course, the most obvious advantage of using plug-ins is that other companies (or even ordinary people like yourself) can create plug-ins for Illustrator. In the following sections, I have listed plug-in packages from several vendors and have written short descriptions outlining their features.

Extensis VectorTools

Extensis VectorTools is probably the best collection of plug-ins on the market. A perfect mix of production-oriented and special effects plug-ins, VectorTools is a collection no serious illustrator should be without. VectorTools includes a Magic Wand Selection tool for selecting multiple objects with similar attributes, and it also enables you to edit colors using curves, just as in Photoshop. You can also turn 2D art into 3D art, set up object style sheets, and more.

Extensis Corporation

http://www.extensis.com

MetaCreations' KPT Vector Effects

KPT Vector Effects is part of the famous Kai's Power Tools suite of plug-ins and applications. Although its interface is just a tad different, KPT Vector Effects offers quick ways to create cool effects in Illustrator, including embossing, soft shadows, 3D, envelope distortion, and more.

MetaCreations

http://www.metacreations.com

HotDoor CADtools

CADtools is a great collection of over 34 drafting and dimensioning plug-ins. Even if you don't do drafting work, these plug-ins can really be useful. A good example is the

Arc tool, which enables you to draw arcs easily—a lot better than drawing whole circles and then deleting the parts you don't need.

HotDoor, Inc.

`http://www.hotdoor.com`

MAPublisher

If you are a cartographer or work a lot with maps, MAPublisher is for you. A suite of plug-ins, MAPublisher enables you to work with Geographic Information System (GIS) data directly in Illustrator. It also offers support for DXF files.

Avenza Software

`http://www.avenza.com`

Vertigo 3D Words

Vertigo is a company that makes 3D tools for use on powerful Silicon Graphics workstations. Recently, it began making plug-ins for use on Power Macintosh computers with Photoshop and Illustrator. 3D Words enables you to create true three-dimensional text and paths right in Illustrator.

Vertigo Software

`http://www.vertigo3d.com`

ILLOM Toolbox 1

Toolbox 1 is a wonderful collection of plug-ins that add some really great (and really cool) features to Illustrator. First of all, a Lasso tool lets you marquee-select objects by drawing a path—just as in Photoshop. It also has Search and Replace for objects (so you can search for red stars and change them to yellow circles, for example) and text style sheets. Plug-ins for time tracking and enhanced transformations round out this excellent package.

ILLOM Development AB

`http://www.illom.se`

Preparing a File for Output

21

NEW TERM If you are sending your file to a service bureau for film output or separations, you should make sure that it prints right—the first time. Keeping your files clean, as I mentioned earlier, is the first step in your quest for perfect film. Streamlining your files makes them print faster (some service bureaus charge for processor time) and more reliably. Messy files have a tendency to crash or hang a *RIP*, the software that interprets files so they can be output on an imagesetter.

Including Typefaces and Linked Images

For anyone to print your file, that person needs the typefaces you used as well as copies of any linked (placed) images. In many cases, you can avoid the typeface problem by converting your text to outlines. In fact, converting your text to outlines whenever saving logos or mastheads that will be used repeatedly is usually a good idea; you might forget about the typeface, thinking it's just a picture, when working in QuarkXPress or PageMaker.

To check quickly which fonts and linked images are in a particular file, choose Document Info from the File menu. Here Illustrator gives you an exhaustive list of your file's details and attributes, including linked and embedded images, as well as fonts used. You can save this information as a text file that you can then send to your service bureau. This information might help the service bureau work on your file faster and more efficiently. Of course, you should also use the Links palette to track all your linked images as well.

Outlining Paths

Let me tell you about an important precaution. As you know, when scaling objects in Illustrator, you have the option to scale strokes as well as the rest of the object. If your art or logo has strokes of a specific weight, and then somebody scales the image without scaling the strokes, you might have a slight problem on your hands. By using the Outline Path function, you eliminate the possibility of such a nightmare.

Blends and the Pen and Ink Filter

Two features in Illustrator can really add a special touch to your document: Blends and Pen and Ink fills. These two Illustrator features also cause the most printing problems. Both the Blend tool and the Pen and Ink filter create hundreds of objects to achieve their unique appearance, which can really tax even the latest RIPs. When using the Blend tool, you have an option to specify how many steps the blend should be. If you are creating a small blend that covers only a short distance, 40 objects may be sufficient, and very rarely will you need to create a blend with 255 objects (which is the default setting). As for the Pen and Ink filter, use it on smaller objects if possible, or try to avoid using it excessively.

Working with Linked Images

You already know that you can place a raster image in Illustrator and have it linked to a file outside your Illustrator document. If you've worked in QuarkXPress or PageMaker, you should already be familiar with this concept. You should also be familiar with the capability to update your linked images to reflect changes made to them after they're placed in an Illustrator file—a command missing from Illustrator. But fret not my dear friend; I'll tell you how to do it. You can use two workarounds to update linked images in Illustrator:

1. After you update and save your raster image in your favorite raster application (such as Photoshop), return to your Illustrator document. Then select the placed image you want to update. Choose Place from the File menu, and choose the file you just updated. After you click the Place button, Illustrator asks whether you want to replace the currently selected image. Choose Yes, and Illustrator replaces the old image with the updated one. Any transformations you had previously applied to that image such as scaling or rotating will be applied to the new image as well. (Note: This approach works only if the new image is still in the same file format as before, such as TIFF or EPS.)

2. After you update your raster image in your favorite raster application (such as Photoshop), save it with the exact same name. Then return to Illustrator. Save and close your document, and then reopen it. Your images are then updated automatically.

Summary

In this hour, you learned a whole lot of tips and techniques on how to be more efficient when working with Illustrator files. You learned how important it is to save files with easily recognizable names, and you learned how clean files can save you a lot of aggravation. Plus you learned all about some really cool plug-ins available for Illustrator, as well as how to re-create scanned art. After this chapter, you have what it takes to add the title "Production Artist" to your business card.

Workshop

The Workshop contains quiz questions to help you solidify your understanding of the material covered in this hour and exercises to provide you with experience using what you have learned. You can find the answers to the quiz questions at the end of the hour.

21

Quiz

1. Which palette do you use to automate Illustrator?

    a. Actions palette

    b. Pathfinder palette

    c. Transform palette

2. Saving your files often is important because

    a. a computer will crash when you least expect it to

    b. you never know when you will need it

    c. just because

3. The best way to get clean, sharp logos in Illustrator is to

    a. use the Autotrace tool

    b. create them from scratch

    c. buy them in a store

4. Linked images are always automatically included with the Illustrator document.

    a. True

    b. False

Exercises

1. Load all the preset actions that ship on the Illustrator CD-ROM, and learn what each one does. See whether any of them can help you work faster during your very busy work day.

2. Practice scanning and tracing logos from scratch. This exercise is good practice for becoming even more familiar with the Pen tool and the Pathfinder functions.

Term Review

Plug-in—An extension or addition that adds new functions to the application.

RIP—Software and/or hardware that converts your document into exactly the resolution required for a chosen output device.

Stray Point—A single anchor point that stands alone, with no path associated with it.

Answers to Quiz Questions

1. a
2. a
3. b
4. b

21

HOUR 22

Printing

You've designed a beautiful piece of art, and now you're ready to print it. Then you can show it to your mother, who will be very proud of you and hang it on the refrigerator door (although she still doesn't know exactly what you do).

Printing is an important part of the design process. If what you are designing will be used in print, seeing how it looks on paper as opposed to onscreen is a good idea. Sometimes visualizing your art onscreen is difficult, and you can get a better grasp of it when you view it on paper. This tip is especially true with type. It might look okay at 12 point onscreen, but when you print it on paper, you realize that 11 or even 10 point would be much better. These subtle aspects often cannot be picked up onscreen.

In this hour, you will learn about the following:

- Printing your files
- Producing color separations
- The PostScript language
- Troubleshooting tips

Printing Files

One of the most basic functions of your computer is the Print command, and it works the same way in Illustrator as it does in just about any other program. To print a document, choose Print from the File menu (see Figure 22.1), or press (Command+P)[Control+P].

FIGURE 22.1

Choosing Print from the File menu.

Document Setup/Page Setup

In Hour 2, "Customizing Illustrator," you learned about the different settings in the Document Setup dialog box. Illustrator also has a Page Setup dialog box specific to your printer and print driver software. You can access this dialog box through the Document Setup dialog box.

First, choose Document Setup from the File menu. On the far right of the dialog box, under the Cancel button, locate the button to open the Page Setup dialog box (see Figure 22.2). Your Page Setup dialog box contains settings for what paper tray to use and in what orientation the page should print (portrait or landscape—tall or wide). Page Setup is Illustrator's direct link to your printer, so the dialog box is different depending on which printer drivers you are using (Laserwriter 7, Laserwriter 8, and so on), and the options available also depend on the printer you are using.

FIGURE 22.2

The Page Setup button in the Document Setup dialog box.

Tiling with the Page Tool

NEW TERM Not everything can fit on an 8.5×11-inch sheet of paper. When you have artwork that is larger than what your printer can handle, you can print the artwork in pieces and then paste the pieces together after the entire file has printed. This process is called *tiling*.

To indicate which part of your file gets printed, you use the Page tool (H) (see Figure 22.3). After you select the Page tool, press and hold down the mouse button, and an outline appears onscreen (see Figure 22.4). Whatever is inside the borders of the outline will print. The artwork in your file is not affected in any way; you are simply instructing Illustrator as to which part of your document to print.

FIGURE 22.3

The Page tool.

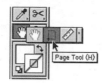

FIGURE 22.4

Indicating which part of a document should print by using the Page tool.

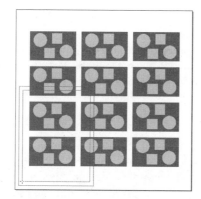

Color Separations

NEW TERM Before color artwork can actually be printed on press—be it CMYK, spot color, or *Hexachrome* (see note)—it must be separated. Each color therefore is printed on a separate page. If, for example, you are printing a four-color process job, you need to have four pages or plates—one each for cyan, magenta, yellow, and black. The process of making these plates is called *color separation* (see Figure 22.5).

FIGURE 22.5

A separated file.

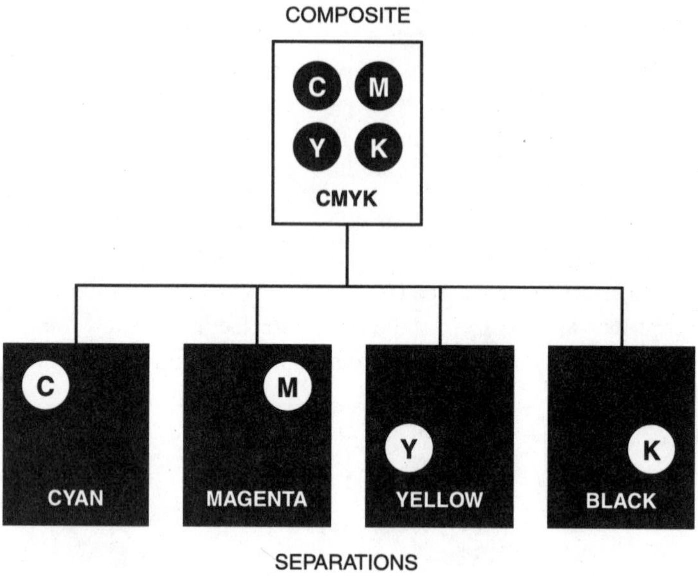

COMPOSITE

C M
Y K

CMYK

C
CYAN

M
MAGENTA

Y
YELLOW

K
BLACK

SEPARATIONS

Hexachrome was developed by Pantone to address one of the main short-comings of CMYK printing: difficulty in printing bright and vibrant colors, specifically in the orange and green areas. Because two more colors, Orange and Green, are added to CMYK, a much larger gamut (range of colors) is attainable. Essentially, this addition results in a six-color job (CMYKOG)—hence, the name Hexachrome.

In most cases, you send your files to a service bureau that prints the separations for you on film and provides you with a Matchprint (a high quality color proof, made directly from the film). However, not every job needs to go to film, and sometimes printing separations on your laser printer is adequate. Sometimes I also print separations to my laser printer to make sure they print correctly. Over the years, this shortcut has saved me thousands of dollars in potential film costs.

Printing Separations

If all this talk about magenta and film is making you nervous, put down the book, take a deep breath, sip a beverage, and pick up the book again. Now let me tell you that printing separations is really easy when you use Illustrator. You can open Illustrator's Separation Setup dialog box in two ways:

- Choose Separation Setup from the File menu (see Figure 22.6).

FIGURE 22.6

Choosing Separation Setup from the File menu.

22

• Click the Separation Setup button in the Print dialog box (see Figure 22.7).

FIGURE 22.7

Choosing Separation Setup from within the Print dialog box.

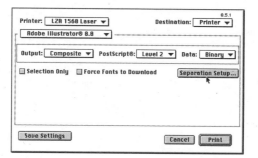

After you choose one of these methods, the Illustrator Separations dialog box appears (see Figure 22.8). Here, you can specify how the separations should be made, as well as specify which colors should be separated and how.

FIGURE 22.8

The Separations dialog box.

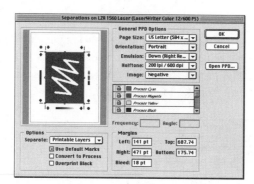

Now, follow these steps:

1. Open a PPD file. A PostScript Printer Description file contains information about your printer such as resolution, available page sizes, and line screens.

> On a Macintosh, your PPD files are located in a folder called Printer Descriptions. You can find this folder in the Extensions folder in your System folder.
>
> In Windows, your PPD files are located in the Windows subdirectory.

2. To specify a PPD file (if one is not already specified), click the Open PPD button (see Figure 22.9), navigate to where your PPD files are, and click the Open button.

FIGURE 22.9

The Open PPD button.

3. After a PPD file is loaded, you can specify options for your separations such as Page Size, Orientation, Emulsion, Halftone, and Image (see Figure 22.10). If you don't know what specifications you should use, consult your printer or production expert.

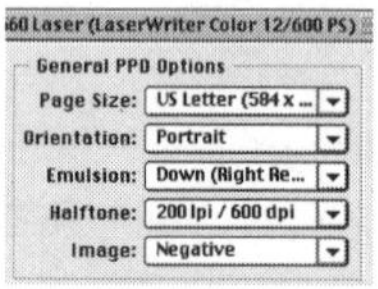

FIGURE 22.10

General PPD options.

Specifying Colors to Be Separated

The most important part of separating a file is choosing which inks will print and how they will separate. In the center of the Separations dialog box is a list of colors that are used in your document. A printer icon in the box to the left of a color indicates that the color will print to its own plate (see Figure 22.11).

FIGURE 22.11

In this example, magenta and black print, but the yellow plate does not.

To print spot colors, uncheck the Convert to Process check box (see Figure 22.12). Otherwise, spot colors are converted to process and separated as a process color, as indicated by a process color icon (see Figure 22.13).

FIGURE 22.12

The Convert to Process check box, located in the lower-left corner of the Separations dialog box.

FIGURE 22.13

In this example, the icon indicates the spot color brown will be converted and will print as a process color.

Positioning the Plate

You also can adjust the position of the separation on the paper or film by grabbing the edge and moving it, as shown in Figure 22.14.

FIGURE 22.14

Positioning the artwork on the page by grabbing the crop-marks and dragging.

Setting Cropmarks

NEW TERM *Cropmarks* are very important. They indicate to your friendly press operator at the print shop where to trim the paper around your artwork. If your artwork contains bleeds (where the artwork goes past the edge of the paper), then cropmarks are the only indication as to where the page should end. Follow these steps to create accurate cropmarks:

1. Draw a rectangle that exactly matches your trim size.

2. Position your artwork within the rectangle (or position the rectangle over the artwork).

3. Choose Object➡Cropmarks➡Make (see Figure 22.15).

FIGURE 22.15

Making cropmarks.

You cannot move or edit cropmarks after you make them unless you select Object➡
Cropmarks➡Release. If you do not have a rectangle selected when you choose Make
Cropmarks, Illustrator draws cropmarks based on the page size.

> Remember that in Hour 17, "Vector Filters," you learned about a filter
> called Create Trim Marks. Trim marks (which you create by choosing
> Filter➡Create➡Trim Marks), however, and Cropmarks (which you create by
> choosing Object➡Cropmarks➡Make) are different. Trim marks are simply
> lines that Illustrator draws for you. They can be edited in that you can color
> them, change their thickness, and even delete individual lines. Cropmarks,
> on the other hand, cannot be edited, and you can have only one set of crop-
> marks in a single document.

PostScript

NEW TERM   At the heart of Illustrator is the *PostScript* printing language. Developed by
Adobe, PostScript is probably responsible for the success of the desktop publishing industry, as well as the use of computers for graphic design services.

The emergence of the PostScript language as an industry standard has created an environment that allows designers and prepress operators alike to achieve a consistent workflow throughout the design and print process. Therefore, when you print a file on your
PostScript printer and send it to a service bureau that uses a PostScript imagesetter, you
get consistent results.

Because PostScript is an actual computer language, you can open any PostScript file in a
word processor and see the actual commands. If you know PostScript, you can even edit

22

the code itself to make changes. Sometimes when files won't print or even open in Illustrator, experts can open these files in a word processor and try to fix the PostScript code itself.

To take advantage of Illustrator's capabilities, you must use a PostScript printer. If a printer does not have PostScript or a PostScript interpreter, you get undesirable results, such as noticeable jaggy edges, and the printed colors may not match what you see onscreen.

Troubleshooting

Although everyone hopes it never happens, sometimes a file fails to print because of an error. Many times, the error occurs because the document is too complex for the printer on which it is being printed, or a software incompatibility exists. If such an event occurs, try the following tips:

- Use the Split Long Paths option, which you learned about in Hour 2. You can find this option in General Preferences.

- Use the Compatible Gradient Printing option, which you examined in Hour 2. You also can find this option in General Preferences.

- Save the file in an earlier Illustrator format. Some older versions of programs may have problems with Illustrator 8 files. Saving in an older format, such as Illustrator 6, may help. Use the Save As command from the File menu so that you don't over-write the original file.

- Isolate the culprit. Delete parts of your illustration one by one, starting with placed images first, sending your file to the printer until it prints. Sometimes a file may become corrupted, or a particular shape may cause a problem.

- Copy and paste your illustration into a new document. Sometimes a file may become corrupted, so the only solution is to destroy it.

Summary

You finally got to see what your art looks like on paper this hour. You learned how to prepare color files as separations in both spot and process colors, so now you can sound more intelligent when you talk to your service bureau and press shop. You also learned all about the PostScript printer language and how important it is to the design industry.

In the next hour, you'll stray a bit from the print world and jump headfirst into the Internet and the World Wide Web.

Workshop

The Workshop contains quiz questions to help you solidify your understanding of the material covered in this hour and exercises to provide you with experience using what you learned. You can find the answers to the quiz questions at the end of the hour.

Quiz

1. The Landscape page orientation is used
   a. To print the page in wide format
   b. To print the page in tall format
   c. To print rolling hills and a sunset

2. Tiling refers to
   a. Printing repeating patterns
   b. Printing your artwork in sections
   c. Ceramic walls in your bathroom

3. The "M" in CMYK stands for
   a. Magenta
   b. Mystery
   c. Mauve

4. A spot color refers to
   a. The color of your dog
   b. A custom color
   c. A color used sparingly in your illustration

5. PostScript was developed by
   a. Apple
   b. Adobe
   c. Microsoft

Exercises

1. Create an illustration using custom colors, and print as spot color separations. Then print the same illustration as CMYK separations using the Convert to Process option in Separation Setup.

2. Create an illustration and use the Cropmarks feature. Then remove the cropmarks and print the same file. Observe the differences between the two printouts, and notice how difficult it is to determine how to trim the one without cropmarks.

3. Create an illustration, and use the Page Tool to indicate tiles to print different sections.

22

Term Review

Cropmarks—Marks or lines that indicate to a press operator or trimmer where to cut the paper.

Hexachrome—A six-color printing process developed by Pantone, Inc.

PostScript—A programming language developed by Adobe Systems for printing and page layout purposes.

Separations—The individual color plates for printing.

Tiling—Splitting up a large page into smaller parts for printing purposes.

Answers to Quiz Questions

1. a
2. b
3. a
4. b
5. b

Hour **23**

Web Graphics

At first, everyone thought the Internet was just a fad, but recently it—or more specifically, the World Wide Web—has become a part of nearly everyone's daily life. Email addresses and URLs are exchanged as often as street addresses and phone numbers. Although the Internet has been around for quite some time, the World Wide Web turned the Internet into what it is today because of two essential features: images and links. Illustrator puts the power of these two features into the palm of your hand.

This hour, you'll examine topics such as the following:

- Dealing with Web-safe color issues
- Assigning URLs to objects
- Exporting in Web-compatible formats
- Working with animation

Designing for the Web

I mentioned earlier that the Web offers two powerful features: images and links. As the old saying goes, "a picture is worth a thousand words," and using images to convey your message can be very effective. You can easily create images in Illustrator for use on the Web (see Figure 23.1).

FIGURE 23.1

Creating eye-catching illustrations for the Web is easy in Illustrator.

Hot Stuff!

NEW TERM   A *link* is something on a Web page that, when you click it, takes you to another page. A link can be specified in your HTML document as either text or a picture (see the following Just a Minute). A picture can also have multiple links, meaning you can specify different links for different parts of your image (see Figure 23.2). This is called an *imagemap*. Illustrator can create Web-ready graphics, but before you begin making your art, you need to know a few things about the Web.

FIGURE 23.2

By defining an imagemap, you can specify a different link setting for each button in this image.

HTML documents are created in a text editor or an HTML editor application. HTML, which is short for Hypertext Markup Language, is the standard programming language used on the World Wide Web. If you're squeamish and don't want to get involved in "writing code," you can find plenty of WYSIWYG (What You See Is What You Get) HTML editors, such as Adobe PageMill and Claris HomePage, to do all the programming for you.

Color on the Web

When you design a brochure that will be printed, you have control over how the final product appears. You specify exact colors and papers to give a precise look and feel to the brochure. On the Web, however, you have very little control as to how your art appears to the different people who view it. Some people might have small, cheap monitors that display only 256 colors. Other people may have large high-resolution monitors set to millions of colors. And if that weren't enough, different browsers such as Netscape Navigator and Microsoft Internet Explorer have different settings, so what looks perfect on your screen may look completely different on someone else's.

Dithered Colors

NEW TERM When you create an image on a computer with millions of colors, what happens when you view that image on a computer that has only 256 colors? Well, the results can be horrifying at times. If a computer does not have a certain color in its palette, it tries to approximate the color by arranging a variety of pixels in the same vicinity to give the appearance of that color. This process is called *dithering*. Sometimes the dithering is presentable, but usually it creates odd and distracting patterns and can also make text unreadable (see Just a Minute).

Dithering is a lot like screening in traditional printing. When the screens are rotated just right, you get a nice rosette, but if the screens do not line up properly, you get an ugly moiré pattern.

Using the Web Palette

NEW TERM As Douglas Adams would say, "Don't panic." You can do a few things to ensure that your art looks great on the Web—on any machine. The first thing is to use the Web-safe color palette. As you learned in Hour 9, "Coloring Objects," computer monitors use the RGB color model. The *Web palette* is a collection of 216 RGB colors that will not dither when viewed onscreen.

How did someone come up with a number such as 216? Well, it's like this: The majority of people out there have monitors with 256 colors (VGA is 256 colors). These 256 colors are in what's called the system palette, which is built into your operating system. The Windows system palette and the Macintosh system palette, however, differ slightly. To be exact, 40 colors do not match up between the two system palettes. So, if you eliminate those 40 colors, you are left with 216 colors that are identical on both platforms (see the following Just a Minute).

If you are creating artwork for an intranet, where you know the type of computers people are using, you can take advantage of that knowledge by using more resources. If, for example, everyone who will be viewing your art has a Macintosh, you can use the Macintosh system palette that contains 40 more colors than the Web palette does.

Now, if you create artwork by using only colors from these palettes, you can be sure that the colors will not dither when viewed on the Web. By now, you're wondering, "Great! Where do I sign up?" and the answer is easy. Adobe has included system palettes for both Windows and Macintosh as well as a color-safe Web palette—all right inside Illustrator. Simply choose Swatch Libraries from the Window menu, and make your choice (see Figure 23.3). The palette, which opens in a new swatches-like floating palette, cannot be edited (see Figure 23.4). If you want to edit colors, you must drag those colors to the Swatches palette first and then edit them.

FIGURE 23.3

Opening the Web palette.

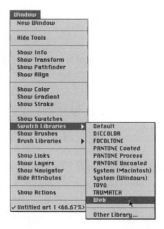

FIGURE 23.4

The Web palette looks and acts similarly to the Swatches palette. Notice the little icon in the lower-left corner, indicating the palette cannot be edited.

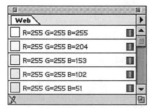

Because the Web and the technology that it brings are constantly changing, dealing with every aspect of Web color can take up an entire book in itself. Because many issues and techniques are beyond the scope of this book, you might want to look into books that delve deeper into Web color, such as *The PANTONE Web Color Resource Kit* or *Creating Killer Web Sites*, both published by Hayden Books.

Assigning URLs to Objects

23

I mentioned before that a single image, otherwise known as an imagemap, can contain multiple links. Using an imagemap allows a user to follow different links, based on where he or she clicks in a linked image. Before Illustrator, you had to create an imagemap in a third-party application, which was usually a tedious task. And if you made a change to your image, you would have to redefine the imagemap as well. Now, with Illustrator, you can do it all in one application, and in one easy step.

You create an imagemap by assigning a URL (uniform resource locator) to an object in your illustration. A URL, which is a fancy word used for a Web address, usually looks similar to this: `http://www.adobe.com`. To create an imagemap, you must know the URL of the page you are linking to.

To assign a URL to an object, open the Attributes palette (by pressing F11). Select an object, and type the correct URL in the Attributes palette (see Figure 23.5). After you enter a URL, it is added to the pop-up list in the Attributes palette, so you can choose from a list as you create more links (see Figure 23.6).

FIGURE 23.5

Entering a URL in the Attributes palette.

FIGURE 23.6

Choosing a link from the pop-up menu in the Attributes palette.

If you have a Web browser such as Netscape Navigator or Microsoft Internet Explorer and an Internet connection, you can click the Launch Browser button in the Attributes palette to check your links.

Web File Formats

You must save your file in a certain file format before it can be used for the World Wide Web. The most popular formats, GIF and JPEG, can be saved right out of Illustrator, and each has its strengths and weaknesses. Another file format, PNG, is slowly making its way into the limelight as well because it offers some features not found in GIF or JPEG. Basically, all these formats use a compression method to make the files smaller so that they take less time to transfer over a modem.

All documents saved in these formats are converted to pixels when they are saved. Always be sure to keep a copy of your original Illustrator documents in case you need to make changes to your images. Also, when you save your Web art, be careful that you give appropriate names to your images. Use only lowercase letters, no spaces, and use the appropriate three-letter extension (.gif, .jpg, .png) so that a browser can identify it.

The GIF89a Format

NEW TERM The GIF89a format (created in 1989, hence the .89a extension) is probably the most popular file format used for images on the Web. Developed by the people at CompuServe, *GIF* uses a lossless compression scheme called LZW. Lossless means that no information is lost when the file is compressed. The GIF format is best used for images with flat color, such as logos and illustrations. For art with gradients or photos, the JPEG format does a better job because the GIF format supports a maximum of only 256 colors (JPEG supports 24-bit color).

Exporting a GIF

You can export a GIF file as follows:

1. Choose Export from the File menu (see Figure 23.7).

FIGURE 23.7

Choosing the Export command.

2. Choose GIF89a from the pop-up menu (see Figure 23.8).

FIGURE 23.8

Choosing the GIF89a file format.

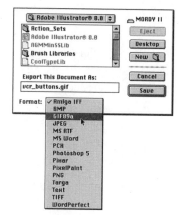

3. Give your file a name (don't forget the .gif extension), and click the Save button.

4. Choose your options from the GIF89a Options dialog box (see Figure 23.9) and click OK.

FIGURE 23.9

The GIF89a Options dialog box.

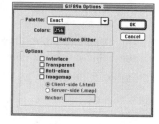

NEW TERM Now take a closer look at some of the options presented in the GIF89a Options dialog box. First, you can select a palette of colors to be saved with the file (see Figure 23.10). Choose either the Web palette or the *Adaptive palette* to get even fewer colors. The GIF format supports any number of colors up to 256. The fewer colors in the palette, the smaller your file size. You then have four options: Interlace, Transparent, Anti-alias, and Imagemap.

FIGURE 23.10

Choosing from different palette options.

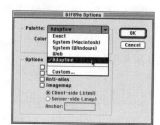

23

- Interlace—Selecting the Interlace option enables your image to appear gradually onscreen when it appears in a browser window. This option gives the viewer an idea of what the image looks like as it loads.

- Transparent—Using Transparent makes the background of your image appear as though it were filled with nothing, letting colors that appear behind it show through. This option is important with irregularly shaped or oval images, which would otherwise appear with a white background.

- Anti-alias—As I mentioned with the Rasterize command in Hour 17, "Vector Filters," this option smoothes out jaggy lines and curves, making the image look better onscreen. Try to avoid using this option with small font sizes because it tends to make the type too blurry to read.

New Term   Finally, if you have assigned URLs in your file, you can export an imagemap along with the GIF file. You can choose to create either a *client-side* imagemap or a *server-side* imagemap. Client-side imagemaps are generally better and are more common in today's Web sites.

The JPEG Format

New Term   The *JPEG* format (pronounced *jay-peg*) uses a lossy compression scheme, meaning that information is thrown out to make the file size smaller. This compression affects the final quality of the image, and you are able to specify how much information is lost during compression (of course, the more you throw out, the smaller the file becomes). JPEG is used primarily for photographic images or complex illustrations with gradients because the JPEG format can support 24-bit color (millions of colors).

Exporting a JPEG

Follow these steps to export a JPEG file:

1. Choose Export from the File menu.
2. Choose JPEG from the Format pop-up menu (see Figure 23.11).
3. Give your file a name (don't forget the .jpg extension) and click Save.
4. Choose your options from the JPEG Options dialog box (see Figure 23.12) and click OK.

In the JPEG Options dialog box, you can set the image quality, which also controls the amount of compression (see Figure 23.13). By selecting a higher quality file, you also create a larger file. To change the quality, simply drag the little triangle slider to the left or right, or enter a number from 1 to 10 in the box.

FIGURE 23.11

Choosing JPEG from the Format pop-up menu.

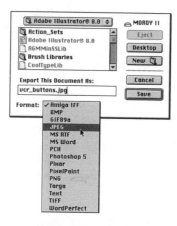

FIGURE 23.12

The JPEG Options dialog box.

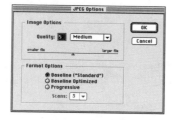

FIGURE 23.13

Setting the image quality.

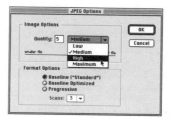

Recently, a new kind of JPEG format, called progressive JPEG, has begun to spread and is supported by the latest versions of popular Web browsers. Progressive JPEG is essentially the same as an interlaced GIF, in which the file loads gradually, enabling the viewer to get an idea of what the image is as it loads. I have even found that Progressive JPEGs are usually a few kilobytes smaller than Baseline (standard) JPEGs.

The PNG Format

NEW TERM The *PNG* format (pronounced *ping*) was initially created to address the shortcomings of the GIF format. Using a completely new compression algorithm, it avoids any legal problems concerning the LZW compression scheme (see the following Just a Minute). PNG also supports 24-bit color, as well as the use of alpha channels for masking. The format, however, is relatively new on the scene and is supported in only the most recent browsers, such as Netscape Navigator/Communicator 4.0 and Microsoft Internet Explorer 4.1. The image will not appear in a nonsupported browser.

> The GIF format utilizes the LZW compression scheme that was developed by Unisys Corporation. A few years ago, after a long legal battle, Unisys began to charge software developers a royalty fee if they created software that implemented the LZW compression algorithm (end users are not charged, only developers). The PNG format was developed as an alternative to the GIF format, to avoid having to pay royalty fees to Unisys.

Exporting a PNG

You can follow these steps to export a PNG file:

1. Choose Export from the File menu.
2. Choose PNG from the Format pop-up menu (see Figure 23.14).

FIGURE 23.14

Choosing PNG from the Format pop-up menu.

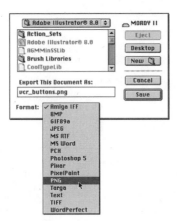

3. Give your file a name (don't forget the .png extension) and click Save.
4. Choose a resolution from the Resolution Options dialog box (see Figure 23.15) and click OK. Because your art will be viewed on the Web, 72dpi is fine.
5. Choose your options from the PNG Options dialog box (see Figure 23.16) and click OK.

FIGURE 23.15

The Resolution Options dialog box.

FIGURE 23.16

The PNG Options dialog box.

23

NEW TERM PNG's *interlacing* scheme is called Adam7, or you can choose to have no interlacing. You can also choose from several filters, which are different compression methods. The Adaptive method is most effective for Web images.

Making Animations

Illustrator's Blend tool can help you create great-looking animations for the Web. The GIF89a file format supports multiple images in a single file, enabling animation. Almost all of today's Web browsers support GIF89a animation.

Basically, an animation is a string of images or frames, and each frame is different from the last. When the frames are viewed one after the other, the image appears to move. You can use Illustrator's Blend tool as follows to help create the different frames:

1. Create two objects: One is the object in its original state, the other in the state you eventually want it to be (see Figure 23.17).

FIGURE 23.17

Two different objects.

2. Select both objects.

3. Choose the Blend tool (W) from the Toolbox (see Figure 23.18).

FIGURE 23.18

Illustrator's Blend tool.

Blend tool

4. Click one point from the first object (see Figure 23.19).

FIGURE 23.19

Selecting the point to blend from.

5. Click a corresponding point on the second object (see Figure 23.20). A blend is then automatically created.

FIGURE 23.20

Selecting the point to blend to.

6. To edit the number of steps or phases you want in your animation, choose Object➡Blends➡Blend Options. Under Spacing, select Specified steps, and enter the number of steps you want.

7. After you create and edit your blend, select Object➡Blends➡Expand to turn the blend into separate editable objects.

You can then tweak each object individually (see Figure 23.21). To create the actual animation file, you need to export each frame as a separate GIF file and then combine them in a third-party animation program such as GifBuilder (for Mac OS) or GIF Construction Set (for Windows).

FIGURE 23.21

After the blend is performed (top), you can tweak and edit each object (bottom).

You also can use the Blend tool to create airbrush effects by creating more steps. Experiment by blending small, light-colored objects within larger, dark-colored objects to create highlights and shadows. Keep in mind that blends can create a lot of shapes that make for slower print times and larger file sizes. For more information on using the Blend tool, see Hour 21, "Working Smart in Illustrator."

Summary

In this hour, you became a techie Web-head! You learned about using "safe" colors when designing for the Web to prevent dithering. You also learned how to create imagemaps by assigning URLs to objects right in Illustrator. And if that weren't technical enough, you learned how to make your images Web ready by saving them in a variety of Web-compatible formats. Heck, you even covered animation!

You'll wrap things up next hour when you learn all about cross-platform issues, so get ready for the home stretch!

23

Workshop

The Workshop contains quiz questions to help you solidify your understanding of the material covered in this hour and exercises to provide you with experience using what you learned. You can find the answers to the quiz questions at the end of the hour.

Quiz

1. A picture with multiple links utilizes

    a. An imagemap

    b. Utter confusion

    c. A single URL

2. The process a computer uses to simulate a color it does not have is

    a. Color matching

    b. PANTONE

    c. Dithering

3. How many colors are in a Web-safe color palette?

    a. 256

    b. 16.7 million

    c. 216

4. The GIF format is best used for images of

    a. Photographs

    b. Logos

    c. Multi-colored gradients

5. Which Illustrator tool is great for creating animations?

    a. The Blend tool

    b. The Free Transform tool

    c. The Zoom tool

Exercises

1. Save an illustration in both GIF and JPEG formats. Then open your Web browser, and observe how they are different in quality. Also, take note of their different file sizes.

2. Create an imagemap for an illustration. Then try reassigning the URLs to different objects.

3. Try creating an animation where the letter "A" transforms into the letter "B." Remember that you must convert the letters to outlines before you can blend them.

Term Review

Adaptive palette—A table of a specific number of colors that are derived from the best possible match in an image.

GIF, JPEG, PNG—Image file formats that are universally accepted on the Internet and World Wide Web.

Imagemap—A list of coordinates that, when referenced to a graphic image, enable users to follow different links, depending on where they click on the image.

Interlacing—The process of loading an image gradually, increasing in resolution and detail as it appears in the browser.

Web palette—A table of 216 specific colors that can be reliably used in any browser and on any platform.

Answers to Quiz Questions

1. a

2. c

3. c

4. b

5. a

Hour 24

Cross-Platform Issues

As you begin the last lesson of this book, remember that the beauty of working with a computer is that anything you create can be worked on not only on your machine but others as well. Whether you're working with a coworker, a client, a service bureau, or even just moving files between your office and computer at home, becoming familiar with moving your files around is a good idea. As I mentioned before, Illustrator is cross platform. This means the program works the same way on both Macintosh and Windows computers, and more important, it means that you can open the same file on either platform as well.

This cross-platform capability sounds really nice on paper, but you should remember that it doesn't always work like that in real life. You should keep in mind several important issues when working with files that will be used on both Macintosh and Windows platforms. Throughout this hour, you will explore these issues, including the following:

- Naming files
- Fonts
- Drag and drop
- Color management

Naming and Saving Files

Be careful when naming your files. The Mac OS supports long filenames (more than 12 characters), as does Windows 95/98, but Windows 3.1 and DOS support only 12 characters in the form XXXXXXXX.XXX.

NEW TERM If you are saving a file on a Macintosh for use on a PC, name the file with the appropriate *file extension* preceded by a period (.EPS, .TIF, .GIF, .JPG, and so on). If your file will be opened in Illustrator for Windows, save it with the Illustrator extension (FILENAME.AI); otherwise, Illustrator will not open the file. (Although Macintosh can tell the kind of file from the file resource type, Windows relies on the three-letter extension to identify the file type.)

If you are copying your file onto a disk or a removable media cartridge, such as a ZIP disk, be sure the disk is formatted for the computer it will be used on. Although support for PC disks is built into the Mac OS, you need a special utility to mount Macintosh disks on a Windows machine (MacinDOS is one such utility).

Patterns and Gradients

Expand your gradients and patterns where possible (you learned how to use the Expand command in Hour 10, "Fills"). You can take this precaution to ensure the integrity of your gradients or patterns in a file. Doing so is especially important when you are transferring files to a computer that uses an older version of Illustrator than what you are currently using. Patterns and gradients as you know them now did not exist in versions prior to version 5 on the Macintosh and 4.1 on Windows.

Drag and Drop

NEW TERM *Drag and drop* is a feature in today's operating systems that greatly increases productivity. Instead of having to copy and paste something from one application to another, you can simply drag your selection right into another application window. If, for example, you are working in Illustrator and want to bring some artwork into Photoshop, you can simply drag the object from the Illustrator window right into the Photoshop window.

Of course, to take advantage of these drag-and-drop features, you must have enough RAM in your computer to run both Illustrator and Photoshop simultaneously (or any other programs that you want to drag objects into or from).

You can drag a bitmap image from Photoshop 4 into Illustrator, but it will be converted to a 72dpi RGB image regardless of what the settings were for that file in Photoshop.

When dragging selected Illustrator objects into Photoshop 4, you can hold down the Shift key to place the object in the center of the active layer, and you can also hold down the (Command)[Control] key to have the Illustrator art placed as paths in Photoshop (for use as clipping paths and selections).

You can also drag objects directly to your desktop. On a Macintosh, doing so creates a clipping file (PICT), and in Windows, dragging objects to the desktop creates a scrap file (WMF).

Font Issues

The two leading font technologies in the world of publishing are TrueType and PostScript Type 1. TrueType was developed by both Apple and Microsoft, and PostScript Type 1 was developed by Adobe. A few years ago, a showcase showdown occurred between these two technologies, and when the dust settled, PostScript remained the standard on the Macintosh platform, but TrueType became the de facto standard on the Windows side.

This use of two font technologies can create some problems when you're switching documents between platforms—especially in documents with kerning or justification. Whenever possible, you should convert your text to outlines to avoid any problems. Of course, if the type must be edited, then converting the type to outlines won't work for you. Just be prepared to see different line breaks and letter spacing when moving the file between platforms.

To ensure that fonts appear identically across platforms, make sure the font names are identical and that they are from the same type foundry (Adobe Garamond from Adobe is very different from ITC Garamond from Adobe).

Compatibility

Cross-platform compatibility gets better with each version, and Illustrator supports many different file formats. Of course, whenever possible, try to keep your file in EPS format, because doing so keeps the file in a scalable format and ensures that your file prints reliably from any PostScript printer.

Color Management

You learned about color management back in Hour 16, "Working with Raster Images," but I think it is necessary to repeat this information again. In all probability, what you see on a Macintosh screen will vary greatly from what you see on a Windows screen. If

24

possible, try to use standard defined colors, such as those from the PANTONE collection, and use a printed swatchbook to proof colors.

Summary

To be successful in today's growing world of computer design, you must be able to work across platforms. You already knew that Illustrator was a cross-platform application, but this past hour you learned all about the little things—the things that matter most—to help ensure a smooth transition between both Macintosh and Windows platforms.

Well, I had a lot of fun, and I hope you did, too, as you learned all about Illustrator. Because the computer field is ever changing, visit my Web site at `http://www.mordy.com` for the latest information on Illustrator. And don't forget to send me email at `mordy@mordy.com`.

Workshop

The Workshop contains quiz questions to help you solidify your understanding of the material covered in this hour and exercises to provide you with experience using what you learned. You can find the answers to the quiz questions at the end of the hour.

Quiz

1. DOS filenames are limited to

    a. 10 characters

    b. 12 characters

    c. 32 characters

2. The term *cross-platform* refers to

    a. Similarities between Macintosh and Windows

    b. Switching to the east-bound local train

    c. Dragging objects directly to your desktop

3. The TrueType font format was developed by

    a. Adobe

    b. Bitstream

    c. Apple and Microsoft

4. Colors appear exactly the same across all platforms.

    a. True

    b. False

5. You can drag objects from Illustrator right into an open Photoshop document.

    a. True

    b. False

Exercise

Close the book and calmly put it down. Then spring out of your chair, pumping your fist emphatically in the air while yelling "YES!" You finished the book, and now you know Illustrator! Woo hoo! Go out and celebrate!

Term Review

Drag and drop—The process of copying items between applications or open windows by simply dragging the selected items without using Copy and Paste commands.

File extension—Following the period in a filename, up to three letters that identify the file type, such as EPS or TIF. (This term applies to PCs only. Mac OS uses a file resource located within the file to determine the file type.)

Answers to Quiz Questions

1. b

2. a

3. c

4. b

5. a

INDEX

Symbols

+ (plus sign), text blocks, 228
~ (tilde) key, 54

A

Acrobat PDF files, 312
actions, 320-321
Actions palette, 320-321
Adam7, interlacing, 355
Adaptive palette, 351
Add Anchor Point tool (Toolbox), 12, 122-123, 169
Add Arrowheads filter, 292
Adjust Colors filter, 275
Align palette, 213
alignment, 213
   baseline shift, 34-35, 243
   grids, 36-37, 40-42

guides, 40-42
indents, 246
justification, 245
point text, 226
points, 130
rulers, 40
Amiga IFF file format, 316
anchor points, 28
   adding, 122-123
   Bézier paths, 106
   combination, 114-115
   control handles, 115
   Convert Direction Point tool, 123
   deleting, 12, 123
   Direct Selection tool, 122
   direction, 12, 123
   dragging, 113
   manipulating, 121-124
   paths (printed), 106
   positioning, 115, 122
   Roughen filter, 281

smooth, 110-114
straight corner, 108-110
Zig Zag filter, 284
angles
   constraining, 31
   default, 31
   guides, 38
animation, 355-356
Anti-aliased Artwork preferences, 32
antialiasing, 352
   preferences, 32
   raster images, 262-263
Area Select, 31, 78
area text, 227-228
Area Type tool (Toolbox), 12
area types, 12
arranging, 81-82
   anchor points, 122
   floating palettes, 16
   layers, 93
   palettes, 16

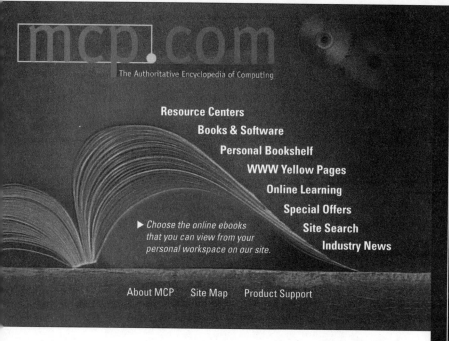

Illustrator Type Magic

Greg Simsic

Every page of *Illustrator Type Magic* makes a visual promise: You will be able to create this! The book 's highly effective, recipe-style approach walks you through the procedures of creating special effects with type, and the stunning four-color illustrations are sure to inspire any designer.

ISBN: 1-56830-334-3   *$39.99 USA/$56.95 CAN*

Illustrator 8 Classroom in a Book

Classroom in a Book, the world's best selling series of hands-on training workbooks, helps you learn the features of Adobe software quickly and easily. The book is self-paced, so you can learn Adobe Illustrator wherever and whenever you choose, in whatever time you have available. *Classroom in a Book* covers a wide range of features, tools, and techniques of Illustrator 7. Even if you are familiar with Illustrator, take the time to review all the lessons you'll be surprised at how much you learn! You can follow the book from start to finish or do only the lessons that correspond to your interests and needs. There is plenty of room for exploration and experimentation!

ISBN: 1-56830-470-6   *$45.00 USA/$59.00 CAN*

Sams Teach Yourself Adobe Photoshop 5 in 24 Hours

Carla Rose

A fast tutorial for people new to Photoshop or looking for a quick introduction to the new features of Photoshop 5. In just 24 sessions of one hour or less, you will be up and running!

ISBN: 0-672-31301-4   *$19.99 USA/$28.95 CAN*

Sams Teach Yourself Adobe Photoshop 5 in 21 Days

T. Michael Clark

In just three weeks, you'll understand the fundamentals of Photoshop 5, master professional imaging techniques, learn how to effectively use all the tools and features, and get tips on creating spectacular designs quickly and easily. Using the step-by-step approach of this easy-to-understand guide, you'll be up to speed with Photoshop 5 in no time!

ISBN: 0-672-31300-6   *$39.99 USA/$56.95 CAN*

Photoshop 5 Type Magic

Greg Simsic

This is the perfect resource for typographers, designers, and Photoshop users looking to spice up their work. Every page makes a visual promise: You will be able to create this exciting artwork! The book's highly effective, recipe-style approach walks you through the procedures of creating special effects with type, and the stunning four-color illustrations are sure to inspire any designer.

ISBN: 1-56830-465-X   *$39.99 USA/$56.95 CAN*

Inside Adobe Photoshop 5

Gary David Bouton and Barbara Bouton

Inside Adobe Photoshop 5 reads like a knowledgeable neighbor who has dropped by to show you the way around the world's most popular image editing program. The Boutons' easy-to-follow style and technical know-how provide comprehensive coverage of Photoshop's newest and traditional features.

Whether you're a professional or a hobbyist, after your intimate visit with the Boutons you'll walk away with the skills needed to accomplish fantastic, advanced image manipulation.

ISBN:1-56205-884-3   *$44.99 USA/$64.95 CAN*

Using Adobe Photoshop 5

Dan Giordan and Steve Moniz

A task-based reference that puts the answers to professionals' problems at their fingertips. Learn to create stunning graphics, correct and enhance the tonality and focus of your images, and achieve professional results quickly with concise, step-by-step directions.

ISBN: 0-7897-1656-9   *$29.99 USA/$42.95 CAN*

Photoshop 5 Classroom in a Book

Classroom in a Book, the world's best selling series of hands-on training workbooks, helps you learn the features of Adobe software quickly and easily. The book is self paced, so you can learn Adobe Photoshop wherever and whenever you choose, in whatever time you have available. *Classroom in a Book* covers a wide range of features, tools, and techniques of Photoshop 5. Even if you are familiar with Photoshop, take the time to review all the lessons—you'll be surprised at how much you learn! You can follow the book from start to finish or do only the lessons that correspond to your interests and needs. There is plenty of room for exploration and experimentation!

ISBN: 1-56830-466-8   *$45.00 USA/$59.00 CAN*

Add to Your Sams Library Today with the Best Books for Programming, Operating Systems, and New Technologies

To order, visit our Web site at www.mcp.com or fax us at

1-800-835-3202

ISBN	Quantity	Description of Item	Unit Cost	Total Cost
1-56830-334-3		Illustrator Type Magic	$39.99	
1-56830-470-6		Illustrator 8 Classroom in a Book	$45.00	
0-672-31301-4		Sams Teach Yourself Adobe Photoshop 5 in 24 Hours	$19.99	
0-672-31300-6		Sams Teach Yourself Adobe Photoshop 5 in 21 Days	$39.99	
1-56830-465-X		Photoshop 5 Type Magic	$39.99	
1-56205-884-3		Inside Adobe Photoshop 5	$44.99	
0-7897-1656-9		Using Adobe Photoshop 5	$29.99	
1-56830-466-8		Photoshop 5 Classroom in a Book	$45.00	
		Shipping and Handling: See information below.		
		TOTAL		

Shipping and Handling

Standard	$5.00
2nd Day	$10.00
Next Day	$17.50
International	$40.00

201 W. 103rd Street, Indianapolis, Indiana 46290   1-800-835-3202 — FAX

Book ISBN 0-672-31354-5